Publications on the Near East

Publications on the Near East

Poetry's Voice, Society's Song: Ottoman Lyric Poetry
Walter G. Andrews

The Remaking of Istanbul: Portrait of an Ottoman City in the Nineteenth Century
Zeynep Çelik

The Tragedy of Sohráb and Rostám from the Persian National Epic, the Shahname of Abol-Qasem Ferdowsi
Translated by Jerome W. Clinton

The Jews in Modern Egypt, 1914-1952
Gudrun Krämer

Izmir and the Levantine World, 1550-1650
Daniel Goffman

Medieval Agriculture and Islamic Science: The Almanac of a Yemeni Sultan
Daniel Martin Varisco

Rethinking Modernity and National Identity in Turkey
Edited by Sibel Bozdoğan and Reşat Kasaba

Slavery and Abolition in the Ottoman Middle East
Ehud R. Toledano

Britons in the Ottoman Empire, 1642-1660
Daniel Goffman

Popular Preaching and Religious Authority in the Medieval Islamic Near East
Jonathan P. Berkey

The Transformation of Islamic Art during the Sunni Revival
Yasser Tabbaa

Shiraz in the Age of Hafez: The Glory of a Medieval Persian City
John Limbert

The Martyrs of Karbala: Shi'i Symbols and Rituals in Modern Iran
Kamran Scot Aghaie

Ottoman Lyric Poetry: An Anthology, Expanded Edition
Edited and translated by Walter G. Andrews, Najaat Black, and Mehmet Kalpaklı

Ottoman Lyric Poetry

An Anthology

EXPANDED EDITION

Edited and translated by
Walter G. Andrews, Najaat Black,
and Mehmet Kalpaklı

UNIVERSITY OF WASHINGTON PRESS
Seattle and London

This edition published with the assistance of a grant from the Ministry of Culture and Tourism of the Turkish Republic.

Originally published by the University of Texas Press, 1997
Printed in the United States of America
11 10 09 08 07 06 5 4 3 2 1

University of Washington Press
P.O. Box 50096
Seattle, WA 98145-5096, USA
www.washington.edu/uwpress

Library of Congress Cataloging-in-Publication Data

Ottoman lyric poetry : an anthology / edited and translated by
Walter G.Andrews, Najaat Black, and Mehmet Kalpaklı.– Expanded ed.
p. cm. – (Publications on the Near East)
Poems in English translation and original Ottoman Turkish.
Includes bibliographical references.
ISBN 0-295-98595-X (alk. paper)
1. Ghazals, Turkish—Translations into English.
I. Andrews, Walter G. II. Black, Najaat, 1955- III. Kalpaklı, Mehmet, 1964–
IV. Publications on the Near East, University of Washington.
PL235.O87 2006
894'.35108—dc22 2006002201

The paper used in this publication is acid-free and 90 percent recycled from at least 50 percent post-consumer waste. It meets the minimum requirements of American National Standard for Information Sciences-Permanence of Paper for Printed Library Materials, ANSI Z39.48-1984.

Contents

Contents

Preface to the 2006 Expanded Edition

Ottoman Lyric Poetry was a publishing success for a book of translations from Ottoman Turkish. According to an unscientific survey of our colleagues, it was widely used in classes ranging from history to world literatures. It also attracted readers and reviewers from outside academia, and, as a result, the paper version sold out in a surprisingly short time. It remains the only book of its kind and a significant number of scholars whom we respect have urged us to bring it back into print. The result is this expanded edition undertaken by the University of Washington Press.

This new edition comes at a time when the part of the world once dominated by the Ottomans is, perhaps, more at the forefront of general awareness in the English-speaking world than it has ever been. However, because this increased awareness is rooted in unspeakable tragedies, it will do little to heal our world unless it helps to generate a mutual understanding that reaches beyond surface divisions and enmities to a core of love and spiritual yearning that we all share. One may not be able to achieve such an understanding solely by struggling to appreciate Ottoman love poetry, but it is not a bad place to start.

We would be remiss if we did not mention that, in addition to the resources mentioned in the Introduction, we (Kalpaklı and Andrews) have published *The Age of the Beloveds*, a far-ranging study of early-modern Ottoman love and love poetry in a comparative European context, that serves well as a companion to this volume. Prominent among other recent resources for encountering Ottoman poetry in English are Victoria Holbrook's translation of Şeyh Galip's mystical narrative *Beauty and Love* (translation) and *Hüsn-ü Aşk* (text), and Shirine Hamadeh's forthcoming study of eighteenth century Ottoman architecture, which contains copious translations of poetry about architectural products. We hope that such resources, combined with our Anthology, will enable more teachers to offer courses in English on Ottoman literature and to include Ottoman literature in more general literature courses as well.

Preface to the 2006 Expanded Edition

The harsh economic realities of publishing in 2006 did not allow us to revise or re-edit the original text. The main body of the text will be exactly as it was in the 1997 edition. We thought long and hard about some of the questions raised about certain translation choices in reviews by respected colleagues and decided that we could live with our original translations without denying the possibility of other correct, or even better, interpretations of what is manifestly complex and ambiguous verse. This we accept as part of the risky business of translation. However, although we could not revise, we were able to add examples from manuscripts and printed sources of Ottoman script versions of some of the translated texts. We hope that this will enhance the usefulness of the *Anthology* for those who are in the process of learning to read Ottoman poems in their original form.

Walter G. Andrews
January 2006

Acknowledgments

THIS ANTHOLOGY has been many years in the making and owes much to many people. All projects of any scope are joint projects. The work of putting together a finished book could not have been done without the financial support of the Translations Program of the National Endowment for the Humanities. We thank those who have made such grants possible, the kind and helpful staff of the Endowment, and the volunteer readers and evaluators who worked with our proposal. We would add a very special acknowledgment of the invaluable contribution of Professor Victoria Rowe Holbrook, who acted as our consultant on the project and shared her considerable expertise in the form of a very detailed and helpful reading of our manuscript. She made our work better without trying to impose her own style. This is not an easy task!

We would also like to express our gratitude to the faculty, students, and staff of the Department of Near Eastern Languages and Civilization and the Middle East Center of the University of Washington who have been our colleagues, friends, and teachers over the years and who have been ever generous with their encouragement and advice. Among them, Kemal Silay very ably helped to proofread our Ottoman texts, and Theresa Truax did her usual positive, insightful, and effective job of critiquing our work.

There are many others. Michael Beard, an accomplished translator and source of wise counsel, carefully read many of our translations and was unstinting in sharing his expertise with us. Talât Halman, María Rosa Menocal, and Jerome Clinton all contributed readings, support, and criticism. Professor Ali Alparslan, Turkey's greatest living calligrapher in the Ottoman tradition, most kindly contributed the priceless examples of Arabic script.

Acknowledgments

None of us could do so much without the consistent support of family and friends.

Walter would like to give special thanks to Melinda, Inez Shultz, and his brother Jim. He dedicates this book to his parents, Walter G. and Louise S. Andrews and to the memory of his Turkish parents, Melda and Rasih Tanberk.

Najaat Black would like to thank her mother and father. Also Donna, Ted, and her many other friends. Thanks to Dell for good words in the early years. Sweetest thanks to Rhiannon and Malik.

Mehmet Kalpaklı would like to thank Yeşim and Sinan.

Finally, we would like to recognize the people we may have forgotten to name—forgotten only at this moment when we must put our gratitude in writing. Please forgive us and accept our thanks.

And please remember, we are committed to our own vision of how Ottoman poetry could be translated. The people mentioned here are responsible for much that is good about our book, but we also rejected a lot of good advice.

Thanks to all.

Poet's Preface

"AT THE GATHERING OF DESIRE . . . " was the first line of the first Ottoman poem I translated over seven years ago. What began as a small collection of poems grew slowly into the present anthology, to include biographies, notes, and illustrations. Originally, I felt translator and poet were one profession. Since then I have seen them fragment into two, with one (translator) absolutely dependent on the other (poet), but the poet corralled by the original work.

I must add that I am not a scholar of Ottoman Turkish. Only through the intricate knowledge and approval of my collaborators was I able to reconstruct these poems.

This was not easy, although often wonderfully enjoyable, like a very difficult puzzle.

Sometimes it was impossible.

Nowhere, however, was the translation process more challenging than in the case of gender. Turkish uses the same word for "he" and "she." English does not. Fixing the gender of anyone's beloved is beyond my responsibility. I stand aside, only left wishing there was an English equivalent which had the delightful ambiguity of the Turkish pronoun.

With that, I would like to dedicate these poems to the men and women who wrote them, and to all lovers and beloveds, everywhere.

Najaat Black

A Note on the Pronunciation and Transcription of Turkish

TURKISH IS quite easily pronounceable by English speakers. The few phonetic differences are slight and restricted mostly to vowels. Today's Turkish uses a modified Latin alphabet as it has done since the 1920s. Although the Turkish modifications to the alphabet are quite easily learned, we have decided to retain the English orthography in the case of "sh" ("ş" in Turkish) and "ch" ("ç" in Turkish) when representing Ottoman Turkish names and titles in the translations, introduction, and biographies for the convenience of readers who know no Turkish. The only case where this is a problem is when "s" and "h" come together as in the name İshak (pronounced "Iss-hock"). We will mention that this is happening where it occurs. We also use "j" for the sound Turkish represents by "c" (the initial sound in "jam" or "jug").

In the notes and in the analysis of the poem by Zâtî in the introduction, where Turkish words are cited in italics, we will use the Turkish spelling with Turkish characters.

The letters peculiar to Turkish are as follows:

â	(either a long "a" or when following "k" or "l" a palatalization of the preceding consonant. Therefore "kâ" is pronounced "*k*^{y}â")
c	(the "j" in "jug")
ç	("ch")
ğ	(a glide between vowels: "iği" = "ee-ee," "oğu," "oh-woo")
ı	(can be formed by saying a long "u" ["oo" in "boot"] and then unrounding the lips [smile!])
j	(the sound "zh" as in the French "je" or "Jacques")
ö	(a rounded "eh" sound: like the vowel sound in "her")

ü	(a rounded "ee" sound: say the vowel in "beet" and pucker)

The transcription of Ottoman Turkish also includes representation of several letters of the Arabic alphabet which Turkish does not distinguish phonetically but which operate as phonemes in Arabic and Persian words. Because "short" vowels generally do not show in the Arabic script these letters are sometimes used in Ottoman Turkish to indicate what kind of vowel follows. This is especially true of the letters "ṣ" (the velarized Arabic letter *ṣâd*) and "ḳ" (the back letter *ḳâf*), which represent "s" and "k" when they precede "back" vowels (a, ı, o, u). The other Turkish vowels are pronounced more or less as follows.

a	(the "a" sound in "father" or the vowel in "hot")
â	(the vowel sound in "ah")
e	(the vowel sound in "bet"; when final the vowel sound in "hey")
i	(the vowel sound in "bit"; when final the sound in "key")
î	(the vowel sound in "key")
o and ô	(the "o" sound in "hotel")
u and û	(the vowel sound in "boot")

The system we use for the romanization of Ottoman Turkish corresponds to a more or less standard Turkish usage and is as follows:

ا â	ب b	پ p	ت t	ث s̱	ج c
ح ḥ	خ ḫ	د d	ذ ẕ	ر r	ز z
س s	ش ş	ص ṣ	ض ż	ط ṭ	ظ ẓ
ع '	غ ġ	ف f	ق k	ل l	م m
ن n	ه h, e/a	و u,v	ى î, y	*hamze* '	

The representation of Ottoman Turkish names is especially troublesome. There is no general consensus and no widely accepted rule to follow. We have chosen to apply the following rules.

Although Modern Turkish does not have final voiced consonants— for example, "b" becomes "p" when final—we retain the voiced consonants (Gâlib instead of Gâlip, Ahmed instead of Ahmet, etc.).

For Arabic compound names—for example, names beginning in *'abd* (slave of), ending in *dîn* (of the Faith)—we will follow the Modern Turkish convention but retain the long vowels and the signs for *ayin* (') and *hamze* (') ('Abdülbâkî, Jelâleddîn, Sa'deddîn, Sheyhülislâm). Those who do not know Turkish should not be put off by the long vowels or unfamiliar signs; the *ayin* and *hamze* are not pronounced and the long vowels are familiar to English speakers and are pronounced as indicated above.

All other Ottoman names including the names of the poets follow the same rules: retained voiced consonants, marked long vowels, retention of *ayin*.

It is important to note that in the present Turkish convention for Ottoman names no discernible agreed-upon rule obtains. Various authors do different things and are often inconsistent within the same work. We have simply chosen the form that seems to be the most commonly used.

All other transcription of Ottoman Turkish follows the generally (although not universally) accepted method used for the edition of Ottoman poetic texts. Except in the "Ottoman Turkish Texts" section at the end, the diacriticals indicating Arabic letters are not used.

OTTOMAN LYRIC POETRY

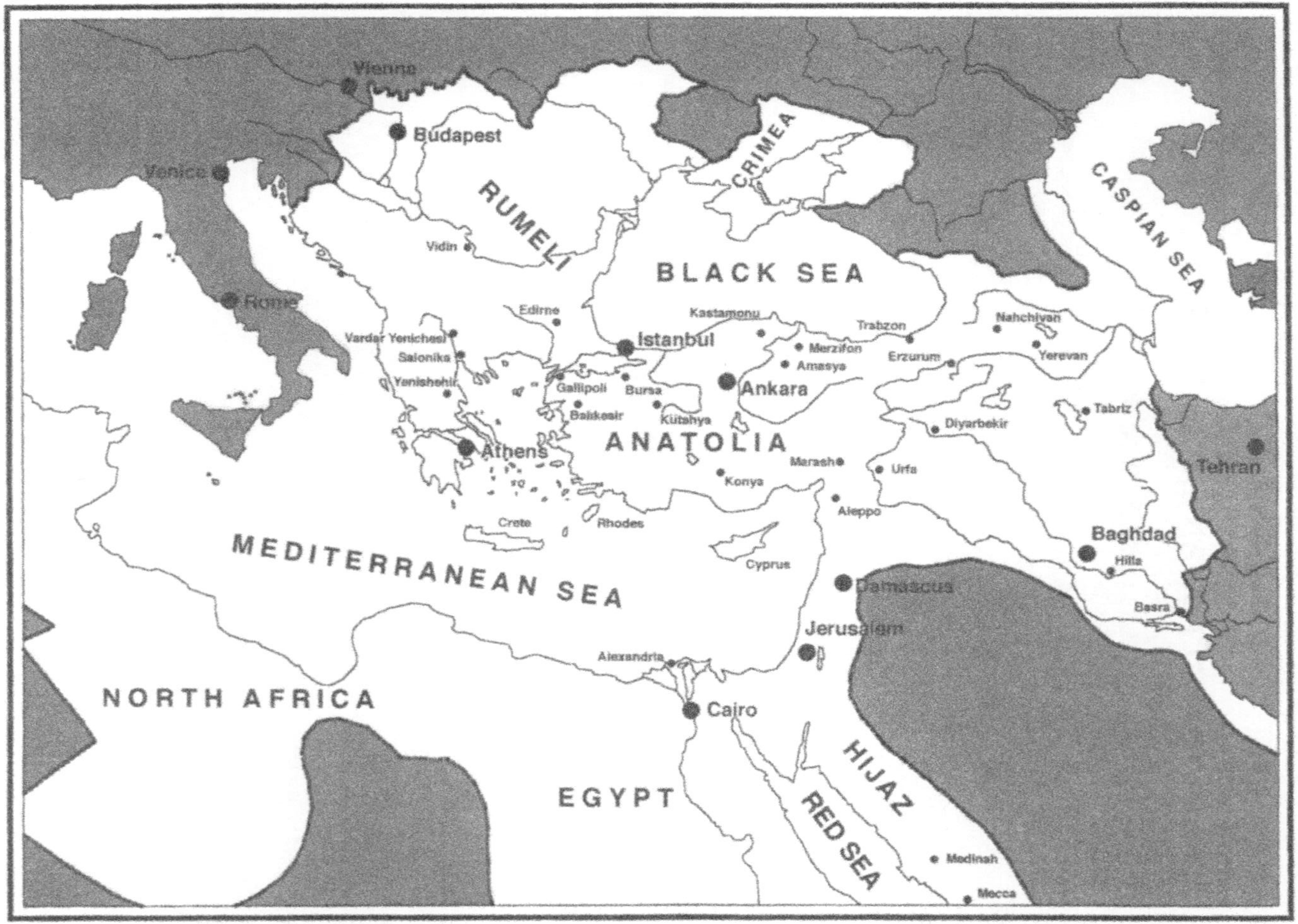
Vienna
Budapest
Venice
RUMELI
CRIMEA
CASPIAN SEA
Vidin
BLACK SEA
Rome
Edirne
Kastamonu
Trabzon
Nahchivan
Vardar Yenichesi
Istanbul
Merzifon
Saloniks
Amasya
Erzurum
Yerevan
Yenishehir
Gallipoli
Bursa
Ankara
Tabriz
Balikesir
Kütahya
Diyarbekir
Athens
ANATOLIA
Merash
Urfa
Tehran
Konya
Aleppo
Crete
Rhodes
Baghdad
MEDITERRANEAN SEA
Hilla
Cyprus
Damascus
Basra
Jerusalem
Alexandria
NORTH AFRICA
Cairo
HIJAZ
EGYPT
RED SEA
Medinah
Mecca

Ottoman Lyrics: Introductory Essay

Walter G. Andrews

OTTOMAN POETRY AND WESTERN RECEPTION

I KNOW of no one who argues seriously that Ottoman Turkish poetry is *not* a neglected literary phenomenon. Outside of Turkey it is so rarely a part of any canonical collection or representation of "world" literature or culture or civilization that it might as well be invisible.

The Ottoman Empire itself was not invisible at all. It was one of the most powerful and significant forces (arguably the single most significant force) in the politics of East and West for a period extending from the middle of the fourteenth century to the early years of the twentieth century. At one time or another, it controlled vast territories from the borders of Poland in the north to the tip of the Arab Peninsula in the south, from the shores of the Caspian Sea in the east to Morocco in the west and held the entire coast of the Black Sea and three quarters of the Mediterranean coast. It was the rival in all things—war, trade, religion, culture—to the great empires and imperial ambitions of Europe. The Ottomans were the standard-bearers of a militant and expansionist Islam that by the sixteenth century emerged in a tide of conquest that ebbed only at the very gates of Vienna and whose passing, in the nineteenth and twentieth centuries, left a residue of turmoil in Eastern Europe and the Middle East that troubles the world up to the present moment. Even though the story of the Ottoman Empire is often told badly—reduced solely to the tale of the Ottoman war-machine in conflict with Europe—the story of the state *is* told by historians and does find its way into textbooks and "world" histories.

There are also things we in the West know about the Ottomans without really knowing that we know. Much of what we commonly perceive as "Islamic" or "Middle Eastern" is a product of the great Ottoman synthesis of the many ethnic and cultural strains that coexisted under the umbrella of their rule. Our popular impressions of Middle Eastern food, music, architecture, decoration, dress, and the like are, in many cases, derived from Ottoman models. Likewise, in the United States, many of our own ethnic communities with Middle Eastern or East-European roots (for example, Sephardic Jews, Armenians, Greeks, Albanians, Hungarians, Slavic groups, Arabs) originated as former Ottoman subjects who came to escape the catastrophic disruptions attending the disintegration of Ottoman hegemony.

Nonetheless, despite the obvious and profound impact of the Ottomans on our past and, residually, on our present, we only know them incompletely, as a reflection in the distorting mirror of age-old enmities. Because they were the great rivals of the West in the period of Western ascendance to power, we know the Ottomans by their armies, their weapons, the splendor and mystery of their palaces, mosques, and public buildings. We know them by the outward face of their religion, by the bureaucratic curtain that distanced outsiders from their centers of power, and by a host of uninterpreted differences from what we believe to be proper and true. But, as with all enemies, we have had little interest in knowing those things that imbued their lives with meaning and passion, the things that made their lives reasonable and ordinary, their humor, their tender moments, their moments of despair, the things they valued, their deeply felt aspirations, their fears and tremblings.

For many, if not most, educated Ottoman elites literature was a central or at least quite important aspect of their lives. For them there was no major medium of cultural expression other than literature and by and large the art of literature to them meant the art of poetry. It is all but impossible to convey to present-day audiences in the West how wide-spread, how important, how meaningful poetry, especially lyric poetry, was to Ottoman culture. For us, poetry is a peripheral art; for them it was *the* central literary activity without rival or peer. Poets and would-be poets abounded at all levels of society. From love to the most profound search for spiritual truth or to impassioned pleas for employment or largesse, all manner of things that touched people deeply were expressed in poetry. People also played with poetry, did tricks with poetry, showed off their talents with poetry, were funny and insulting and naughty in poems. Poets routinely left collections of many hundreds or even thousands of poems, and almost everyone, from the ruler to the peasant, from the religious scholar to the rake and drunkard, aspired to be a poet.

These are some of the reasons why Westerners might have noticed Ottoman poetry. The reasons why we have not noticed it are equally numerous and not nearly as straightforward. As I already mentioned, there have been obvious advantages to seeing the Ottoman enemy always as an implacable warrior and never as a sensitive poet. In addition, however, our notions, both theoretical and practical, of such things as a universal literary history, universal literary values, pure national languages and cultures emerged and developed at a time when the Ottomans were imagined to be a striking example of all that Europe was not.

For those who would understand more, in fascinating detail, about how a huge and vital literary tradition can be made simply to disappear, I would recommend two books, both of which appeared in 1994. The first is María Rosa Menocal's *Shards of Love: Exile and the Origins of the Lyric*. *Shards* is not about the Ottomans at all (except for traces of the history of my early and peripheral encounters with the author). It is the brilliantly written story of how the writing of literary history in the West came to take its present form, of how the Petrarchian project of constructing a smooth narrative of descent from the pure, originary classical languages and cultures to the equally pure and unary national languages necessitated the writing out or obscuring of the in-between period that we call the medieval. Menocal reads the medieval not as a moment of past time since transcended but as a metaphor for a kind of literary practice that defies the national culture paradigm. This kind of literary practice and the milieu in which it becomes possible are visible today as "postmodernism" but can more broadly be seen as a potential that reasserts itself in many times and places including, in my reading, the Ottoman. When we are exiled from the order and unities of culture, language, ethnicity that make up the great smooth national narratives of history, we are cast out into a multicultural, multi-lingual, multiethnic "non-nation," an empire that frustrates our need to narrate a descent from origins and forces us to confront the lyrical unevenness of our lives. This is a confrontation that from time to time, for good or for ill, we try hard to avoid. And the history of Ottoman literature is in large part the history of that kind of avoidance.

The second book I recommend—the best study of Ottoman Turkish literature I have ever read—is Victoria Holbrook's *The Unreadable Shores of Love*. In the course of talking about Sheyh Gâlib's eighteenth century lyrical romance *Beauty and Love*, Holbrook weaves a discussion and analysis of the creation of the modern literary history of the Ottomans. Her introductory remarks include a telling paragraph:

> The "Middle East" is euphemism for what was the Ottoman Empire, a euphemism that disappears the Ottoman west. The Empire left behind many modern nation-states, probably as many politically individual entities as any polity ever has. Most of them determined themselves in contradistinction to the empire they participated in for centuries, and all of them, including the Republic of Turkey declared in 1923, have had reasons to marginalize the Ottoman cultural past in their histories.

In a situation where no one (including the Turkish Republic, its actual descendant) had an interest in claiming or seeking origins in Ottoman culture, it is not surprising that Ottoman literature remains on the distant margins of "world literature." Even the rediscovery of Ottoman culture by the Turks of today, as anxiety about infection by Ottomanist political ideology has waned with time, is complicated by projects of populist "Islamists" and elitist Ottoman-revivalists to recuperate Ottoman literature as part of an anti-national, anti-western, anti-modernist program.

In the West and especially the English-speaking West, the most powerful preserver and definitive "source" for Ottoman poetry has been Elias John Wilkinson Gibb's *History of Ottoman Poetry*. Begun in the last years of the nineteenth century and completed posthumously early in the twentieth century by his friend, the Persianist E. G. Browne, Gibb's six-volume grand narrative has dominated the reception of Ottoman poetry to the present day. In the absence of scholarly and institutional support for the study of Ottoman literature, Gibb's massive narration, rooted in Western, nationalist, positivist discourses and the perspectives of ardent Turkish revolutionaries and reformers dominates what we know. It preserves Ottoman poetry indeed, but ironically does so in a form that authoritatively rationalizes its invisibility. Victoria Holbrook in *Shores* gives a rather detailed account of Gibb's narrative and its influence, so I will merely point out that Gibb, very much in the Orientalist tradition, locates Ottoman literature in relation to its supposed origins in Arabic and Persian literatures—of which it is portrayed as the degenerate descendant. He chronicles both its decadence and its decay and eagerly celebrates the birth of the new literature which replaced it. And, quite ironically, all this is done very much as a labor of love, love for an object on which he lavishes his mature life, which he studies and translates profusely, and which he fixes and frames for permanent exhibit.

The difficulty that Gibb presents for those few of us who persist in reading and studying Ottoman poetry is that his undeniably valuable work is almost all there is and his story is the major obstacle to telling any other story. The museum Gibb created of Ottoman poetry has been too fixed, too static, and it is past time to do something else.

The need to do something else makes it difficult to step open-eyed into the trap of characterizing Ottoman poetry. Characterization means that we are encouraged to start where we have always been. It also conflates variety, change, history into simple generalizations on a quite vast complexity. But because we must begin somewhere, let me start with some of what I think I know.

The Ottoman elites were possessed of formidable poetic tools. They had inherited a living tradition of poetic forms and themes common to a Perso-Arabic tradition in an Islamicate context. By the fifteenth century, that poetic mode had already transcended Persian and Arabic and was spreading east and north into the classical Chaghatay Turkish tradition and west into Ottoman Turkish-speaking lands. Subsequently, the same late-Islamic poetic tradition would echo in the Mughal courts of India and flourish in Urdu culture.

Ottoman poetry was highly developed, complex, and sophisticated. It built upon shared knowledge of previously employed themes and cultural motives using lexical tools capable of fashioning the most intricate metaphors, the most perplexing ambiguities, and the most mind-boggling hyperboles. Yet for all its reliance on established codes, for all its preoccupations with artistry and poetic craft, Ottoman lyric poetry has as its wellspring the intensely experienced passion of love. From a center at which sexuality and spirituality merge, the poetry radiates into all the primary relations that engender intense emotional responses. On one extreme it extends toward a panegyric awareness of a transcendent ruler/sultan figure. On the other extreme it merges into a mystical-allegorical tradition and employs the symbology of real-life passion as a guide to self-immolation in divine unity. Thus poetry becomes a vital synthesis of the emotional content of relations to the ultimate temporal, spiritual, and personal foci of intense desire.

The formal features of the poetry are quite firmly fixed. In general, the basic unit is a couplet of two equal half-lines that adhere to one of about a dozen set rhythmic patterns. Each couplet is, by convention, self-contained in grammar and theme and is not required to have any necessary or overt connection to other couplets of a multi-couplet composition.

Most often compositions made up of numbers of couplets will have one rhyme throughout, the only exceptions being some stanza forms and the rhyming couplets used primarily in longer narrative poems. Overwhelmingly, the favorite lyric form was the *gazel*, a short poem of more or less sonnet length—five to seven lines with some longer and shorter exceptions—a rhyming first couplet and the same rhyme in the second half-line of each following couplet. By convention, the last or second-to-last line of most lyric poems will contain the pen name of the poet.

As seems to be generally true of pre-modern cultures, Ottoman culture is a culture of variants. Originality is highly prized, but it is not an originality that demands a poem unique in all its features with a discernible origin in a particular author. This is a more recent concept. The situation of Ottoman poetry more closely resembles that of improvised jazz, rock, or hip-hop, where masters of the art render common themes in unique and original ways and the less accomplished only mix and match familiar riffs. At first, the more Ottoman poetry one reads, the more it will begin to sound the same to our ears. But if we consider how the tenth or ten thousandth rendition of *The Basin Street Blues* can all of a sudden be stunningly original, we can get a feeling for how a poem can be made new in an ages-old culture of variants.

As we approach the question of translation it is also important to note that many or most of the features of Ottoman poetry seem to conspire against its being understandable outside a context marked by a huge amount of shared knowledge and many unspoken expectations. This is another point at which Gibb's narration has had great power. His *History* embeds his translations—including a separate book of translations—in a mass of biographical, historical, and philological detail that then appears necessary in order to make the meaning of the poetry accessible, especially in translation and to outsiders. By making it difficult and hence dependent on scholarship to replace what once made it understandable, Gibb and the scholarly reception based on his work created the illusion of a cultural and temporal abyss separating Ottoman poetry from the kinds of contemporary readings that we give to premodern European literature. As Holbrook cogently points out, *difficulty* itself then becomes a political sign for the failure of the elite, courtly, high-culture literature of the Ottomans and the success of a pure, national, egalitarian Turkish literature. This is an immense problem for readings and translations of Ottoman literature—when readings of poems are themselves read as positions on the Ottoman state and its republican successor.

THE TRANSLATIONS

Translation is always more problematic and more simple than it seems. It is problematic because translation clearly cannot do what many people believe it proposes to do: it cannot move a linguistic something from one language and culture to another. It is not even a matter of losing something in the moving process—a "noise" problem as information science would have it—it is a matter of losing *everything* in the process and then trying to reconstruct another language's and culture's impression of what the lost thing might have been. What is simple is that the translation is really a reading of a poem, a poem about a poem.

For this reason, an endless number of different translations are possible for any given poem—depending, of course, on what one wants to say about the original. For example, E. J. W. Gibb (1901, 115) wanted to say about Ottoman poems that they are archaic, something we have passed by; they are focused on formal features (rhyme, rhythm, etc.), "difficult" language, obscure references, trite sentiments, and rhetorical trickery. So he says this by translating as follows:

> Before thy form, the box-tree's lissom figure dwarfed would show;
> Those locks of thine the pride of ambergris would overthrow.
>
> Who, seeing thy cheek's glow, recalls the ruby is deceived;
> He who hath drunken deep of wine inebriate doth grow.
>
> Should she move forth with figure like the juniper in grace,
> The garden's cypress to the loved one's form must bend right low.
>
> Beware, give not the mirror bright to yonder paynim maid,
> Lest she idolater become, when there her face doth show.
>
> Baqi, doth he not drink the wine of obligation's grape,
> Who drunken with *A-lestu*'s cup's o'erwhelming draught doth go?

The result here is plainly verse—a quite skilled attempt to reproduce in English rhythm a combination of Ottoman metric feet formed by alternations of long and short syllables. However, for all their replication of formal features of the Ottoman originals, Gibb's translations have few enduring poetic merits and certainly do not conform to the tastes and expectations of present-day audiences. Nonetheless, wherever we find a translation of Ottoman poetry it will likely be one of Gibb's or similarly "Gibb-erish." This is usually because what Gibb wanted to say about Ottoman poetry is also what many anthologists and representers of Ottoman poetry want to say (when they could not just forget about it altogether).

More recently, Professor John Walsh of Edinburgh University wanted to say something a bit different: that Ottoman poetry may have been formal and stylized but it was also enjoyable and readable and possessed of beauties that might touch us now. So in a group of translations published in the 1978 *Penguin Book of Turkish Verse* (103–104), he represented Ottoman poetry as in this example (see poem no. 52 for our rendition of the same poem by Nâ'ilî):

My tears were as the streams which make the garden places sweet;
Forth flowed my heart like water to a roguish sapling's feet.

A strange Mejnun am I! The spectres of my Sweetheart's eyes
Surround me like distraught gazelles in never-ending suite.

Your eyelashes, like witches, change their colour; all in black
They plan to raid my heart by night and crush it in defeat.

My heart's become a tree of sighs; inspired by your svelte form,
It waves about the garden like a cypress trim and neat.

The brilliant aspect of my virgin verses, Nailî
Derides the mirror of the sun, like love's moon-faced elite.

The poem is still heavy on the rhyme, in part because most Ottoman poetry rhymes just like that: a rhyme in both half-lines of the first couplet and the same rhyme in the second half-line of each following couplet. Walsh is a scholar and does not want to wander too far from the feel of poems as he reads them in Ottoman Turkish. But his poems are also far less archaizing than Gibb's, lighter in touch, standing alone without needing to float on a sea of footnotes. There have been some other sensitive translations more like Walsh's: Talât Halman's (1987) translations of Sultan Süleymân's poetry are a good example. Nonetheless, other than Gibb, there has been no major translation project since Victorian times and certainly not enough minor projects to represent even a minimal range of stylistic and interpretive options.

So what do we want to do with *our* translation project, what do we want to say? Well, first of all, we do not intend to replace Gibb with another definitive representation. We would like to begin a proliferation of translations of many kinds. We would like to take issue with the notion that there is or can be a "true" translation that is scholarly enough and poetic enough to make transparent everything that was of real value about Ottoman poetry.

Above all, what we want our translations to say about Ottoman poetry is that it was poetry. This is in large part why we are working as a team. For me, and for Professor Kalpaklı, Ottoman poetry is something we have learned to approach as scholars. Between us we know a lot about the words and the tropes and the contexts. Often when we try to translate we get caught up in formal features—in multiple meanings, rhetorical tricks, and erudite allusions—and poetry goes out the window. So Najaat Black made poetry out of our scholarly musings about poems and let go what must be let go of in order to write a poem about a poem. We argued all the time: "No, Najaat, you just made that up, it's beautiful but there's nothing like it in the poem we are translating!" "That's an ugly word and I won't use it!" "This poem just doesn't work in English." But in the end we have arrived at a sample of poems that come as close as we can make them to telling the story we would like to tell about Ottoman poetry.

If we can say what we want to say, people who read these translations will get a taste of the intense emotional involvement that flavors this kind of poetry, a whiff of the delight that its extravagant imagery can produce. We would have readers today begin to sense why this was such a popular form of entertainment and enlightenment among educated Ottomans for such a long time. In the pursuit of these goals we have been willing to jettison some poetic cargo that other translators have thought quite important. The rhyme is mostly gone; it is not something we do much in poetry these days and it got in the way of producing good English poems. Occasionally readers will find clear traces of *redîf*, the practice of including a word or phrase that is exactly repeated after each rhyme, but the rhyme itself is most often absent. We have usually kept the couplets. They did not interfere and felt right to us. But some poems just did not come out well in couplets, so for them we dropped the couplets too. Rhetorical complexities went, where they had to, along with obligatory notes.

As a result, our translations are quite risky and will be difficult for many of our scholarly readers. We have been willing throughout to take great liberties in order to express our understanding of the meaning and emotional impact of the originals. Our interpretations and the manner of their rendering will, of course, always be subject to someone else's notion of a "better" or "more correct" reading or more appropriate style of translation. In fact, a lively debate about how Ottoman poetry should or could be translated is one of the things we hope will result from this anthology.

When we first thought about this book, we wanted to do something radically new, to produce an anthology of translations of Ottoman poetry without scholarly notes. So we decided to replace notes and background and commentary with something more like a milieu. There are short biographies of the poets, both reflecting and translating the kinds of things contemporary biographers of poets would have said or did say about them. There are retellings of some of the popular romantic tales referred to in the lyrics. There are little excerpts from Ottoman writing and tidbits of information intended to give some idea of the breadth and character of Ottoman literary culture. (It should be noted that these pieces were translated by Andrews and Kalpaklı, who rendered the poetry in them in a very straightforward and less poetic manner than will be seen in Najaat Black's renditions of the anthologized poems.) And then there are pictures—many taken from or based on Ottoman miniatures—of things that attempt to give an idea of how certain themes and scenes were represented to Ottoman audiences. We even included texts of the original poems so that scholars who want to use the anthology for teaching can do their own commentary, and even "correct" our translations.

There are also notes. In the end, it was not possible to receive financial support for the project without promising to include notes. So there are notes—separated from the poems so that the anthology can be read without them—and they have turned out to be a welcome addition that takes the pressure off us scholars a bit by letting us show now and again that we knew what we were leaving out.

Because we did not want the notes to be crucial, we tried to select poems that translate well into English and do not need much additional explanation. This often meant omitting poems that depended on instances of homonymy, derivation, or reference that are peculiar to Ottoman Turkish. We also tended to avoid poems that turned solely about an uncommon point of Islamic myth or historical wisdom. It did not seem necessary to introduce either obscurity or obligatory glosses into our translations in order to give a reasonable overview of Ottoman lyric poetry.

The selection of poems also makes a significant gesture toward poems that have been anthologized or selected or commented upon by Turkish scholars for Turkish audiences. It should be mentioned that Turkish general audiences now read Ottoman poems only with the help of paraphrase-style translations and commentaries. This gesture is intended partially to offset the cultural bias inherent in choosing poems that work well in English and partially to begin a new translation effort by creating a shared experience for English-speaking and Turkish audiences. This also means that we have translated a number of "famous" poems which were also translated by Gibb or Walsh or others. The danger—a danger to which we are painfully sensitive—is that biases ingrained in the received scholarly tradition will simply be perpetuated. We only hope that our overall selection will dissipate some of the effects of any such bias.

Although we do not give examples of every possible lyric form used by the Ottoman poets, we have tried to represent a variety of forms. Here again our choices were driven mostly by the suitability of particular poems for translation into English. Most of the examples are *gazels* and some are stanzaic forms (*muhammes, sharkı*, etc.)—a distribution that generally reflects relative preponderances. In addition, we hope to have touched upon most of the main themes of Ottoman poetry: for example, the madnesses of love and intoxication, the pain of love, love and intoxication as metaphors for mystical-religious experience, advice and admonition.

Lastly we have tried to select poems from the work of major poets spanning a period from the fourteenth through the nineteenth centuries. Here the selection procedure is most problematic. No one will deny that the poets represented are for the most part major poets, but they are not the *only* major poets. There will be poets that some like better or consider more important that we will have left out. We have also included poetry by women, who, as a class, were not in a position to be considered major poets. Nonetheless, any anthology will reflect the interests, expertise, and tastes of its compilers. And so it is with ours.

Another area that demands some explanation is the actual state of the original texts. The situation of texts in Ottoman Turkish studies is largely anomalous. Since the alphabet reform of the early 1920s, most editions of Ottoman texts have been edited, not in their original Arabic script form, but as transcribed by editors into a modified modern Turkish (Latin letter) orthography. This means that the base, "edited" text is not a "version" of the original or an original but an editor's version of an already interpreted transcription of a manuscript or set of manuscripts. The obvious problem here is compounded by the fact that some scholars and anthologists have transcribed their own versions from single manuscripts and those versions are a variance with later "editions" representing an editor's reconciliation of a number of manuscripts.

The issue is even more complex because, especially in the case of major poets, the manuscripts do not unequivocally resolve many of our problems. A major poet's *dîvân* or collected works may well exist in anywhere from ten to one hundred different manuscripts each with quite reasonable variants for many poems. Thus we must establish a text for any poem by reliance on an "expert" judgment about a reasonable reading. In the case of the poems included in this anthology, we have selected poems that have been edited in one of the manners mentioned above. Where possible we have compared available versions with the idea of locating the version that most accurately represents the text agreed upon by the scholarly community. In a few cases the texts represent our own editing work. It is important to note, however, that it is not the purpose of this anthology to question or correct the received textual tradition for well-known poems by major poets.

A NOTE ON GENDER

Ottoman poetry is, at its core, love poetry. Even when the object of love is a beloved ruler or patron or the Deity or the Deity's reflection in a physical being, there is always a subtext that reflects the overwhelming emotions of intense erotic attraction. And for a number of reasons the nature of Ottoman poetic eroticism is an immensely sensitive subject. What everybody who knows Ottoman poetry understands quite well and what is very seldom discussed is that the beloved is often, if not most often, by convention and in a tradition antedating the Ottomans, a young man.

The reticence of Turks on this subject is understandable. As a general rule the West has often avoided responsibility for its own feelings and behaviors by attributing homoerotic desires to a degenerate and depraved "East." If Turks wish to avoid participating in this kind of distortion—even in the name of some sort of scholarly truth—it is not surprising. In the face of the relentless repression of similar behaviors by Western elites—the suppressed eroticism of the male-only British public and American private school, for example—it is quite rightly feared that such "truths" will be construed to reflect badly on Turks or the "East" or Islam. Nonetheless, the fact that the Turkish language does not distinguish gender either by endings or by pronouns allows Turks an honest avoidance of the issue that is not permitted to English translators. We were required to assign gender to the beloved. And what we have chosen to do, where we cannot leave gender ambiguous, is to represent the beloved as a woman.

The Ottoman society of the poetry-producing and -consuming elites was structured in a way that was highly conducive to a naturalized eroticism that did not distinguish between male or female objects. Public institutions—the army, the bureaucracy, the palace, the educational system—were entirely male. In general theory and at some times and places, women were severely restricted in their public appearances; for a woman to be visible or talked about was most often considered to be scandalous for the family involved. Unrestricted women were usually either members of minorities or thought to be prostitutes. Young men, from shop boys to elite slaves to the sons of the elites, however, were quite visible and often educated in the conventions of poetic eroticism. Where it was risqué but tolerable to make poetic comments and erotic advances to a boy, it would be far more serious (and insulting and dangerous) to direct such attention toward a woman or girl.

Moreover, in a situation—in no way restricted to the Islamicate East—where a huge power disparity existed between women and men, even the most powerful women were only able to wield power by the manipulation of men, who, in turn, were the only ones able to act directly in the public sphere. Among the cultural elites, this, combined with the social separation of men and women from a relatively early age, meant that many men viewed women as quite different and dangerous creatures. The male-centered dominant ideology considered men to be intelligent, straightforward, and relatively guileless, focused on spiritual concerns and broad ethical goals. In contrast, it saw women as generally devious, manipulative, deceitful, and concerned with the mundane surface of life and its frivolous adornments. The material world was often described as a woman: attractive on the surface but malignantly enticing men from appropriate otherworldly and intellectual concerns. So, in the light of this misogynistic fantasy, it is not surprising that there existed an often expressed notion that true and open intellectual, spiritual, and erotic relationships were far more possible with a male partner.

Accordingly, several poets wrote love poems about specific shop boys and other famous youthful male beauties and there are quite a number of poems (*shehrengîz*) consisting of brief, clever descriptions of the most attractive boys in some city. There are only a few such poems we know of that describe young women (always young women of the lower classes). We must also remember that poetic conventionality and traditionality allowed poets to distance themselves from responsibility for words and behaviors that would not have been tolerated in any other context. Poets could, in a sense, claim that they were only reenacting behaviors that had been permitted to poets for centuries without causing any calamity to society as a whole.

This is not to say that poets never wrote about female beloveds. There are any number of examples including some very tender poems addressed by Sultan Süleymân to his wife, Hürrem (see Halman 1987) and poems to powerful women of the court. Moreover, in the romantic narrative poetry, which is often concerned with rulers and dynasties and thus with families, male-female romance is predominant and includes love poems addressed from men to women and from women to men (see *The Story of Leylâ and Mejnûn* following poem no. 24), and the women protagonists of these narratives are often powerful, heroic, and sympathetic. However, even in these clearly gendered love poems the beloved is in no manner distinctly female and conventional terms for a young male beloved are often used even when the poet obviously has women in mind.

As time passes, by the eighteenth century at least, women have become more visible in the public lives and entertainments of the Ottoman elites and the presumption of a female beloved becomes more likely. Nonetheless, the conventions show only very minor changes and there is still no way to tell the gender of a beloved from the internal evidence of the poem. Thus there is always an ambiguity, an ambiguity that convention shades toward a reading that includes a young male beloved.

It is important to remember that the slightest reference to gender in Ottoman poetry raises issues for us today of homoeroticism and homosexuality and the historical contexts of discourses about both, which are sensitive and vexed issues that demand entire books of their own. We must consider, at least, that the discourses in which "homoeroticism" and "homosexuality" are meaningful did not exist for most of the Ottoman period and so are not part of the consciousness of Ottoman poets in the ways our own contexts might lead us to expect. (An excellent demonstration of the complex nature of Western discourse on Middle Eastern homoeroticism is Boone 1995; see also Andrews 1989.) We would urge our readers to remember that gender in Ottoman poetry is ambiguous and that they are welcome to read the gender of lover and beloved in any way that pleases them.

AN OTTOMAN POEM UNDER THE MICROSCOPE

The ways in which Ottoman poets and their audiences understood their poems, enjoyed, and created them are often quite different from what poetry-lovers are accustomed to today. Almost always these differences cannot be represented by a translation. So, for those who are curious, what follows is a dissection and microscopic look at one Ottoman *gazel*. The poem is from the *dîvân* of Zâtî (Tarlan 1970, 639), whose biography you will find in the Poets section. It was chosen because, like many of Zâtî's poems, it is unusually full of the peculiar things that Ottoman poets liked to do. The first couplet, which the Ottomans called the *matla'* (the place where a heavenly body rises), goes like this (if you want to try pronouncing the Turkish, see the above Note on the Pronunciation and Transcription of Turkish).

> Ġarîbem ġurbete düşdüm göñül âvâre yârum yoḳ
> Benüm âh etdügüm 'ayb eylemem kim iḫtiyârum yoḳ

First let us look at some of the elements of form. The rhyme in this couplet is complex, as is the case with many Ottoman poems. The rhyme itself is in *âr* (e.g. *yâr* and *ihtiyâr*). The *-um* after the rhyme is a possessive ending (my) and will be the same in every rhyme. The *yok* (it isn't, there isn't any, it does not exist) is the *redîf*. The word *redîf* originally meant "a person who rides into battle on the back of someone else's saddle," so the *redîf* rides behind the rhyme and is the same in every rhyming line. The first couplet (*matla'*) has two rhymes; the rest of the lines will have the same rhyme but only in the second half-line.

And now for the rhythm. The half-line is the largest rhythmical unit and is made up of a number of rhythm-feet, which the Ottomans (and Arabs and Persians and others) represented by word-patterns made up from the root *f–'–l* (where the backward apostrophe represents the consonant *'ayin*, which does not exist in our phonetic repertoire). As I mentioned above, a foot is made up of long and short syllables. A long syllable is either a closed syllable (consonant–short vowel–consonant) like *bab* or a consonant with a "long" vowel like *bâ*. A short syllable is a consonant and a regular or "short" vowel. Some vowels can be read either "long" or "short." The pattern of the rhythm of this poem is *mefâ'îlun, mefâ'îlun, mefâ'îlun, mefâ'îlun*: *short, long, long, long* (⏑ – – –) repeated four times. So the first half-line would divide rhythmically as follows:

> Ga-rî-bem-gur // be-te-düş-düm // gö-nül-â-vâ // re-yâ-rum-yok

Note that the syllable *te* in the second foot has one of the vowels that can be read either long or short. Here it is long. You can now scan the rest of the lines.

Ottoman poets like to emphasize and build upon relations between words. One way to do this is to use words that come from the same Arabic root as in the case of *garîb* and *gurbet* both of which come from the root *g–r–b* (this is the rhetorical figure the Ottomans call *ishtikâk*, "derivation"): *gurbet* is "exile, being away from home" and a person who is *garîb* is a stranger, or a person who acts strangely (not knowing how people around here are supposed to act). So the line begins "I am a stranger [or I act strangely], I have fallen [*düşdüm*] into exile [I am all of a sudden without a home]." Words may also be related by belonging to a group of related concepts (the figures *tenâsüb* or *mürâ'âtu'n-nazîr* "observing the similar"), as in the case of *âvâre* which means "vagabond or homeless person" as does *garîb*. So the rest of the line reads: "the [my] heart [*gönül*] is a vagabond, I have no beloved [*yâr*]." The sense of this is that the beloved is like a home or homeland to the heart, and one who has no beloved has a homeless heart.

However, Ottoman poets also love to include the possibility of a less obvious reading that makes a line interestingly ambiguous. For example, here *gönül âvâre* (period) is a sentence: "the heart is a vagabond." But if one reads *gönül–âvâre–yârum* then *gönül âvâre* becomes an adjective modifying *yâr* (beloved) and the line reads ". . . I have no vagabond-hearted beloved." This is to say, there are no beloveds around with unattached hearts who could make a home with my heart.

This ambiguity does fascinating things to the reading of the second line of the couplet which seems at first to read: "Don't make a fault/sin [*'ayb etmen*] out of my sighing [*âh etdügüm*] for I have no free-will [*ihtiyârum yok*]." This refers to the general principle of Islamic Law that a person cannot be held blameworthy in instances where free-will is lacking. So making a fool of oneself by moaning and groaning in public should not be considered a fault in this case. However, the second reading of the first line conjures up another reading of the second line. The word *ihtiyâr*, which means "free-will," also means "choosing, or the ability to choose between alternatives." So the second line can also be read: "don't make a fault out of what I am sighing about [thinking that it is my beloved], what I am really sighing about is that there are no unattached beloveds to choose a lover from [and this is not the sort of affront to polite society that moaning about a particular beloved would be—when a particular person and that person's family would be shamed by being identified as a beloved]."

The second couplet moves on to another image that seems related to the first only by the general theme of wandering and instability.

> Şu ḳarşuġı ḳara ṭâġdan geçem mi ebr-veş yâ Râb
> Hevâ-yı zülf-i yâr ile benüm bunda ḳarârum yoḳ

On the surface the couplet reads something line this: "Should I pass over [*geçem mi*] that black mountain [*kara dağ*] like a cloud [*ebr-veş*], oh Lord [*yâ Râb*] // With my [because of my] passion [*hevâ*] for my lover's [*yâr*] lock of hair [*zülf*] I have no stable place [no home] here/on this." However, Zâtî has employed another favorite rhetorical tool of the Ottomans that we recognize because the imagery in the second line does not *seem* to have any generic relation to that in the first. That is, the "passion" and "lovelock" do not seem to have much to do with the "mountain" and the "cloud". But the word *hevâ* which means "passion/infatuation, or the first [and most powerful and dangerous] degree of love," has a homonym *hevâ* that means "weather or atmosphere." So the poet invokes the figure *tevriye*, in which a word with two distinct meanings is used in a context where it could have either meaning and where the least obvious meaning gives the most interesting reading. Thus the lover is like a cloud—an image that builds indirectly on the previous couplet. He is like a cloud because of his instability but also because he is associated with the sigh (*âh*) that traditionally is depicted as a cloud of black smoke issuing through the chimney of the throat from the fire of the burning heart (or more commonly liver, which is the organ that burns with passion for the Ottomans). This black cloud is like a dark rain cloud that, like a lover, weeps as it wanders the earth. In this case the cloud, or lover turned into a cloud by sighing, wishes to cross an insurmountable obstacle (the black mountain) or, more likely, to hover over the mountain as clouds often do over high peaks. Thus the beloved's black hair is a mountain over which the lover wishes to hover, but the (stormy?) atmosphere/weather (*hevâ*) in her vicinity simply does not allow any such hovering. (Of course the weather in the vicinity of the beloved's locks is usually windy, which tousles the locks in an irresistible manner.) We must also remember that these multiple readings are not an either/or matter: all of the readings are implicated in the sense of the couplet.

It is in the third couplet, clearly the "couplet of the *gazel*" (*beyt'ül-gazel*) of the poem, that Zâtî took the play on double meanings to a bewildering extreme:

Raḳîbe ṣadr gösterdüñ ol fitneye ulu
Benüm bir it ḳadar veh veh ḳapuñda i'tibârum yoḳ

A first reading of the couplet would likely be: "You showed [*gösterdün*] the rival [*rakîb*] to the place of honor [*sadr*] and called [*dedün*] that troublemaker [*fitne*] Great One [*ulu*] // [while] alas alas [*veh veh*] I don't even have the respect [*i'tibâr*] of a dog [*it*] at your door [*kapu*]. This would be an unremarkable couplet were it not for the poet's stunningly clever use of multiple double meanings. In fact, this couplet became rather famous for exactly this reason. The sixteenth-century biographer of poets, Latîfî uses it as an example, without mentioning the author, in his discussion of the poems of Ahmed-i Dâ'î (ed. Cevdet, 86) and Gibb reproduces the passage from Latîfî in his *History of Ottoman Poetry* (vol. 1, 258 n 3) at the end of the nineteenth century.

Again the second reading is generated in part by the audience's understanding that an Ottoman poet will tend to group like things (*tenâsüb*). The comparison of the rival/protector (*rakîb*) to a dog is an old and standard one. But what if we go looking for more "dog things"? Well, Latîfî points out that the word *fitne* (troublemaker) can also, in the dialect of the common people, mean a kind of small dog. It doesn't mean that anymore so far as we can tell, and neither we nor Gibb have run into any other usages like this. Nonetheless, the common street language of the sixteenth century is not very well known to us and none of Latîfî's contemporaries take issue with this reading, so there is good reason to conclude that it is a reasonable or possible one. If we keep hunting, we see that the word *ulu*, which as a noun/adjective means "great/great one," can also be the imperative form of the verb *ulumak*, which means "to howl." Further along, the reduplicate *veh veh* (alas alas) is also a common onomatopoeia for the yapping of a dog. And while we are hunting double meanings, it should be pointed out that the word *sadr* that means a place of honor in the phrase "you showed [*gösterdün*] the place of honor [*sadr*]" is also the word for "chest/breast."

Thus the couplet implies another reading that says: "You showed your chest to the rival and told that little mutt, 'Howl!' while I have less respect than a dog [i.e., that dog/the rival] going yip yip at your door." There is also the implication that the beloved exposed him/herself in some way to the rival and set him to reciting poetry, which Zâtî, the great poet, compares to the yapping of a little dog. Rivalries among poets were at least as intense as rivalries among lovers.

The next two couplets move on to fill out the poem pleasantly without such extravagant excursions into multiple meaning.

Benümle olmasan gelmez nigârâ yanuma şâdî
Melâlet deñlü fırḳatde benüm bir ġam-güsârum yoḳ

This couplet reads: "If you are not with me [*Benümle olmasan*], oh beloved [lovely as a work of art], joyousness [*shâdî*] never comes to be with me // In separation [*fırkat*] [from you] I have no friend to drive away grief [*gam-güsâr*] like depression [*melâlet*." The rhetorical tool employed here is not collecting like things but creating oppositions (*teẓâd*). There is also a "folded" parallelism: you (beloved)—joyousness // depression—a friend (that drives my grief away). So the idea is that the beloved is equivalent to joy, and when the beloved is not there, the most joy that her replacement can offer is depression. This is also an example of the kind of artistic exaggeration that Ottoman poets are so fond of.

The last line is the "signature couplet" (crowining couplet or *tâj beyt*). It contains the pen name of the poet and, in this case, echoes some of the rhetorical features of the rest of the poem.

Dedi yârum ṣıyam bir gün sınıḳ göñlüñ gibi başuñ
Eger 'ahdi bütün olursa Ẕâtî inkisârum yoḳ

One reading of the couplet might be: "My beloved [*yârum*] said, I will break [*sıyam*] his head [*baş*] one day [*bir gün*] like his broken [*sınık*] heart [*gönül*] // But if her oath [*'ahd*] is whole [*bütün*], oh Zâtî, I will not be down-hearted." There is both a gathering of like things here (*tenâsüb*) and a reference to a double meaning. The word represented here by "down-hearted" is *inkisâr* which comes from the Arabic root *k–s–r* which has the sense "to break." Hence *inkisâr* also means "to be broken". So a reading of the line focusing on the *tenâsüb* might be: "My beloved said, I will break his head one day as I broke his heart; if her promise remain unbroken, oh Zâtî, I won't be broken up about it." What non-Ottomans might miss about this is the exaggerated devotion the poet implies by saying, "If she will just keep her promise and pay enough attention to me to bother breaking my head, I will be happy."

Not every Ottoman poem is so rhetorically intricate. Zâtî is notorious for the complexity of his verses, a characteristic that made it difficult to find poems of his suitable for our style of translation. Nonetheless, this *kind* of complexity was valued by Ottoman poets and their audiences and should be recognized as more than accidental when it also shows up in our translated versions. One of the things that Ottoman poets could do because they worked with limited, stable, conventional components was to take wild flights of rhetorical fancy and revel in subtle allusions and barely perceptible connections. This is exactly what we cannot do. Our poetic universe is highly individualistic and unconventional and today lacks even the sources of generally understandable reference that the Bible and the Greek/Roman "classics," for example, provided for the poetry-consuming elites of previous generations.

PERIODS AND THE CANON

The issue of periodization is, for the Ottomanist, a vexed and quite vexing one. For many years scholars have blithely assumed that there *was* an entity corresponding to "the Islamic/Middle Eastern literatures" that could be periodized as if the peculiar story of development told about European literature were universally applicable. Thus we have had "classical Islamic/Middle Eastern literature" and "medieval Islamic/Middle Eastern literature" and "modern" Turkish, Arabic, Persian literature, the latter no longer "regional" or "religional" because the modern must be "national" and not defined by an area or religion. Gibb's periodization of Ottoman poetry is even more bizarre, combining political periods (e.g., "the Süleymânic Age") with uniquely European notions (e.g., "romanticism," "classicism") and periods determined according to supposed influences from more competent literatures (e.g., "the first, second... Persianizing period"). In this manner, the whole project has become so contaminated by an almost ludicrous ethnocentrism that it seems fraught with peril even to attempt a synthetic overview of the development of Ottoman poetry. I believe that we are simply not ready to do so adequately. We lack reasonable, agreed-upon criteria for talking about development. We also lack the specific studies from which such criteria could be derived.

This is not to say, however, that we Ottomanists have no sense of development. Clearly, something happens to literature in the Ottoman dialect about the time of Ahmed Pasha and this something starts being done quite well after Nejâtî. The Zâtî and Bâkî kind of rhetorically powerful poetry is vastly influential through the time of Nef'î. The "Indian school" manifests itself strongly from Nef'î, Nâ'ilî, and Neshâtî through

Sheyh Gâlib. There is a noticeable shift of focus in Nâbî and a revolution in Nedîm that ferments in those who come after him until it bursts into our consciousness with the "modernizing" literature of the late nineteenth century. But these are not "periods" as such; they cannot be narrowly delimited by this century or that or confined to influences of the work of a few canonical poets. As one looks at the literature of the whole central Islamic world after Timur (the early fifteenth century) it is even difficult to see a reasonable pattern of literary history that confines itself to the literature of one particular language. Poets easily and regularly transcend languages. A single Ottoman poet might write in Turkish and Persian and Arabic and Eastern Turkic (Chaghatay). So also do poets transcend styles and influences. And when we have looked for parallels to this in narratives about our own historical poetic experience to help us sort things out we have distorted the Ottoman experience immensely.

So we are going to begin with this much said. Our work is, after all, a compromise driven by the wish to reintroduce Ottoman poetry to as many audiences as we can. We would like it to be more possible to teach a course on Ottoman poetry in translation, to include Ottoman poetry in a course on Middle Eastern literature, or world literature, or Ottoman history. And we would like to give people who read poetry just for the love of it an opportunity to acquaint themselves with a fascinating and all but invisible poetic tradition.

When the last word must be written and the book sent to press, one becomes painfully aware of all that could not be done. But if this book is a beginning of things, it will be enough. If it should be a last word then it would be inadequate even were it ten times longer.

The Gathering of Desire

1. Nesîmî

d. ca. 1404

Oh my idol of the temple, in the dark of night,
    in the early dawn, far from you—I burn
And when I long for our desired union,
    within an even greater fire—I burn

The searing fire of love, with desire's flames,
    has laid waste to my soul
See how brilliantly I burn, like the sun,
    like the moon

The pain of being far from you causes me
    to bleed
From deep within me blood pours
    from my eyes—I burn

The image of your sun-cheek always appears
    before me, shining
From its heated brilliance, one ray falls
    upon me—I burn

Grief for you has thieved from my hand
    both patience and peace of heart
I'm not burning from winds of passion,
    from truest grief—I burn

Smoke rises from within me, coloring
    the wheel of the skies
Look! I am in flames! See my burning!

This is not hidden—for the beloved,
    I burn
If she wishes in her cruel heart
    to set me flaming—I burn

Those who speak ill say Nesîmî is burning
    with grief, it's true
For he who burns with grief, the beloved
    loves him deeply—so deeply I burn

2. Ahmed-i Da'î

d. ca. 1500

The torture of the beloved is no punishment
    at all
Thank God for the faithfulness of your cruelty

There are many beloveds with cypress-bodies,
    witch-eyes, and trouble-making brows
But not one of them has been so enticing
    as you!

If those who thirst for the wine of your rubied lips
    gave one thousand lives
One thousand lives for just the dregs—
    it would be cheap!

No matter how much I am separated from you,
    no matter how far
Your image remains constant within my soul

Oh my beloved, why do you withhold our union?
It does not befit you to torment your slave
    this way!

Do a favor for the lovers, bring joy and captivate
    their hearts
One must be faithful, for we know beauty
    does not last

From my heart, I love you dearly,
    more than life itself
Believe me, God knows there is no error
    in what I say

3. Sheyhî

1375–1431

Your sun-face is a mirror of the soul
I know
An image of both worlds is found within
I know

The artist who could paint one point
on the circle of your beauty
Would be famed as a master in this world
I know

Your glance says, "I will lay waste to the city
of your heart!"
This is a royal order from the Sultan
I know

I can't understand the deceits of your eye
and brow
One is sedition, the other disaster
I know

You've recognized your slaves with the favor
of torment
But it's been long since you've thought of me
I know

Oh sufi, who sees goodness in your hypocrisy
Abandon such thoughts, it slanders the faith
I know

Oh Sheyhî, you need the garden, the beloved,
wine and the *saz*
All that's left is the life of this moment—
grief and sadness
I know

The garden, the beloved, wine, and the saz

From the *Dîvân-i Hâfiz*, Süleymaniye Kütüphanesi, Hâlet Efendi 647 (fol. 25b)

4. Sheyhî

It's the season of spring, let us be
    cheek to cheek with the east wind
Let us be friends with the rose,
    and companions of its scent

It is the time of the wild tulip—
    with pure hearts let us take up the cup
Like the narcissus, let us be drunk
    without pretense

Like the rosebud, keep hidden the secrets
    of your fate
But like the blooming rose, let your heart
    be open to the pleasure of the field

Jem said the cup is the key, throwing open
    the gates of the city
Come, let us be disciples of the cup
    that reveals the secrets of this world

Let us await God's mercy, for we have sinned
If we expect rewards for obedience—
    forgive us

Oh Sheyhî, the wise say it is madness
    to ask God's forgiveness in the spring
Today, let us know the pleasure of the season,
    tomorrow we may bow as saints

5. Ahmet Pasha

d. 1497

Ask about my wailing from the prayers
    of the bird of dawn
Ask about my suffering from the wounded heart

Ask the letter, damp with tears, about the fire
    of my sighs
Ask the burning pen as it writes the tale
    of my grief

I know desire for your shining cheeks
    from the candle of the moon
Ask about the pleasure of your lips
    from sugar and from honey

Ask about emptying the purse of my life
    for your sake
Ask the bowl of the skull when my body
    has turned to dust

If you don't believe I've turned to dust
    ask the east wind
Ask the wind returning home with dust
    upon its feet

Oh wind, who is my herald, go ask
    that love-thief
Ask her why she sent me, weeping,
    out of sight

In the valley of exile your slave Ahmed
    has fallen to his knees
Ask the cycle of the moon about the torments
    he suffered along the way

The *Mejlis*: Gathering of Desire

The Ottoman lyric can be many things, but most often it is a song, a song of longing and desire expressing itself in the setting of a gathering of dear friends. This gathering—the *mejlis*—with its cast of characters, its locations, its food and drink and music and dance, is central to lyric poetry as lyric poetry is central to it.

If there were to be an ideal gathering, with all that this party should have, it would be set in the evening of a springtime, on the warm lawn of a garden caressed by gentle breezes. The company of close friends would be gathered within the garden walls, each a brilliant conversationalist, a poet, emotionally sensitive, open, spiritually aware. By the light of perfumed candles they would partake of delicious foods, roast meats, fruits and nuts and candies of every kind, accompanied by the purest wines in crystal bowls. And these would be served by the loveliest of youths, in whose features the beauties of the garden reflect: rose cheeks, bud lips, hyacinth hair, lawn of cheek-down . . . Musicians would play, dancers dance, and sweet-voiced storytellers recite the tales and poems of love, and through all this would run the threads of sparkling conversation. Thus, their hearts freed by intoxication and passion, the truest of partygoers would spend all night in their revelry and greet the dawn with yet more wine and the embrace of a beloved now languid-eyed with drink and sweet fatigue.

There would be occasion to recall that the intoxication of the mystic opens the heart to experiencing the divine, that the Prophet's Son-in-Law, 'Alî, called together the Forty Perfect Saints in Paradise, where a gathering was held in which all became intoxicated by the juice of a single grape and danced the archetype of mystical dance. Within the sanctuary of friendship and trust, there would also be a harsh word or two for those who censure the party: the bigots, the ascetics, the religious literalists and dry moralists, those who renounce beauty and pleasure without ever understanding what they mean. They are like the beloved's protectors who would bar the lover's pursuit of passion and the joy of union.

Even the Sultan had his own gathering. A precious few of the most brilliant, witty, and talented of the Empire's elites would be appointed *musâhibs* (conversational companions) to the ruler. As such they were allowed behind the public façades of the palace into the private quarters of the Sultan where they would enact with him the party of which the poems and poets sing. As the ultimate of earthly beloveds, focal point of worldly desire, the Sultan radiated power onto his lovers and close friends. So too would access to the intimate gatherings of any power-holder promise fulfillment of material needs, and thus, at the core of many "political" or "economic" relations were relations of love, companionship, and trust.

There were many parties, parties in the full bloom of summer, in the fall, indoors during the winter, picnics, boating parties, drunken debauches and refined soirées. But they all share a great deal and what they share is consistently referenced in the poetry. And if, as we read an Ottoman lyric poem, we remember the party, its characters and characteristics, then the often bewildering shifts of focus from line to line might begin to resolve themselves into the scripting of conversational flights in the context of a familiar gathering.

6. Ahmet Pasha

Is there any heart not bleeding
  from the arrows of your glance?
Is there any life not sacrificed
  to the bow of your brow?

A life spent without you is a life
  lived in vain
If your true love is absent,
  your own soul has fled

My beloved, with her glance,
  she slays one thousand lovers
Yet that's nothing compared
  to the trouble she might cause!

That idol has covered her woman's tresses,
  but not abandoned her pagan ways
She has cut the belt around her delicate waist,
  but not yet become a Muslim

I have wept so much blood longing
  for your rubied lips
Every door and wall of your town
  are made coral from my tears

When the moth of my soul recalls
  the shining lamp of your beauty
There is no party not warmed
  by our passion, our verse

All our hearts are gathered in your dark curls—
  what if the wind unbinds them?
Will there be any of us not disheveled
  and crazed with thoughts of love?

At dawn Ahmed catches the scent of the rose,
  and in his anguish sighs, ahhh!
There's not a nightingale in the garden
  whose heart is not burned by love

7. Nejâtî

d. 1509

Those glances rain down arrows on the country
  of the spirit
Like the black Tatar shaman bringing rain
  with a magic stone

Separated from you, my eyes rain water
  and then rain blood
They scatter your path with pearls
  and then with coral

The people of the world know of my weeping
  by the smoke of my sigh
They know when the black wind blows
  there will be a deluge

I have wept so many tears, now only blood
  will flow
From this day on, the torrent will be red
  'til it runs dry

The saki, with her Jesus-breath, pours down
  life from the bowl of her lips
Saying to the gathering of friends,
  "This is *your* drink of wine!"

Those on your threshold will spill tears
  when they hear my sighs
When the south wind blows from Mecca
  heavy rains are known to fall

The bow-browed one rains down arrows
  with her sharp glances
The shafts of anger pointed with hailstones
  of disaster

Upon seeing the hearts caught on the points
of your dark curls
One would suppose some great serpent were pouring
fire from its jaws

Oh Nejâtî, is there a price to be put on your
jewel-scattering pen?
Every drop rained down from that black spring cloud
becomes a pearl

The saki (lovely wine-pourer) and the gathering of friends
From the *Dîvân-i Hâfiz*, Süleymaniye Kütüphanesi, Hâlet Efendi 697 (fol. 15b)

8. Nejâtî

The heart is pleased when black down covers
your shining cheek
The sun of the love-thief rises when the moon
is dark

My beloved, is it fitting that you long
for the empty steppe?
There your glance will become a thief,
your eye a wild gazelle

Oh my idol, when there is the dust of the places
you have been
To say "Paradise!" would be using sand to cleanse
for prayer, when there is water

Since I became a lover, I eat only trouble
and torment
When one falls sick, he craves food
of the strangest kind!

Following the path of the beloved, I shout
"yâ hû"!
And hope that loving spirit will turn
and give her glance to me

The east wind told the musk of China about the scent
of your dark curl
Saying, "Why go to Anatolia when the perfumed one
is there?"

Don't call me crazy when I don't follow
your advice
Those who are wise will mind their
own affairs!

Oh my heart, how am I to put my mind
    at ease?
When I see her, I lose my senses, without her
    I lose my life!

Oh Nejâtî, who will invite you
    to the party of friends
Now the beloved has said, "I won't go
    if he is there!"

9. Nejâtî

Those tulip-cheeked ones—what they dared do
in the garden!
Beside them, the cypress could not sway,
nor the rosebuds open

They wouldn't let the wild tulip into the
conversation of the roses
Saying it was a stranger from the distant
steppes

The custom of the beautiful ones is tyranny
and torment
But they've never ruined anyone the way
they've ruined me!

What about those brows like a bow,
those pointed glances?
They left their arrows in my breast,
wouldn't allow my heart to beat

There are a thousand beauties
as lovely as Joseph
But they are never sold, never seen

So praise God for our sakis, with their
life-giving wine!
They don't let us thirst for the water of life,
nor for the rivers of Paradise

Hey Nejâtî, have patience, what can you do?
Who among the lovers has not learned torment
from the beauties?

The young and beautiful Joseph is sold into slavery
From Fuzûlî's *Hadîkatü's-sü'edâ*, Süleymaniye Kütüphanesi, Fâtih 4321 (fol. 38b)

10. **Nejâtî**

Spiraling, the sparks
 of my sigh
 reach the skies
Where the heart of the lamp
 of the heavens
 burns, turning.

Does the one hanging
 by the noose of your curl
 touch his feet to the ground?
With delight
 he surrenders his life
 twisting,
 twirling.

The pigeon returning
 circles with this message:
 the black Damascus
 of your curl
 has destroyed
 the Egypt of my heart.

If your door
 were not the Kaaba
 the sun and moon
 would not forever,
 like holy pilgrims,
 circle around it.

The mirrors, turning,
 those hopeful eyes,
 constantly watching the ones
 who come and go.

Those mirrors, suspended,
    the facets of their eyes
    shining—
    maybe the one they see
    is you!

You rise, you dance
    spinning,
    I bow my head
    I submit.
And yet—it's your twisting curl
    that embraces your silver breast!

Oh Nejâtî
    at this royal party
    it would be pleasing
    for the musician to dance,
    before the Sultan,
    before the beloved, turning,
    reciting this fresh new verse.

Iskender/Alexander, Hızır, and the Fountain of Eternal Life

The hero Iskender, as he and his adventures appear in Ottoman poetry, is a mixture of Alexander the Great and the mysterious Zu'l-Karneyn (most likely "He of the Two Horns" or "He of the Two Epochs" or "Lord of East and West") mentioned in the Quran (Sura XVIII, The Cave, verses 83–101). The Quranic parable is brief and without details of context, so a huge folklore has grown up to explain and expand upon it.

The character of Hızır binds together a vast number of stories and several other characters. He is often associated with the prophet İlyâs (Elias). The two are sometimes joined in one person (Hızrellez or Hızr-i İlyâs) and at other times they are depicted as partners. Also in the Quran (Sura XVIII, 60–82), is a parable in which Moses is guided by a person called just "One of Our Servants." This person is taken to be Hızır, who is therefore considered to be the ultimate spiritual guide. In popular Turkish culture, Hızır is the immortal man who has the power to bring the dead to life and who shows up at the last moment to rescue the deserving hero from hopeless situations. The Arabic word *ḫıẓr* is a sign for "green," which further links Hızır to immortality and the wide-spread folklore character known as "the green man."

The story of Alexander and Hızır that echoes most often in Ottoman poems goes more or less as follows (in a very much abbreviated version).

When Darius the Persian captured Anatolia, he turned it over to his vassal Philip, whose daughter he married before returning to his capital. The daughter gave birth to a son who was to be the heir to his grandfather's lands, a boy whom the stars heralded as a future conqueror of the known world. Under Philip's guardianship, the lad, named Iskender (Alexander), was educated by the greatest philosophers of the day: Plato, Hippocrates, Aristotle, and Socrates. When Iskender reached the age of fifteen, his grandfather died and he succeeded to the throne. After converting to Islam with the help of Hızır who appeared mysteriously in disguise to set straight the materialistic Greek philosophers who had taken the boy's education as far as they could, Iskender has a vision which is interpreted as granting him lordship over all the earth.

The young ruler's ambitions are opposed by his father's successor and the invincible armies of Persia and its allies are brought against him. Nonetheless, the brave and cunning youth wins a surprising victory and adds all the Persian realms to his domain. He then turns his attentions to India, which he also conquers. Upon this there follows a long series of adventures and conquests that bring the hero into contact with all the strange and wonderful legends of the earth: the mount of serpents, the land where gold grows like grass, the amazons of Wak Wak, dragons and monsters and odd creatures in great profusion. However, out of these many exploits a few take on a poetic life of their own.

In one episode, an expansion of the Quranic parable mentioned above, Iskender is traveling in the East when he comes to a great range of mountains with a pass between two peaks. The people who live in the shadow of these mountains complain to the world-conqueror that two tribes of vicious barbarians live on the other side of the pass, from which they descend now and again to pillage and plunder. So Iskender has a huge dike built in the pass, piling it with chunks of iron and some precious metals—this was, after all, a pious deed! He then causes large fires to be built and fanned with giant bellows until the metal melts and forms an impenetrable coating over the dike. Thus the tribes of Gog and Magog (Jûj and Majûj) are shut up behind the "Dike of Alexander" until the Last Day, when they shall be released upon the earth.

Iskender goes on to defeat the demons of Mazenderan and in Egypt sets up his famous "Mirror of Alexander," which, like the "Cup of Jemshîd," reflects all of good and evil that happens in the world.

In the end, however, having seen all the wonders of the earth and having conquered all that he possibly could, Iskender faces the realization that the future holds nothing for him but loss and inevitable death. A wise man seeing his sorrow informs him of the existence of the Water of Life, of which one sip will make a man immortal. Iskender is again energized and sets out on his last great adventure accompanied by his vizier, Hızır. They travel to the uttermost East, passing through many more adventures, dangers, and opportunities to gain spiritual wisdom. Finally they arrive at the city of Fulfilled Desire (Shâdkâm) where dwell only women, who promise to help the hero in his quest.

Alexander in conversation with Plato

From Emir Husrev Dihlevî's *Mesneviler*, Süleymaniye Kütüphanesi, Aya Sofya 3776 (fol. 57b)

The Fountain of the Water of Life, the women say, lies not far away in the midst of an impenetrable darkness. Their hostesses guide them to the edge of the darkness and the conqueror, his armies, and his vizier plunge in. Wandering in the dark, the band is caught in a great storm that separates them each from each. As they all grope about in the murk, Hızır chances upon the fountain, drinks from it, and is made immortal. He then vanishes, never to be seen by Iskender again.

Finally the hero and his men emerge from the darkness, having failed to find the fountain. Iskender is discouraged, struck by the futility of all his conquests. He grows sad and ill; when even Plato cannot cure him, he dies and is buried with one hand unshrouded to tell the people of the world that even the greatest conqueror of the age left this life as empty-handed as he came into it.

11. Mihrî Hatun

d. 1506

I opened my eyes from sleep, and suddenly
raised my head
There I saw the moon-face of the love-thief,
shining

My star of good luck had risen—I was thus
exalted
When in my chamber I saw this Jupiter rise
to the evening sky

He appeared to be a Muslim, but by his dress
an infidel
And divine light poured from the beauty
of his face

I opened, then closed my eyes, but he had
vanished from my sight
All I know of him—he was an angel
or a faery

Now she knows the water of life,
Mihrî will not die until the Judgement Day
For she has seen that visible Alexander
in the eternal dark of night

12. Mihrî Hatun

At times, my longing for the beloved slays me
At times, union with him and the passing
of time slay me too

My enemy laughs at my condition, but I cry
on and on
How can my spirit endure this sorrow which kills
us all?

Oh you who doctors the sick heart with his image
The trouble is medicines, like poison, kill me

This day, all my friends and enemies, come crying
I've not yet met my fated end, but these perplexities
kill me

Oh my rival, if Mihrî dies on the thorn of love,
why grieve?
You dog! The grave-keeper stones you, but the
rose-mouthed one slays him too

13. Mihrî Hatun

My heart burns in flames of sorrow
Sparks and smoke rise turning to the sky

Within me, the heart has taken fire
like a candle
My body, whirling, is a lighthouse
illuminated by your image

See the rope-dancer of the soul, reaching
for your ruby lips
Spinning, descending the twist of your curl

The sun and moon came to your quarter,
circling in the sky
Bowing to you, faces in the dust
before your feet

Oh you with the bright face, radiant as Venus
The moon twisted into a crescent to resemble
your arching brow

When longing for an image of your lips
had befallen my heart
Oh Mihrî, then my heart burned
in flames of sorrow

An Ottoman rope-dancer

From the *Surnâme-i Vehbî* miniatures by Levinî Osman, Topkapı Palace Museum Library, Ahmed 3593 (fol. 54a)

14. Zeyneb Hatun

late 15th century

Remove your veil and illuminate the earth
    and skies
Make this elemental world more brilliant
    than any paradise

When your lips stir, the rivers of Paradise
    come to boil
Uncover your curls of ambergris, so the entire world
    may be perfumed

The black down of your cheek wrote a royal
    command to the east wind
It said—go quickly to Cathay and captivate all
    of China with your sweet scent!

Oh heart, the water of life is not your lot,
    nor sadly is the kiss of your beloved
Even if you wait one thousand years, searching
    like Alexander in the darkness

Oh Zeyneb, go simply, bravely,
    surrender all decoration
Abandon your love for this adorned
    and deceiving world

15. Revânî

d. 1524

What do you say about that cypress body
    that hunts the heart?
What do you say about that hyacinth curl,
    along with those cheeks of rose?

Oh Nâsih, let's not speak of the mole, the curl,
    and the black down of her cheek
What do you say of her brow with its alluring way?

Oh pious one, there is no place for you
    in this world!
What do you say of us, fallen in the dust
    with love?

Oh my beloved, the beauties make so many promises
    to the lover
Put aside their promise, what about the thigh
    that warms the thigh?

The zealot says, "Give up the cup!"
    He says, "Give up the wine!"
By God, Revânî, what do you say
    to such a trouble-making one?

16. Lâmi'î

1472–1532

Yesterday I saw that sun-faced beauty
gowned in sky-blue
I longed to lie before her like a shadow,
but she fled

I believed it was nightfall, that beloved sun
disappeared so quickly
Or clearly she was lightning, flashing
from a cloud

In fear of my rival, that dog, she longed
for her place of sleep
That deer-eyed beauty mistook her lover
for a wolf, and fled

My eyes sought the beloved, but she eluded
my thought
That lovely one, she is a faery or some vision

In a moment of joy, she revealed
her face and vanished
Perhaps she was the bird of fortune flying,
a shadow come and gone

Losing all restraint, I set the falcon
of my heart upon that pheasant
Now I have neither one, nor the other

Oh Lâmi'î, I have learned from the ways
of that faery
This wretched world is but an image
glimpsed in sleep

17. Zâtî

1477–1546

Oh heavens, why do you cry? Is your beloved seen
in all places, but never by your side?
Do you have a shining moon that wanders everywhere,
just beyond your reach?

Oh garden, has the season of autumn made your
face so wan?
Or do you have a swaying cypress who looks beyond
the wall?

Oh nightingale, you're always weeping and crying out
with every breath
Do you have a laughing rose that shares one shadow
with the thorn?

I cried, "Oh beloved, I must sacrifice my life
for your sake!"
With a thousand angers, she replied,"Your life!
Have you not already spent it?"

Oh Zâtî, like the beloved's curl you are
once again disheveled
Are you endlessly oppressed, or do you have a lover
as haunting as a jinn?

The Pleasantries of Zâtî

It was a fact of life for Ottoman poets and the people of their milieu that skill in witty conversation and the art of poking fun with apt verses was highly prized. Moreover, poets were expected to be rewarded for their cleverness—especially those poets who lacked wealth or high position. A splendid example of a poet who lived by his wits and made no pretense of desiring an official job of any sort was Zâtî who became famous during the apogee of Ottoman glory in the reigns of Süleymân (the Magnificent to Europeans) and his father, Selîm, in the sixteenth century. Zâtî collected a number of his most famous witticisms in a form that survives today. For the most part, they contain crude and amusing sexual references in the setting of very refined verse—a striking contrast to the delicate and often ethereal character of serious poetry. The following are two examples of more (or less) presentable vignettes which give some indication of relations between the poets and their patron-audiences and also point to the power of poets to wound by ridicule.

> At one time I was in conversation with a brilliantly lovely youngster of noble birth. In the course of our companionable chat I had let fall pleasantries of every description and that lantern of the gathering of the spirit was quite aroused by these witticisms. On his back he wore a smoke-colored European kaftan and he said to me, "My lord Zâtî, this kaftan is yours; come over tomorrow and get it from my room." I showed up the next morning and he said, "It has been put away in a trunk for you, but no one is home and my mother has the key. Don't trouble yourself to come back, I'll send a servant with it." "Lovely," I said and left. About a month passed, and I realized that he wasn't going to send the kaftan. So I composed a couplet and dispatched it to him. As soon as he saw it he sent me the kaftan's price. The couplet was this:
>
> Why bestir yourself so tardily in sending the cloak to us
> Had I been some donkey's dangle you'd clothe it without fuss
>
> At another time, one of the scions of nobility invited several high- born youths to his auspicious abode that they might, the same evening, enjoy an excellent party. They had also sent word to this guileless well-wisher of yours inviting him to come as well. When evening came, I arrived at the door of their blessed domicile and from within a poor unfortunate [servant] emerged to say, "Welcome sir, but the gathering has been postponed until tomorrow evening. If you would come tomorrow. . . ?" I accepted this as

true, turned, and departed. As a matter of fact, there had been someone attending who had been offended by me [in the past] and this person had said, "If he comes, I'm leaving!" And so they drove this poor fellow [me] away. The next day I accidentally learned what had happened. So I dashed off a bit of verse and sent it to them. They were so affrighted that they collected fifty silver pieces each— it came to eight hundred pieces in all—and dispatched them to me, saying, "Do us a favor and don't write anything else [about us]!" The verse was this:

I don't know what the lesson is, but from their gathering
Some bad actors drove Zâtî off last night with a trick

They dance about changing from face to face by turns
Playing magic lanterns by inserting a candle stick

18. Hayretî

d. 1535

We are not slaves of Süleymân, nor the captives
of Selîm
No one knows us, we are slaves of the shah
of generosity

One who is the servant of love has never bowed
to the nobles of this world
We are the Sultans of another world—
Hey look, whose slaves are we?

Don't think we thirst for the sweet water
of the rivers of Paradise
We eat sorrow and we gulp blood continuously
at our place of suffering

Oh my sultan of love, don't think we kneel
to the new beauty of youth
We are slaves of the ancient allure of your
radiant face

Oh Hayretî, we gave up the silken cloak,
we quit the dervish cap
We are only slaves of the coarse robes
of this world

19. Figânî

1505?–1532

My sad heart is burnt black in the fire
of my breast
My tears mirror your lip, red as blood-colored
wine

Above the torrent of my tears, the sphere
of Heaven turns
Just like a mill-wheel above the flooding
stream

Since that hard-hearted one destroyed the province
of my heart
It appears a ruined city, no stone left upon
a stone

The nine vaults of Heaven and the mighty
throne of God
Seem only bubbles on the vast sea of my tears

Oh Figânî, the dust of your body borne by your
cold, cold sigh
Is only a handful of earth cast to the
freezing gale

The Cosmos and the Earth

Although the Ottomans were quite competent and often innovative geographers and astronomers, the poetic and mystical cosmology remained fixed in ancient forms that provided a coherent and unchanging narrative linking all creation and binding it to both the Divine and the fates of human beings. The earth was surrounded by nine circles, nine crystalline domes or spheres. The outermost sphere, the ninth heaven, is called the "Heaven of Heavens [Sphere of Spheres]," "the Starless Sphere," or "the Throne of God." The eighth heaven contains the fixed stars (as opposed to the planets or "traveling stars") and the constellations, it is " the Sphere [Heaven] of Stars" or "the Sphere of Constellations" or "the Footstool of God." These two spheres are the domain of God's eternal commands and hence of an ultimate destiny separate from the day-to-day turns of fortune that befall earthly beings.

The next seven circles are the spheres of the planets, which include the sun and the moon. From the outside in they are the spheres of Saturn, Jupiter, Mars, Sun, Venus, Mercury, Moon. In the sublunary sphere, inside the circle of the Moon is the world of "being and place" (where things come into and go out of existence and where they are fixed by location in space and time). This world is also divided into spheres, the outermost being the sphere of fire, hot and dry. The next is that of air, hot and moist, followed by water, cold and moist, and finally by earth, cold and dry.

As the seven planetary spheres revolve they influence the fortune of human beings and can themselves be influenced. So do the poets often curse and implore the spheres, bewailing their misfortunes and begging for better days. The planets themselves are often personified: the Sun is the sultan of the heavens, the Moon is its grand vizier, Mercury is the scribe, Venus the musician, Mars the general, Jupiter the judge, and Saturn the treasurer. Each planet is also associated with a color or colors: the Moon is green or silver, Mercury blue, Venus white, the Sun yellow or gold, Mars red, Jupiter tan, Saturn black.

Jewels, which are the highest manifestation of the mineral world, are also influenced by the heavens. The ruby, for example, is just a black stone until it is brought from the mine and placed in the light of the Sun, which it absorbs to ignite its internal flame. The carnelian is a dull rock in the Yemen until it is shined upon by the double star called

Süheyl (Argus) and turns crimson. The same is true of all precious minerals: gold is created by the Sun, silver by the Moon, and so on.

The inhabited earth is also divided into seven climes ruled by the seven planets: India (Saturn), China (Jupiter), the Land of Turks (Mars), Northern Iran (the Sun), Central Asia (Venus), Europe (Mercury), the Land of the Bulgars (the Moon). The seven climes are associated with the seven seas and all are surrounded by the Encompassing Ocean and the circling range of the impassable Kâf mountains.

This is but a glimpse of the surface of a vastly elaborated cosmology that serves the Ottoman poet as the source of countless allegories, metaphors, and comparisons.

20. **Figânî**

Your kiss does not satisfy the heart,
    it is crazy with desire for our union
Friend, please forgive me, but this world
    is a world of greed

Your body rises like the dead on Judgement Day,
    you are my promise of Paradise
Alas! You will turn me to dust before
    I have truly died

I fell in love with the moon-faced one
    whose name I cannot mention
Even in Edirne, city of beauties,
    she outshines them all

That which makes me crazy, raving,
    and dressed in mourning clothes
Is she of the black brows and the chestnut eye

Oh Figânî, if you wish to know
    that rose-mouthed one
She is a speaking nightingale in the garden
    of deepest beauty

21. Fevrî

d. 1570

The arrow of your glance pierces my wounded
heart
Separation from your pure ruby troubles
my soul
The thought of the black down on your cheek
turns me to dust
Come, my soul—or separation from you
will destroy me!

By the treachery of the turning skies you are
far from me, oh moon
The seven-layered heavens are colored blue
by the smoke of my sigh
If you have a wish of God, a wish of happiness
in both worlds
Come, my soul—or separation from you
will destroy me!

Since you have gone, the heart has become so
sick from pain
It is unable to speak, and knows not where
it dwells
Let my breast hold you once again—do me
a favor, do me a kindness
Come, my soul—or separation from you
will destroy me!

Pain and grief have made me sick and taken
my strength away
Both my body and my soul may soon
depart
Without you, only one breath in my body
remains
Come, my soul—or separation from you
will destroy me!

The sword of longing has cut this broken heart
to pieces
Into each fragment, the dagger of separation
has put one thousand wounds
It's time for you, through union, to cure
the one who has no cure
Come, my soul—or separation from you
will destroy me!

For so long I have not seen your sun-face
nor beheld your moon-cheek
My heart is ill, and cries and wails
to the sky
If you wish to know the face of God through
kindness, then come to me
Come, my soul—or separation from you
will destroy me!

Oh you, with a cheek like Paradise, since Fevrî
has been apart from you
His soul has been tortured in a hell of suffering
and torment
For the sake of Muhammad, have mercy on me,
the sinner
Come, my soul—or separation from you
will destroy me!

22. Hayâlî

d. 1557

They do not know how to search for the World-Adorner
in their world
The fishes live in the ocean but do not know
what the ocean is

Hey ascetic, don't talk about the tortures of Hell
to the tavern-goers
Those who live for the moment do not know the grief
of the coming day

Covered in dawn-colored blood, lovers do not see
love's wound
They do not recognize the mote in the sunbeam,
they do not know the moon in the sky

Those who tie the bowstring of tears to their bent
bodies
They shoot the arrow of desire, but do not know
for what the bow is made

Oh Hayâlî, those who pull the shawl of poverty
over their naked bodies
Are proud they do not know satin and brocade

A Peri (female Jinn)

From Topkapı Palace Museum Library, Hazine 2165 (fol. 64b)

23. Hayâlî

We are among those who came to be moths
to the candle of beauty
Oh glowing candle, we are among those
who came burning

The orphans of my tears wander your quarter
begging for gifts and favors
Oh my beloved, we are among those who came
for your gift of mercy

Oh beguiling one, to befriend the dogs
who guard your door
We are among those who came to be near you
in an honorable way

Oh ascetic, don't forbid us our wine
and our beloved!
Since the origin, we are among those who travel
this path as drunken friends

Oh Hayâlî, we have bound together a new book
in sweet description of your cheek
Oh my sultan, we are among those who came
to recite our verses before you

24. Hayâlî

When dawn hennas her hands with the blood
of the horizon
Let the new bride of the golden veil uncover
her shining face

Let her make the skies the envy of the pleasure-house
of Jemshîd
Let her brilliant cheek shine to every limit
of the universe

Let Venus make the dazzling ray a string
for her *saz*
Let her make a harmonious song out of the melody
of Virgo

Let the bowl of the sun pour out the dregs
of illumination
Let every mote be drunk and dance upon seeing
her bright face

Let me take that glass in hand and gaze
Until the desired one is mirrored in the magic
of the glass

Should I not stare into the bowl, my eyes
are bubbles floating
In the wine I see both worlds, elusive,
like writing on the water

Oh Hayâlî, they say wine is the brilliance
of the face of the wise
And the full bowl lights the lantern
of the poet's eye

The Story of Leylâ and Mejnûn

The story of Leylâ and Mejnûn, by Ottoman times, was a tale told often, appearing in numerous poetic-narrative versions, including well-known renditions by the famous Persian poets Nizâmî (1140–1202) and Jâmî (1414–1492) The tale was subsequently rendered in Turkish by several poets, such as Hamdî (1449–1503) and the Azeri master-poet Fuzûlî (d. 1556). It also existed in many prose versions in the popular oral tradition. The summary here is adapted from elements of several versions.

The ubiquitousness of this story can be seen by the numerous references in the lyric poetry of the Perso-Turkic tradition to Mejnûn, the crazed lover (*mejnûn* in Arabic means "crazy, mad") and his beloved Leylâ (*Leylâ* is related to the Arabic *leyl*, which means "night"—from which numerous poetic conceits about dark hair, the night of despair, etc. are created). This story is often referred to without elaboration with the expectation that contemporary audiences would fill in the details.

For the mystics, the story of Mejnûn has a special resonance. It is read as an extended allegory of the spiritual progress toward abandonment of self and the final rejection of the worldly, physical object of passion in favor of annihilation in the unity of existence, which is pure passion's true object.

A boy named Kays was born to a well-to-do family belonging to a powerful Arab tribe. This long-hoped-for son was his father's darling and grew to be a handsome child. At school he became acquainted with the young and lovely Leylâ, with whom, despite the innocence of their tender ages, he fell deeply and passionately in love. Leylâ returned his love with equal force and the two grew daily closer and more devoted, until they had time for little else than each other. Thus, Kays became known among his fellows by the name Mejnûn ("the Crazed [with love]").

When the story of this love reached the ears of Leylâ's parents, they were scandalized by the impropriety of the relationship and removed Leylâ from school, secluding her so that she could bring no more disgraceful gossip upon the family. Mejnûn, distraught at finding himself unable to meet with Leylâ, began to haunt her neighborhood, attempting to see her by donning disguises as a beggar or wandering dervish. Thwarted in the end by the vigilance of Leylâ's guardians, Kays begins to appear truly mad and wanders from town into the wilderness, where he lives in solitude for a time.

Meanwhile, Mejnûn's father sets out to search for his son, whom he discovers in the wild, ragged and disheveled, unable to recognize even his own father. Some semblance of sanity seems to be restored to the young man when his father promises to seek out Leylâ as his bride. And so Mejnûn returns to his family but resists all their well-meaning attempts to turn him from his devotion to Leylâ.

After a time, Mejnûn goes secretly with some friends to the place where Leylâ lives and contrives to meet with her briefly at her tent. However, when his identity is discovered, he is driven away. Wishing to help, his father goes to Leylâ's tribe, but when he asks Leylâ's hand for his son, he is told that she cannot be married off to a madman. The father insists that Mejnûn is not mad but merely distraught because of the intensity of his love. He then asks Mejnûn to come forth to prove his sanity. Unfortunately, just at that moment, Leylâ's dog approaches him, recognizing him as an old friend. The wretched Mejnûn, overwhelmed by the knowledge that the dog has recently been with Leylâ, falls upon it with a shower of affection. This display of unbalanced behavior brings the negotiations to a sudden and unsuccessful halt, and the disappointed lover once again flees to the wilderness.

The father again seeks out his son and attempts to cure him, by taking him on a pilgrimage to the Holy City of Mecca. But once there, Mejnûn prays at the Sacred Kaaba, not that he be cured but that his love and its torment be increased. Next his father enlists the intercession of a holy man, who is likewise unsuccessful. The power of religion having failed to cure him of his love, Mejnûn continues to wander the wilderness, writing impassioned lyrics that are repeated by strangers until they reach the ear of Leylâ, who responds in kind by writing poems that she leaves on the road to be picked up and recited by any who pass.

There follow a number of other attempts at intercession by the family, friends, and relatives of Mejnûn, who variously employ stratagems, entreaties, and outright warfare to unite the lovers. None of this is successful, and Mejnûn continues to haunt the desert, befriending the animals, composing poetry, and becoming madder with each passing day.

In one incident, hoping to encounter Leylâ, Mejnûn allows himself to be chained—as madmen were in those days—and led about the country by an old woman who uses him as a partner in her begging. In time they come to Leylâ's dwelling but upon finding himself on her threshold the poor lover's madness only increases to the point at which he bursts his chains and again escapes to the desert.

In time, Leylâ is married off by her well-meaning parents to a wealthy man but refuses to consummate the marriage or renounce her love for Mejnûn. Meanwhile, her maddened lover continues to wander the wastelands, surrounded by bands of shy gazelles, protected in his sleep by lions and panthers, emerging only to weep for a moment at the grave of his father, who has died, broken-hearted at the sorry fate of his beloved son.

Further attempts at a cure for Mejnûn or reunion of the lovers come to naught, and finally, with the death of her husband, Leylâ resolves to seek out Mejnûn. She goes to the desert, where they encounter each other and both faint away from the intensity of their passion. Upon recovering, Leylâ takes Mejnûn to her encampment and the two spend a brief time embracing until Mejnûn's madness returns and he flees again to the wilderness, focused solely on his love, no longer able to recognize the beloved who was once its object.

This rejection and the inescapable fact of her lover's madness shatters the devoted heart of Leylâ, and, after a short time, she pines away and dies in anguish. When Mejnûn hears of her death, his torment is increased. He makes a series of visits to her grave, and finally returns for the last time. Begging death to take him, he throws his now broken and wasted body on Leylâ's tomb and so gives up his final tenuous hold on life.

Leylâ's caravan finds Mejnûn in the wilderness surrounded by wild beasts

From the *Hamse-i Dihlevî*, Süleymaniye Kütüphanesi, Hâlet Efendi 377 (fol. 117b)

25. Fuzûlî

d. 1556

Oh God, don't let anyone be like me,
    crying and disheveled
Oh God, don't let anyone be an addict of love's
    pain and separation's blow

Always I have been oppressed by those merciless
    idols, those beloveds
Oh God, don't let a Muslim be a slave
    to those infidels

I see the moon-faced one, thinking of killing me
    with her love
I'm unafraid, oh God, just don't let her change
    her mind

When they want to draw from my body the arrowhead
    of the cypress-bodied one
Oh God, let it be my wounded heart they take,
    but not her arrow

I'm accustomed to misery and cruelty—how would
    life be without them?
Oh God, don't let my suffering be limited
    nor her tyranny end

Don't say that she shows no justice, that she is
    so unfair
Oh God, let no one but her be sultan
    on the throne of my heart

In the corner of this tavern Fuzûlî found a treasure
    of delight
Oh God, this is a holy place, may it never
    be brought to ruin

26. Fuzûlî

If my heart were a wild bird, it would nest
in your twisted curl
Wherever I am, oh jinn, my love is by
your side

I'm happy with my suffering, take your hand
from the medicine that will cure me
Oh doctor, do not heal me, the poison
that destroys me is your cure!

Don't be shy and pull your skirts from the hands
of those fallen with love—take care!
For the hands which hold your hem, if suddenly
emptied, may pray evilly to the sky

The fragments of my shattered heart lie pierced
on the spearpoints of your lashes
Go to sleep, drunk on your own beauty, and mend
my heart by the closing of your eyes

Separation from you is death, beloved, the end
of life itself
I am bewildered by others who live long
apart from you

The wick of your spirit is twisted
like the hyacinth curl of the beloved
Hey Fuzûlî, you can't hope for release
until you burn like a candle with love's flame

27. **Fuzûlî**

For long years we have been haunting the quarter
of those who call us vagrants
We are the soldiers of the sultan of the spiritually wise,
waiting for God to befriend us

Night and day we crouch in the dust at the threshold
of the tavern
Don't think we are begging, we are waiting for promotion
at prosperity's door

We are not like those vultures, hunting
for the world-corpse
We are the contented Phoenix, waiting
on the summit of Kâf mountain

Our eyes see no sleep, we are troubled by those
who keep us from her
We are the night guard, watching over the treasure
of the secrets of love

Surprised by your love, we stand still as the stones
of the wall
While others wander through the garden, we wait
at our place of torment

We are the caravan on the path of isolation,
we fear danger along the way
Sometimes Mejnûn keeps our vigil, sometimes it is I,
we are sentries through the night

Don't think our nightly crying out is in vain!
We stand sentinel in the tower of devotion
over the country of love

Ferhâd and Mejnûn lay down, drunk
on the full cup of love
Hey Fuzûlî, while they sleep, it's our turn
to speak of the heart

28. **Fuzûlî**

The pointed reproach of the enemy
cannot harm me
The arrowheads of your glances
protect me with an iron skin

I am also safe from the striking stones
of blame
For the chains which bind the madman
are an iron fortress around me

The wounds of your sword have covered me
in a shirt of blood
But my tears have worn the shirt away,
I am naked and ashamed

Oh light of my eye, were my eye not shining
from the candle of your beauty
My worldly vision would be no use to me
at all

The pleasure of wondering when I will be
near you
Keeps me from calling any place my home

Oh keeper of the garden, it is useless to wander
in the rose-garden of many delights
When I burn for union with the cypress
of the jasmine breast

Oh Fuzûlî, let the throne of power
go up in flames!
God knows, far better are homeless nights
in the warm ashes of the hamam

Hüsrev, Shîrîn, and Ferhâd

The stories of Hüsrev and Shîrîn (the Sweet), and Ferhâd and Shîrîn have been told in many versions. The story of Ferhâd and his hopeless love for the Princess Shîrîn, especially, is the subject of several popular tales, in many of which Ferhâd is portrayed as coming from the lower classes. The whole story is tortuously involved, with numerous subplots, characters, and mistaken identities, but some of its basic elements became very much a part of general cultural awareness among the Ottomans. Briefly sketched, the relevant parts of the plot go something like this.

Hüsrev, also known as Hüsrev Pervîn, was a prince of the Sassanid dynasty, son of Hurmuz and grandson of the famed Nûshirevân. Like princes of the Ottoman dynasty years later, Hüsrev was raised under the tutelage of a great and wise scholar named Buzurg-Umîd (Great Hope). As punishment for a youthful misdeed his father had given away his horse, his minstrel, and his belongings, but the young man bore the just punishment without complaint and as a result was granted a vision in which his grandfather promised him a singer named Bârbud with the world's sweetest voice, Shebdîz the swiftest of horses, a beloved named Shîrîn, and a throne. How this prophecy was realized is the substance of the ensuing tale.

Hüsrev, it seems, had a friend named Shâvûr or Shâpûr who had traveled through the country of Armenia, which at that time was ruled by a queen named Mehîn Bânû who by chance had a beautiful niece named Shîrîn and a marvelous black horse named Shebdîz (the Black-Colored). When Shâpûr described Shîrîn to the prince, Hüsrev was struck by the resemblance to his dream and smitten by the reported beauty of Shîrîn. So he sent Shâpûr back to Armenia to plead his case. Shâpûr, a great artist, paints a picture of Hüsrev and leaves it where Shîrîn is sure to encounter it. This she does and falls immediately in love. Learning the identity of the person in the portrait from Shâpûr, she contrives to borrow her aunt's famous horse and, while on one of her usual outings, manages to elude her entourage and set out in pursuit of her beloved.

Hüsrev has been accused of plotting against his father and is forced to flee the capital for a time. He makes his way to Armenia. Meanwhile, Shîrîn—her loss mourned by her aunt—has been wearily searching for her love. While resting for a moment she is attacked by a lion, which she kills, and then, dirtied by travel and struggle, she decides to bathe in a nearby pool. As she bathes, Hüsrev passes by and notices the lovely young woman naked in the pool. He is dumbfounded by her beauty; but when she sees him, he respectfully turns around. The woman rushes from the pool, snatches up her clothes, and, mounting Shebdîz, flees toward the Persian capital at Medâ'in, faintly suspecting that she may have seen the very young man she so ardently sought.

In Meda'în, Shâpûr and Hüsrev's household have been expecting Shîrîn and try make her comfortable, finally building her a palace of her own in the hills. In time Shâpûr returns to Armenia, where Hüsrev has been generously hosted by the queen, who has made him a present of the horse named Gülgûn (Rose-Color), a magnificent animal from the same stock as Shebdîz. When he hears news of Shîrîn, he sends Shâpûr back to Meda'în with Gülgûn so that she might return to Armenia.

Meanwhile there has been a coup in Meda'în and the general Behrâm Chûbîn has killed Hüsrev's father. Hüsrev himself is advised to lie low for a time, and Behrâm in his absence declares himself ruler. So when Shîrîn returns, Hüsrev has already departed, but in time they chance to meet during one of Shîrîn's outings and enjoy a time of merriment in Hüsrev's camp. Shîrîn, however, refuses Hüsrev's advances, telling him that they must wait until he has taken the throne and they have been married.

So the two part again. Hüsrev makes his way to the land of the Byzantines, where he makes an ally of the ruler and marries his daughter. With Byzantine help, Hüsrev defeats the usurper and takes the throne, whence he rules with exemplary justice and mourns the absence of Shîrîn. On her part, Shîrîn has returned sadly to Armenia, where she succeeds to the throne following the death of her aunt.

In her mountain castle, Shîrîn is troubled by her inability to get either milk (in some versions) or fresh water (in others) because the source is blocked by the high peaks. Shâpûr, who learns of her problem, introduces her to his friend Ferhâd, an accomplished engineer. Ferhâd is sorely smitten by the lovely queen and sets about to fulfill her every wish. He begins to work furiously and in a short time has dug a canal through the mountains. Shîrîn is impressed, but the young man will take no reward and instead flees into the wilderness, distraught and maddened by his love.

Hüsrev, however, has heard of this affair, and although both the queen and the engineer have behaved blamelessly, he is tormented by jealousy. He has Ferhâd brought before him and, when the young man will not renounce his love, offers to renounce his claim to Shîrîn if Ferhâd will complete the (impossible) task of cutting a road through Mount Bîsütûn. The young man agrees and begins to work, punctuating his labors with moans of anguished love. The story of his progress and his anguish reaches the ears of Shîrîn, who makes a visit to the mountain to see what is going on. Ferhâd is both crazed by her presence and driven to new heights of effort.

When Hüsrev hears of Shîrîn's visit and sees that Ferhâd may well finish his impossible task, he asks his counselors what he should do. On their suggestion, just as Ferhâd is about to complete his mountain-cutting, an old woman is sent to him with the news that Shîrîn has died. Overcome by grief, Ferhâd throws himself from the mountain and thus dies of his love.

This does not immediately resolve the situation for Hüsrev and Shîrîn, however. She is angry at what happened to Ferhâd and displeased by Hüsrev's marriage to the Greek princess, who has since died. She refuses his advances, and he turns for affection to a courtesan named Sheker (Sugar). In time, through the machinations of Shâpûr, the two are brought together. They reconcile, are married and live happily together for some time.

In the final scene, an older Hüsrev is assassinated in his sleep by his evil son, the offspring of the Greek Princess. The son then declares his love for Shîrîn, who pretends to give in to him. But when the new King has destroyed all Hüsrev's properties and built a magnificent funeral bier at her request, she approaches Hüsrev's body, kisses his fatal wound, and stabs herself in the same place. With a cry of woe, she embraces her dead lover and so dies.

Shîrîn visits Ferhâd as he works to cut a path through Mount Bîsütûn
From the *Hamse-i Dihlevi*, Süleymaniye Kütüphanesi, Hâlet Efendi 377 (fol. 64a)

29. Nisâyî

d. ca. 1550–1560

We are the Mejnûn of our age, we dwell in the wilderness
of seclusion
We have abandoned the many for the one, we dwell
in the loneliness of solitude.
We are companions at the celebration of grief, we await
sweet talk with the *nay*
Oh *zahid*, do not believe we are waiting for a safe path
to Paradise
We are the tormented lovers, we haunt the place
of blame

Like Mejnûn, we have made our home in the wilderness
of freedom
Like the Phoenix, we have made a nest on the summit
of annihilation
We are hidden treasure, and we do not reveal the secret
of the heart
In the retreat free from care, how many treasures
we have found
We have abandoned the dervish crown and throne,
we haunt the place of tranquillity

Heart and soul, drunkard and blame-seeker—we are a pair
of crazy pairs
At the festival of sorrow, with Vâmık and Ferhâd
who died from love
We drink from love's cup, and rejoice
in what may come
We have been enslaved by the wine-makers
for so many a year
Yet we are the sultans of the world, we stand guard
at the gate of good luck

I have abandoned my home and sacrificed my whole life
for your sake
I've shown everyone my tears, I've revealed all
that I am
I won't turn away from you, even if all the world
oppose me
For union with you, the living spirit gives up all
that it owns
Oh *hoja*, we are keeping watch, spending the treasure
of our life on union

We are the Hüsrev of the age, kings of the tears
of blood
With our weeping, we have given Mount Bîsütûn
to the flood
Seen with the hard-hearted one, we appear to be
the mountain-cutter
With the memory of the sweet lip of Shîrîn,
we suffer like Ferhâd
For how long, oh Nisâyî, have we waited
at this gate of afflictions?

Fabulous Birds

Among the legends handed down to the Ottoman Turks and regularly referenced in their poetry are stories of the fabulous birds. Because none of these birds has a close equivalent in the mythology familiar to Westerners, the translations either use the Turkish name or refer to the phoenix which shares characteristics with some of them.

The first of these birds is the *'ankâ*, which in Turkish legend is often said to be a bird with a name but no body. The *'ankâ* has a long history. It was said to have been created by God with all perfections and a long neck (which the name *'ankâ* reflects) but it and its kin burgeoned to the point at which its depredations on the birds and humans of the Arab Peninsula became so great that one of the Arab prophets of the period between the Hebrew Prophets and Muhammad prayed for its destruction and God responded by destroying *'ankâ*-kind with thunderbolts.

In Turkish legend the *'ankâ* is often referred to as "the emerald-green *'ankâ*." It has a human-like face, and flies continuously at great height without ever alighting except at its nest in the vastly high and inaccessible range of the Kâf mountains, which in the legendary geography surround the inhabited earth. The *'ankâ* can be a cruel predator and can also bring good luck or help a worthy person in distress.

The character of the *'ankâ* is often mingled with that of the *sîmurg* also. The *sîmurg* is a central character in the Persian poet Ferîdüddîn 'Attâr's (d. ca. 1230) mystical allegory of the quest of the self for union with the Divine. In this allegorical tale entitled *Parliament of the Birds*, a group of thirty birds led by the Hoopoe sets out to find the mythical *sîmurg*. After a series of adventures that leave them stripped of worldly desire and concern for the physical self they look as though into a mirror and see that they have become what they sought, the *sîmurg* (which, in Persian, means "Thirty-Bird"). Thus the *'ankâ* is sometimes said to have the colors and characteristics of thirty birds.

This mystical connection is the source of many of the conceits involving the *'ankâ* in Ottoman poems. Most often it is a sign for mystical contentment and the lack of desire or need for anything of this world. It roosts on its distant and inaccessible Kâf mountain, the ultimate hermit, cut off from worldly cares and concerns.

The *hümâ* is another legendary bird whose characteristics are also mingled now and then with those of the *'ankâ*. It is also known popularly as the "Bird of Fortune" or "Bird of Luck" or "Bird of Paradise." According to legend, in ancient times the *hümâ*, which was green-winged, yellow-beaked, and little larger than a sparrow, would descend and light upon the shoulder of the person destined to be the next ruler. In later versions, it would fly continuously (like the *'ankâ*), unable to light because it had no feet, and would confer rulership or simple good fortune upon anyone who came under its shadow. In Ottoman poetry, the beloved (who is often associated with the ruler) is identified with the *hümâ* insofar as she bestows unimaginable good fortune on anyone who comes under the shadow of her attention.

The *kaknûs* is a giant multicolored bird whose beak is pierced by three hundred and sixty holes. Out of those holes it can produce every variety of musical sound. Even the sweetest-singing birds are entranced by this music, and when they draw near they are eaten by the *kaknûs*. This bird lives but a year and at the end of its time gathers together a great mound of twigs and other kindling. It stands atop the mound and begins to make music, which so excites and inflames it that sparks fall from its wings and are fanned into a fire that finally consumes the bird. Out of the ashes emerges an egg that will produce another *kaknûs*. This phoenix-like fiery rebirth is often attributed to the *'ankâ* and is the source of numerous metaphors referring to the mystics, who burn away self-concern in the fires of passion. The *kaknûs* is also considered the symbol and source of all music. It is told that the first human musicians learned their trade from the *kaknûs*.

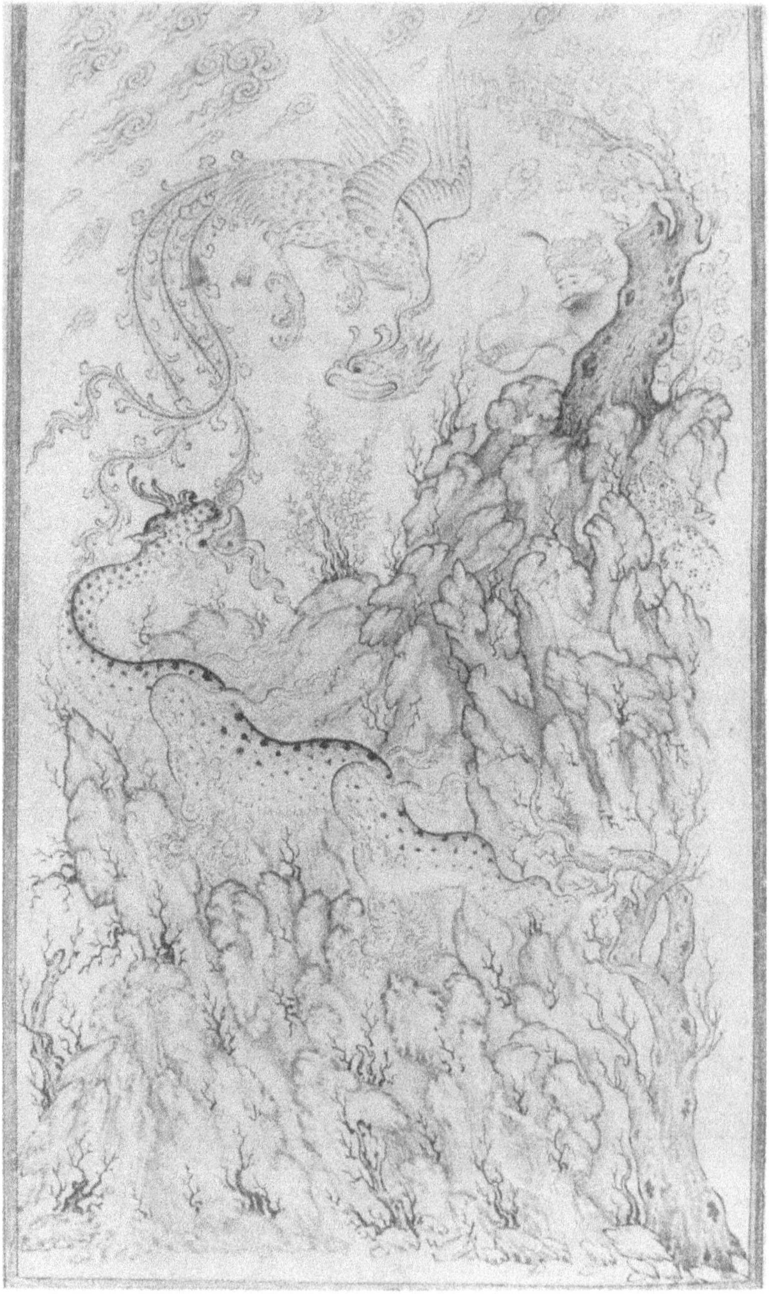

The 'Ankâ fighting with a dragon
From Topkapı Palace Museum Library, Hazine 2163 (fol. 2a)

30. Nev'î

1533–1599

We don't need the cup of pleasure
from the hand of this lowly world
It isn't manly to take game from the hands
of the weak

Don't grieve—fate offers us all the cup
of death
Even Jemshîd drank that poison from the hand
of this miserable world

I saw the page of the heart, and the borders
were full of verse
I know this was written by the beloved's
learnéd hand

The sea is stormy, tormented and distraught
by love
While the still mountains complain of silence
and of patience

To Ferhâd, the stone-cutter, his own body
was the mountain
Or he would not have been helpless at the hands
of his passion, that Bîsütûn

The comb and the tangled curl are never once gone
from my heart
At its hand, my life has gone wildly astray

Nev'î has written a poem about the people
of the pure heart
Sometimes thankful for love and madness,
sometimes crying out in complaint

31. Nev'î

Help me, oh sapling of the tulip cheek,
    in the garden of allure
Pheasant strutting proudly like a partridge
    through a garden of elegance
Oh sultan, commander of those faithless thieves
    of the heart
Do me a favor, spare this blood-scattering eye
    grown pale from weeping
Light of my eye, joy of my heart, all my life!
If you cannot be my friend, at least do not
    be my enemy

Oh monarch on the throne of freedom
    from worldly need
Is it fitting the dark-faced rival follows
    close as your shadow?
Let me, your maddened lover, remain at your feet
    like my tears
I'm blinded by weeping, grieving for your curl
Light of my eye, joy of my heart, all my life!
If you cannot be my friend, at least do not
    be my enemy

I have no path to the Kaaba of desire,
    other than your street
I have no place to pray in the temple
    of this passing world, only your gate
To whom shall I plead, I have only you
    to ask for justice
Oh tyrant, grief has slain me who has
    committed no crime, no sin
Light of my eye, joy of my heart, all my life!
If you cannot be my friend, at least do not
    be my enemy

Oh cherished moon in the sky, if union
is not my fate
I would be happy now and again with a greeting
from afar
If you wish God's blessing, protect yourself,
don't provoke my sighs, my tears
Don't forget this soul lost, wandering the night
of grief
Light of my eye, joy of my heart, all my life!
If you cannot be my friend, at least do not
be my enemy

Oh darling, if the rival speaks harshly
to you of Nev'î, the sinless one
I wouldn't expect you to lower your ear
like a bending rose
I don't know why you turn your face
from your nightingale
What can I do? Since the beginning
separation has been written on my brow
Light of my eye, joy of my heart, all my life!
If you cannot be my friend, at least do not
be my enemy

32. Bâkî

1526–1600

Five Line Stanzas by Bâkî (Mânî?) *on a gazel of* Fuzûlî

That tyrant, is she not persuaded by the tears
of the lover?
Doesn't she know this wailing will find its way
to her once more?
Doesn't she fear the Resurrection? Doesn't
she believe the dead will rise again?
She's tortured my soul—has she never
had enough of this torment?
The heavens are set aflame by my sigh, so why does
my candle of hope not burn?

From time to time that laughing rose looks
at the nightingale of the soul
Strangers are blessed with a share of kindness,
but I with endless pain
She makes others smile, but causes me to weep
a thousand sorrows
The beloved treats all the lovesick ones
with the cure of torment
So why doesn't she cure me—doesn't she know
my heart is sick from love?

My deepest secret is heard by one and all,
and my sighing never ends
My heart has collapsed in ruins, but my soul
will soon be free
My flooding tears pour down and my wails rise
to the sky
In this night of grief my spirit burns, my tears
are red with blood
My screaming wakes one and all, will my black luck
not wake and change?

Since grief conquered my heart, contentment
has abandoned my world
Because of the calamity of love, the rose-garden
seems but ash
How many nights has that silver-bodied one
not had word from her captive?
I've kept my grief hidden, and they said, "Make it
known to her!"
If I were to tell her, would that faithless one
believe me?

Being apart from the rose-scented cheek,
the nightingale grows pale
The turning of fate draws pearls from my eyes,
and the world is filled with my cries
When I see your beauty, oh moon-faced one,
my tears scatter to the winds
When I gaze on the rose of your cheek, tears of blood
pour from my eyes
My darling, in the season of the rose, won't the
flooding waters run dark with blood?

The heedless one who is witness to your cheek
becomes a crazy drunk
It is impossible not to adore you, you are impossible
not to love
No matter how hard, the heart breaks and turns
towards you in the end
I didn't love you, but you bewitched my heart
and mind!
The fool who blames me for my love will know shame
when he sees your shining face!

Bâkî is your slave, he tastes sugar
when he speaks of your lips
His life's devotion is wandering your quarter,
crying out for you in vain
He's a beggar brought to his knees, an exile
in the desert
Fuzûlî is a melancholy drunk, he is shameful
in everyone's eyes!
What black passion is this? He has never
had enough of love's torment!

33. Bâkî

Oh beloved, since the origin we have been
  the slaves of the shah of love
Oh beloved, we are the famed sultan
  of the heart's domain

We are the poppies of this wasteland
  whose hearts are burnt black with grief
Oh beloved, be generous as the cloud,
  don't withhold your water from the thirsty heart

Fate saw we had a jewel inside us and tore
  our hearts apart
Oh beloved, it left our bodies bleeding,
  mined of the precious knowledge of love

Don't let the dust of sadness cloud the waters
  of the fountain of your soul
Oh beloved, for us faces shine bright with pride
  across the Ottoman lands

The poems of Bâkî go around the world
  like the full cup at the gathering of friends
Oh beloved, we are the cup, and we are the cupbearer
  of this turning age

ازلدن شاه عشقڭ بندهٔ فرمانیوز جانا
محبت ملکنڭ سلطان علیشانیوز جانا

سحاب لطفڭ آبن تشنه دللردن دریغ ایتمه
بو دشتڭ بغری یانمش لالهٔ نعمانیوز جانا

زمانه بزده کوهر سزدیکیچون دلخراش ایلر
انکیچون بغرمز خوندر معارف کانیوز جانا

ملکدر قلمسون کرد کدورت چشمهٔ جانی
بلورسن آب روی ملکت عثمانیوز جانا

جهانی جام نظمم شعرباتی کبی دور ایلر
بو بزمڭ شمدی بزده جام دورانیوز جانا

"*Oh beloved since the origin . . .*" *in Arabic script*
Calligraphy by Ali Alparslan, from the private collection of Mehmet Kalpaklı

34. Bâkî

The fountain of my spirit thirsts for your ruby
 mouth, the water of life
Offer a drink from the cup of your lip,
 the fountain of youth thirsts too

My soul desires your red lip, but the beloved
 wants to drink my blood
Lord God, why does the spirit thirst,
 and the beloved thirst too?

Not only does the heart long for the pure water
 of union
The world-sea, dry-lipped from covering the earth,
 thirsts too

Oh saki, the heart and soul are pleading
 at the gathering of grief for you
Shift your hand, your foot, the lovers
 at the wine-party thirst too

Oh my beloved, both the rival and the lovers long
 for the sweet water of union
As infidel and Muslim thirst for the pure
 water of divine mercy

What if she who resembles Leylâ drives Bâkî
 weeping into the wilderness?
The dust of the desert thirsts for the tear
 of Mejnûn's eye

35. Bâkî

If only the bud would open
like the beloved's ruby lips
It would scatter turquoise and the plain
become a field of green

If I were to obey the advice
of the holy man of the town
Then what of spring, the beloved,
and the pleasant wine?

I have drunk blood at every moment,
served by the saki of fate
If only I could open like the wild poppy,
and reveal love's burn within

What if the hearts cry because
of that ruthless hard-hearted one?
And what if that love-thief
were coquettish and alluring?

Oh Bâkî, let the cup pass around again,
see the rose within
Let the beloved be always near,
in revelry along the bank of the stream

36. Bâkî

Sparks from my heart rise
 to the heavens turning
While my tears pour, spinning,
 to the earth

In the fire of your love, the heart
 of the disappointed lover burns
Turning, turning, like a magic lantern

Night after night on the bed of grief
 I see no sleep
Restless, turning, I lament until the dawn

Oh idol, from the grief of loving you,
 my weeping eye is drowned
My sad eye, a small boat, capsized
 by a whirlpool of tears

At the *bayram*, let us hear
 the ferris-wheel weeping
Spinning, let it display
 that silver-breasted one

In a whirlwind, the dust of her threshold
 rises to the skies
Spinning, it anoints the eyes of the stars

Circling the candle of your cheek,
 the heart becomes bewildered
Like a moth burns wing and feather
 in the flame

The jeweler's wheel pierces the pearl
 as fate pierces the soul, spinning
These pearls, these jewels, are Bâkî's tears

37. Bâkî

Your rebellious glance lines up the cavalry
 of your lashes
Soldiers armed with lances, they wait for war,
 row by row

To watch you on the path of the rose garden
Swaying cypresses stand along each side,
 row by row

To combat the throngs of my tear-soldiers
The world sea sends forth its waves,
 row by row

Don't think it's a flock of cranes crying
 in the sky
It's the birds of my heart and soul returning
 to you, row by row

To see who prays with you knee to knee
 in the mosque
The tearful eye, like the water-seller,
 roves from row to row

The people of the heart are drowned
 in your blessings of grief and pain
At the table of your kindness guests await
 your gifts, row by row

If the reed pen sways like a banner
 while telling of your body
Then the books draw up their verses
 like soldiers, row by row

The lovers stand near you on every side
Like the columns of the Kaaba, row by row

Oh Bâkî, they will know your worth
    upon the funeral stone
And your friends will stand before you,
    hands clasped in reverence, row by row

38. Yahyâ Bey

d. 1582

Come wander through the city, drink wine
    from the bowl
Oh ascetic, do the wise run from the tavern
    door?

When I see those languid eyes, I cry out
The black cloud of my sigh pours tears
    on our party like hail

That full moon, if she did not rise one night
    and brighten our hearts
Then would it matter if I-of-the-black-days
    had never been born from my mother?

Learn how to burn from the moth, oh heart,
    from the moth
When it sees a shining face, with desire,
    it sacrifices itself to the flame

Oh poor heart, let me lose my life
    from waiting
Waiting for my calamity to come from her house
    in her alluring way

When I sit side by side with that perfect-bodied one,
    no matter where I am
I make my breast into mother-of-pearl for the sake
    of that unique jewel

The heart said,"Yahyâ thieved a kiss
    from the beloved"
Let it be known this is good news, good news
    from his crazy heart!

39. Yahyâ Bey

Poetry holds the written veil across its face, shyly,
    like Joseph
And speaks, hidden by its own intrigue

The heart-taker would know my plight
    if she could look upon my verse
She would know my pain if she would listen
    to my cries

It is fitting for masters of vision to gaze
    upon the poem
It is a wave on the sea of beauty,
    the brow of the beloved

Like the shattered mountain of Moses,
    poetry has witnessed the divine
It ripped its collar open, tore itself apart

Poetry reveals the pained desires
    of the people of suffering
For the maddened lover my book of verse
    is a declaration of bewildered love

Poetry is revealed from the realm
    of essence
Every line invokes a voice of the unseen
    world

Yahyâ, let the roses, wild with passion,
    tear at their robes
When I recite verses in honor
    of her slender grace

Moses praying at Mount Sinai
From the *Hamse-i Dihlevî*, Süleymaniye Kütüphanesi, Hâlet Efendi 377
(fol. 14a)

40. Rûhî

1548–1605

Curse the thorns of fate, and damn as well its roses
  and its garden
Curse my rivals in love, and damn as well the beloved
  who brings me pain

There is a life made captive by the pleasures
  of wine
Curse the wineseller, and damn as well the wine
  and the drunkard

Since the wasteland of death is home
  to those born to this world
Curse the caravan that crosses this desert,
  and damn as well its guide

What shall we do when fame and glory are bought
  and sold?
Curse the one who sells them to the unworthy,
  and damn the one who buys them

In this world, where the opium-eaters are the knowers
  of mysteries
Curse their whirling trances, and damn as well
  their opium and their secrets

When the intelligent fall upon evil ways,
  and the ignorant become powerful
Curse the good luck of this world, and damn
  its bad luck too

Curse the good fortune brought by the turning
  of the heavens, curse misfortune too
Damn both the fixed stars and the planets

Since both this world and Paradise are forbidden
  to the mystics
Remain with Allah—think not of life, nor pray
  for the delights hereafter

41. Sheyhülislâm Yahyâ

1552–1644

Saki, offer the cup, let them call me a drunkard
Let them say, "Look at the love-crazed one
who misbehaves!"

Everyone here is continuously filling
their cup
From now on, let them call this gathering
a tavern

Destroy the dwelling of the heart, don't leave
a single stone standing on a stone
Do this, and let the travellers call it a ruin

What is an image other than you
doing in my heart?
Would it be fitting to call the Kaaba
a temple of idols?

Yahyâ, words reveal the secret truth
of loving affection
May the friends listen well and say,
"Do not tell them to strangers"

42. Sheyhülislâm Yahyâ

Let the hypocrites practice their way
in the mosque
And you, come to the tavern, where there is
neither hypocrite nor hypocrisy

Don't long in vain, you who thirsts
for the pure cup
They buried the cup of purity with Jem

The beloved has driven away the watcher
from the threshold
And that black-faced rival has come again—
have you seen the calamity?

We could not repel the army of grief,
though we fought like martyrs
What plan of man can overthrow the decree
of God?

Hey Yahyâ, how could I not be crazy
with love?
My beloved is so exquisite that my wild
heart soars

43. Sheyhülislâm Yahyâ

Is there no heart capable of love,
    is there no beloved in this city?
Is there no drunk at this gathering,
    is there no wine, no cup?

Why shouldn't your heart joyously open
    like the bud?
Aren't there any roses in this garden?
    Aren't there nightingales?

We cannot find a heart who speaks
    like a parrot
Is there no one who inspires his verse,
    no one to sweetly recite?

Is the heart worth less than stone?
    Is there no favor-giving sun?
No fortunate star to transform
    the black stone into ruby?

Why do all poets not nurture
    the virgin word?
Aren't there any masters of verse
    like Yahyâ?

The Down on Your Cheek

The down on the beloved's cheek is the source of so many themes and comparisons in Ottoman poetry that it is worth telling the whole story of cheek-down in one place. Under the generally understood rules of love, a person with soft, dark cheek-down—peach-fuzz—is considered an appropriate love-object, which means either a woman or a boy who has not yet begun to grow a true beard. This is an important distinction, because the moment a boy is far enough along in adolescence to grow a beard he is considered a man and is disqualified as a potential beloved. This does not mean that adult homosexual and homoerotic relationships were unheard-of or even that they were universally condemned. However, they were part of the private life of the individual and, like sexual relations with one's spouse, were not appropriate subjects for art or polite public conversation. The distinction between attraction to beautiful young men and boys, which was quite common, and a general homosexual orientation was quite clearly maintained.

The face of the beloved, including the eyes, forehead, eyebrows, lashes, cheeks, lips, chin, mole—everything except perhaps the nose—is subject to minute examination by the Ottoman poets. And the cheek-down is no exception. In addition to the reasons mentioned above, the cheek-down is a favorite topic in part because the word for "cheek-down" (*hat*) is the same as the word for "line, mark, writing, calligraphy." Thus the black marks of down on the cheek of the beloved are compared to calligraphic writing. The dusting of down, for example, is described as the minuscule "Dust" (Gubâr) script of classical calligraphy, or as "sweet smelling herbs" (*reyhân*) after the Reyhânî script. Thus the cheek becomes the written page, a letter, a royal command, or even a calligraphed page of the Sacred Text.

The herbal image is a link to the cheek-down's role in the garden of the face. Many times the down is described not as black but as (dark) green and is compared to both sweet herbs and the grassy lawn of the garden, in which can also be found the roses of the cheeks, the tulip lips, the cypress body/stature, hyacinth hair. In its greenness and its blackness it is also associated with Hızır, the green man of the Alexander legend (see the section following poem no. 10), and with the darkness which surrounds the Water of Life (or the beloved's lips).

In its blackness and sweet smell the down is also often related to black and fragrant musk and hence to China and the land of the Tatars from which musk comes. This initiates a comparison between the darkness of the East and the fairness associated with Rûm (literally more or less Byzantium and usually meaning the cheek). In its greenness, it is sometimes a parrot that hungers for the sugar of the beloved's lip.

The down clustered about the sugar lip is also described as a swarm of tiny ants gathered for a sweet feast.

There are a myriad other comparisons evoked by the cheek-down. They are too many to recount here, and most are understandable if the reader is willing to match wits with the Ottoman poets. This is part of the fun.

44. Nef'î

1572–1635

That black drunken eye has become a tavern
of coquettishness
In every troublemaking corner, you'll find
a drunk is sleeping

Her glance drinks angrily from the cup
of sweet provocation
So what if every drunken look turns the world
upside down?

If the tassel on the turban of the drunk
doesn't sweep the threshold of the tavern
Then he doesn't give lustre to the party
of Jemshîd

So what if Nef'î prays to the beloved
while drunk?
The sins of drunkards are forgiven
by the most generous of the wise

Like the hero Rostam, my beloved's glance
has taken scimitar in hand
And her black lashes are drunken soldiers,
ready to war against me

Helping a drunk at the wine-party

From the *Dîvân-ı Hâfız*, Süleymaniye Kütüphanesi, Lâleli 1739 (fol. 1a)

45. Nef'î

Those who painted my portrait painted me
with cup in hand
When they saw I was drunk on the wine of love,
they drew me as a drunkard

If the *zâhid* were wise, he wouldn't ask me
to give up pleasure
What a shame! They have portrayed me as crazy,
and him as sane!

What you see in the eye of the lover
is not the shadow of her eyelash
They have drawn the darkness of her cheek-down
onto the white of the weeping eye

I am that lover whose fame in humility
has taken the entire city
Those who wrote the story of Mejnûn
have written it in vain!

Oh Nef'î, from the way you speak we see
your heart is burning
When they write your verse, their pens
shall burst in flame!

46. Nef'î

The heart is both the cup and the wine,
    the heart is the alluring saki
The heart is the pleasure-keeper
    for the people of love

So what if I sacrifice my life a thousand times
    for one exquisite vision of your face?
The heart has long been prisoner of its desire

Love is within the heart, so let life and the flesh
    become dust
After death, my heart lives forever in the world
    of eternal signs

The heart is but an atom, yet by the light
    of the sun of love
The heart becomes a medallion on the vast dome
    of time

So what if Nef'î celebrates alone with his heart
The heart is both the cup and wine, the heart
    is the alluring saki

47. Sheyhülislâm Bahâyî

1601–1653

Oh cry, what are you doing, disturbing
 the one who feigns sleep?
The world will be ruined by her discord
 when she wakes

Be merciful, let my wounded heart remain
 caught in the trap of her curl
What are you doing, setting free a bird
 with a broken wing?

Oh doctor of the heart, you have a cure
 for all ailments
What are you doing to those born
 with the madness of love?

Oh wind, you've come and disheveled
 the beloved's curls
Once again you've caused havoc,
 what are you going to do?

Oh glance, my executioner, why do you draw
 your scimitar
Already the universe has been martyred
 by the sword of love

Oh Behzâd, you paint beautifully the mole
 and cheek-down of the beloved
But when it comes to her troubling charm
 what are you going to do?

Oh sad heart, admit you are not capable
 of prosperity and pleasure like Bahâyî
Life is this way—what are you going to do?

48. Nâbî

1642–1712

When we watch the spinning of the sky,
    we no longer think of stars
When we see the furrowed brow of the ocean,
    we forget about the pearls

Once we, too, sought the cup of this world
But when we saw the saki wanted favors,
    we gave the cup away

When we heard he longed for autumn,
    we forgot the boy of the garden
When we saw it on the turban of the rival,
    we gave up the freshest flower

Like a crucible, the heart is warmed
    in the fire of separation
We no longer beg for union with the beloved
    of the silver breast

What is one to do with generosity
    that doesn't bring peace of mind?
Once we knew the scented candle of the burning
    heart, we gave up ambergris

Once we severed the bonds of quarrel,
    we did so with success
We quit the sword, we forgot about the dagger

Nâbî took pleasure with the throat of the bottle
    and the foot of the jug
Then he let go the beloved's skirts, and the collar
    of all desire

49. Nâbî

In the garden of time and destiny, we have seen
both the autumn and the spring
We have seen both the time of joy and the time
of sorrow

Don't be exceedingly proud, for in the tavern
of good fortune
We have seen one thousand drunks intoxicated
on pride

We have seen countless stone fortresses
in the land of worldly fame
And not one could withstand the exploding sigh
of a broken heart

We have seen a flood of tears from the people
of grief
With a roar we have seen the deluge engulf
one thousand homes of luck

We have seen countless swift riders
of this battlefield
Whose only remaining wealth is the life-taking
arrow of love's sigh

We have seen many who are proud
of their high office
Who must one day wait on others, hands folded
by the door

Oh Nâbî, we have seen many wine drinkers
at life's party
Who have exchanged a cup full of their desires
for a beggar's bowl

50. Nâbî

At the gathering of joy, the wine cup
    comes and goes
Just like the ebb and flow of the sea

You opened up to strangers, just like
    the blooming rose
So tells the swift wind as it comes and goes

Even if Jesus came again to the face
    of our earth
There would be no cure for those sick
    with love

Since the sultan of grief became the sovereign
    of my heart
The warriors of passion, on the plain
    of my breast, come and go

For so long Nâbî has been coming and going
    from this quarter—crazed
And not once has that beloved asked,
    "What does this man desire?"

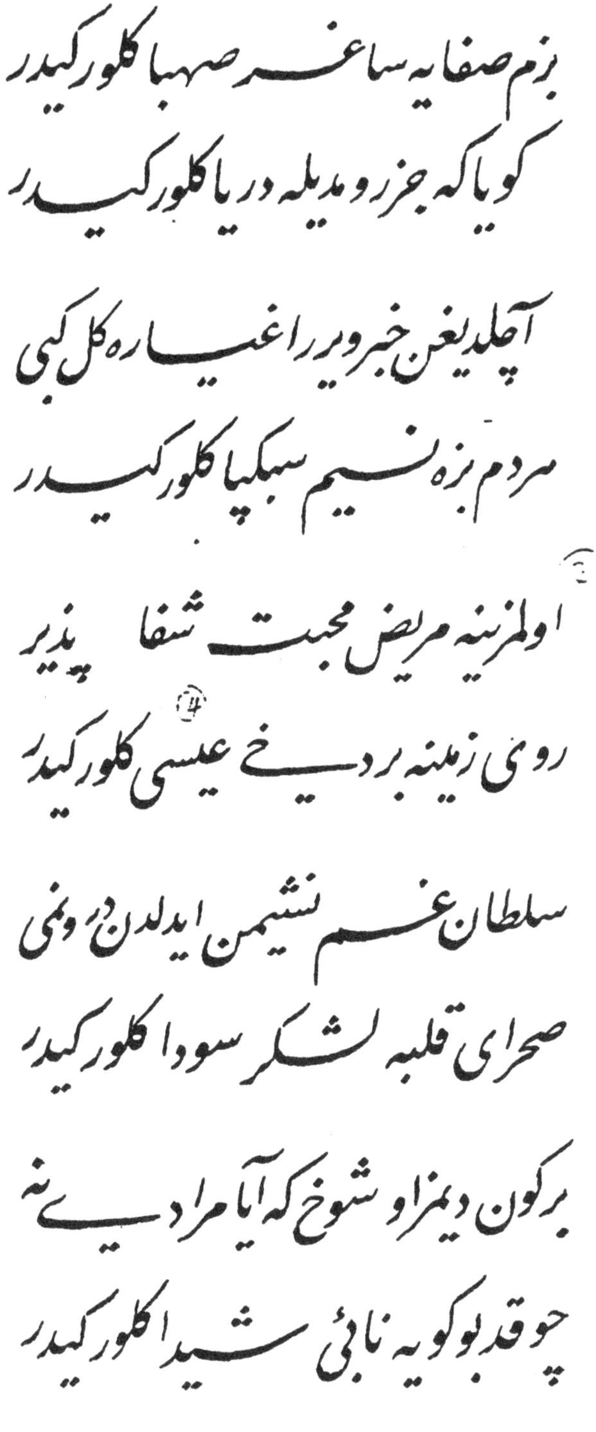

"At the gathering of joy . . ." in Arabic script

Calligraphy by Ali Alparslan, from the private collection of Mehmet Kalpaklı

Rûmî's Mirror

Symbolism of the mirror is everywhere in Ottoman poetry. There are decorative mirrors, round mirrors of many facets, the mirrors held by beggars or begging dervishes so that a gentleman may check his appearance for a small coin, mirrors of silver and glass. But most commonly the mirror is the mystical mirror. The mystics most often begin from the Sacred Tradition (the words of God related by the Prophet but not found in the Quran) that says: "I was a Hidden Treasure and wished to be known." The Hidden Treasure subsumes the attributes of God which can only be known through their reflection in human beings, of which Adam was the first and the perfect mirror. Thus the Divine Attributes are the hidden thing, the secret concealed in human beings as the polished mirror is hidden in a container of felt.

The theory of mysticism for the Ottoman poets had numerous sources but none any more generally applicable than the work of Mevlânâ Jelâleddîn Rûmî (Our Lord, from the title *mevlî* or vulgarly *mollâ*, Glory of the Faith, the Anatolian) often referred to simply as Rûmî (the Anatolian). He was born in Balkh in what is now Afghanistan in 1207. His father, Bahâ Walad, was an important scholar of religious law and a sufi with many followers. When the Mongol armies approached Balkh, Bahâ Walad and many followers set out on a pilgrimage to Mecca from which they never returned. Their road led from the Arab Peninsula to Anatolia and the city of Konya, where they were received warmly by the Turkic (but Persian-speaking) Seljuk rulers of the area. Bahâ Walad soon became known as the outstanding scholar of Konya, and his son Jelâleddîn was raised and educated to follow in his footsteps.

By the time his father died (in 1231), Rûmî's formal education was complete, and he began the spiritual practice of sufism under the guidance of his father's successor. In 1244, when he was already a sufi master, Rûmî came in contact with the mysterious Shemseddîn (Sun of the Faith) of Tabriz (also known as Shems-i Tabrizî, Sun of Tabriz). Shems had a profound influence on Rûmî; the direction of his life altered abruptly from that of a scholar and legalist to that of an ecstatic dervish. Rûmî's life revolved around Shems and continued thus to revolve even after his master suddenly disappeared without a trace, possibly murdered by Rûmî's disciples. In the perfect mirror of Shems Rûmî saw God, and the removal of the mirror did not for him mean the removal of the true beloved that had been reflected therein. He went on to write a vast collection of love poems (*gazels*) to Shems and dropped out of his public life.

When Rûmî died in 1273, he left behind some of the most widely read works in Persian on the theory and practice of sufism, including his collected lyric poems (called the *Dîvân of Shems-i Tabriz*), the famous *Mesnevî* (the general term for a long poem in rhyming couplets, like calling something *The Poem*, *The Novel*), and a prose work called *In It What Is in It* (*Fîhi mâ fîhi*). The *Mesnevî* especially would have a profound effect on Ottoman poetry from its inception to its last days.

Rûmî was succeeded by his son Sultan Veled (the Turkish pronunciation of the Arabic *walad*), who began the process of transforming Rûmî's practice from the center of a limited circle of transplanted Persian mystics to the center of vast, elite, and powerful dervish order, one of the main roots of Ottoman Turkish culture.

Rûmî's *Mesnevî* is a massive collection (about 25,000 couplets) of parables, comments, and interpretations that reaches into all aspects of sufi spirituality. It is so powerful a source that any of the mysticism that permeates Ottoman poetry references it intentionally or not. In these very particular ways we cannot really know Ottoman poetry without knowing something of Rûmî. So, on the subject of mirrors, here is the story from Rûmî's *Mesnevî* of the contention between the Chinese and Anatolian (Rûmî) artists.

> The Chinese said in painting we are the best
> And those of Rûm replied, the power and glory are ours.
>
> The Sultan spoke: I would we make a test of this,
> See which of you can prove his claim.
>
> So China and Rûm began to quarrel
> 'Til from the quarreling Rûm withdrew.
>
> The Chinese said, let there be a room
> Set aside for us and one for you.
>
> And there were two rooms facing door to door;
> One the Chinese took, the other those of Rûm.
>
> The Chinese then asked one hundred colors of the Shah
> Who opened up his treasury that they might have them.
>
> So from the treasury each and every morn
> The Chinese took these colors as a gift.

But the Rûmîs said no color do we need or shade,
Our work demands but that the tarnish be removed.

So they shut the door and set to burnishing;
They became like the sky clean and pure.

There is a way that leads from two hundred colors to colorless;
Color is like the cloud and colorless the moon.

In a cloud, the light you see or brilliance,
Know you, it's from a star or sun or moon.

And when the Chinese toil was done,
They beat their drums for gladness.

And the Shah came in, saw the pictures there
Which as he faced them stole his wits away.

Then after he came to those of Rûm
And they let fall the curtain in between.

Reflection of those images, that artifice
Gleamed in those walls made pure.

All he saw there, here was bettered;
His eye was robbed from its socket.

Oh father, those of Rûm are the sufis,
Artless, unstudied, unread.

But they've polished clean their breasts
Of vengeance, avarice, desire and greed.

That mirror-like purity doubtless is the heart
Which takes in images numberless.

Reflected in his heart's mirror that Moses holds in his breast
The formless infinite form of the Unseen.

Indeed that form is not contained within the spheres,
Not in the Highest Heaven nor Sphere of Stars nor on the Fish.

Though that one can be numbered or has a limit,
Know you, the heart's mirror is limitless.

There the mind's struck dumb or leads to error
Because the heart's with Him or He's the heart.

The reflection of every image shines not forever,
But from the heart, both the many-numbered and numberless.

Without end, each image that comes to it,
Shows itself within flawlessly.

The polishers are free of color and of scent,
They see, at every instant, the beauty of the moment.

They cast aside the form and husk of knowledge,
Raised the banner of certainty's eye.

Thought departed, illumination gained,
They found center and source, the throat and sea of Knowing.

Death, before whom all others live in terror,
This folk makes a target of their jeers.

No one can defeat this people's hearts;
Harm falls on the shell and not the pearl.

Though given up on grammar and learning of the law,
They've taken up on poverty and abandonment of self.

Since the image of the eight heavens shone forth,
The tablet of their hearts has opened to it.

One hundred impressions of Highest Heaven, the Sphere of Stars,
the Void . . .
But what impression this? No! The very sight of God.

Although a long essay of notes would hardly be enough for any passage from Rûmî, a few particulars might need explanation. The Chinese were for the artists of Persia the absolute masters. The term Rûm actually comes from "Rome" (i.e., the Catholic Church, both Roman and Eastern) and refers in Islamic usage to the Byzantine Greeks and the lands they held or once held, particularly Anatolia. Moses here and elsewhere represents the Perfect Man or the perfect sufi. He has made himself the perfect mirror that completely reflects the attributes, the word, and the power of God. The Highest Heaven is called the Throne of God, the next, the Sphere of the Stars, is called the Footstool, and on the Fish rests this Earth. In terms of practice, Rûmî and other sufis say that the polishing of the heart takes place by invocation of the Divine (*zikr*) and meditation (*fikr*).

51. Nâ'ilî

d. 1666

We are the snake hidden in the staff
    in the hand of Moses
Don't believe we are the snake, we are the ant
    crushed beneath the foot

Even if we are reflected in the mirror
    before the face of intellect
It cannot see us, we are hidden
    within its proud gaze

Our place of refuge is in the wild eye
    of Mejnûn
We are the charm of beauty, hidden
    in the cheek of Leylâ

Even were it diamonds, it would not serve us
    as a cure
We are the brand of madness, hidden in the black
    center of the heart

Moses couldn't see us on Mount Sinai,
    nor in the flaming bush
We are hidden in the shining of God's radiant face

We are the sickness, our health is an addict
    of our suffering
We are love, hidden in the secret house
    of passion

We are the changing wand in the hand
    of the trickster of the turning skies
Every moment we are hidden in a thousand
    watching eyes

Oh Nâ'ilî, with our poems we are magicians
    of the image
We are visible in our words, but hidden deep
    in the heart of meaning

52. **Nâ'ilî**

My tears became desire that illuminates
    the rose-garden like a stream
My heart poured forth love like water
    for a shy young tree

I am a strange lover, Mejnûn, circled
    by images of the beloved's eye
Again and again, like bewildered gazelles,
    they wander around me

Your eyelashes matched their dress
    to that of witches
They all donned black for a night-raid
    on my heart

Your sapling body is like the slender *elif*
    in the *âh* of my heart's passion
Just like the swaying, heart-seeking cypress
    in the garden of the rose

Hey Nâ'ilî, from the rising of your verses
    comes luster and a brilliant shine
Which puts to shame the mirror of the sun
    like the moon-face of the beloveds

The letters hâ *and* elif

Left, the Arabic script form of the word *âh*, which means "sigh." *Right*, the tall letter *elif*, often compared to the cypress tree, the beloved's body, and the self-inflicted scratches on the breast of the distraught lover. It also has the numerical value of one and is the first letter in the name of God (Allah) and so comes to be a sign for the divine. The letter *hâ* is compared to the "burns of love" so that the lovers's chest scratched and burned in anguish is written over with the word *âh*. Calligraphy by Ali Alparslan, from the private collection of Mehmet Kalpaklı.

53. Nâ'ilî

Since the thunderbolt of disaster set our
threshing ground afire
The roses in our meadow seem the red coals
of Hell

We are the tormented ones in the sanctuary
of the Kaaba of love
Our home is a hidden corner in the grief-house
of the heart

We are that perfect lover hidden by the veil
of meaning
The veil is our own skirt, stained
by passion's blood

We are the saki, pouring the red blood of the heart,
while cup in hand
The love-thief's drunken glance casts the dregs
of our life to the ground

Oh Nâ'ilî, the symbols written by your pen
are like the talismans of witches
They are words of power that shake the walls
of the lands of verse

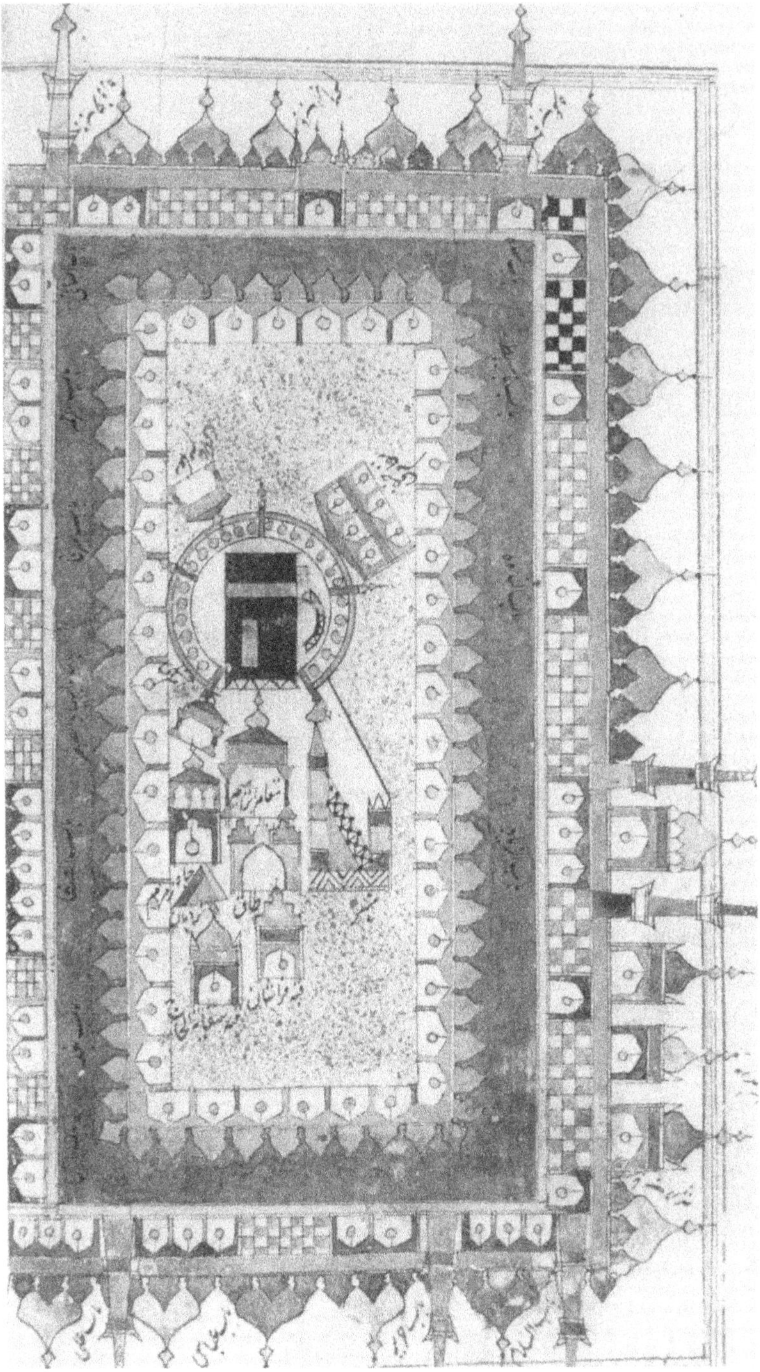

The Kaaba

From Ali Saffetî Lokman's *Fütûhu'l-Haremeyn*, Millet Kütüphanesi, Farsça 1312 (fol. 19b)

54. **Nâ'ilî**

What witch are you, that entangles our hearts
in your curls?
You are a gazelle who sets traps in the holy sanctuary
of the Kaaba

Your lashes are Tatar soldiers, and you the warlord,
Hulagu
Your reign has ravaged the country of the spirit,
the Baghdad of the heart

Both Hîzîr and Jesus have sacrificed themselves
to the water of life of your lip
You are the drink of water for which the soul
of Alexander thirsts

Oh my love, my sun, you are the adornment of the nine
gardens of the skies
You cannot be compared to the beloved's cheek,
you are the wild rose that blooms alone

Oh Nâ'ilî, the beloved's brows scowl
with anger
When you say of her mouth, it is as fine
as the tip of her curl

Poetic Parallels

A Letter to the Sultan

At the height of the reign of Sultan Süleymân in the sixteenth century, Bâkî was the acknowledged master of poets. He was also a noted religious scholar who would, in time, rise to one of the highest religious-legate positions in the land. Sultan Süleymân was himself an avid poet and numbered Bâkî in his circle of friends who gathered for entertainments that included recitals of poetry. The following is a letter from Bâkî to the Sultan on the subject of some poems that the poet had received from his ruler.

This letter also brings up the topic of "parallel poems" (*naẓîre*) which appear to have been quite common in Ottoman times. The composition of "parallels" was the practice of writing a poem using the rhyme, rhythm, and basic imagery of another poet's poem. We have included several examples of parallel poems among these translations: Neshâtî's "We are desire" is a parallel to Nâ'ilî's "We are the snake"; Mihrî's "My heart burns" and Bâkî's "Sparks from my heart" are parallels to Nejâtî's "Spiraling, the sparks." While there was a definite element of competition in choosing to write a parallel, there was also a good measure of respectful acknowledgment—for no good poet would write a parallel to anything but the best poetry. Thus Bâkî's composition of parallels to one of Süleymân's *gazels* is immensely flattering and is said to have been one of the happiest moments of the Sultan's life. If this is true, and there is no reason to doubt that it is, poetry and poetic skill must truly have been highly valued.

It is also worth noting that this letter demonstrates a number of the prominent characteristics of Ottoman formal prose of the high style, including the very around-about manner of addressing the ruler especially in the matter of commenting on his poems. It may be difficult to recognize that Bâkî is saying he has received two poems, that one of them is rather good and contains a couplet with an original usage, and (without saying) that the other is not so good.

> After bowing the face of humble submissiveness to the auspicious earth of his residence and, as is fitting, performing and expressing a prayer that his life be extended and his good fortune be increased from day to day, the presentation of this worthless slave is this: that two noble *gazels*, choice and exceptional, by his Lordship the Monarch have arrived and this miserable

servant, with Divine assistance, has composed two incompetent and error-laden parallels to one of them. In truth, added to the fact that the noble *gazel* is unmatched and without peer in its opening line, its closing line, and all its other noble lines, one couplet, the couplet beginning

If crookedness exist, why wonder at an infidel in the *mihrâb*?

is, in particular—I swear by God most mighty—to such an extent an outstanding couplet that it can have no parallel. For such a long time both the poets of Persia and the poets of Rum [the Ottomans] have spoken ever-so-many words on the topic of the *mihrab* [niche in the mosque indicating the direction of prayer] and it is only at this moment that I have seen something so beautifully delicate. May God Who is Praised and Exalted increase the life and fortune of his Lordship the Monarch and bring his worldly and after-worldly desires from wish to reality... by His Munificence and Beneficence may His remembrance be exalted.
Forever may the Sultan's noble person of angelic temperament be united with the protection and concern of the Lord of Glory, *For He is ever merciful to His servants.*

From [your] poor servant
Bâkî, the humble

[On the margin]

If you should deign to ask, "Why did you [Bâkî] write *two* parallels," there is a famous proverb, *One is never satisfied with a losing game.* If it so happened that I came up with a reasonable couplet, I would do a few couplets more. Yet how could there be Divine Aid sufficient that such a lowly wretch as I would be able to compose a parallel to such noble verses? What has been done is merely an imitation!

The line from Süleymân's poem refers to the fact that the *mihrâb* is usually semicircular and hence resembles the eye-brow. It is "crooked" [curved] like the eyebrow and crookedness is a quality of religious error or sin. So the "infidel" in the "prayer niche" is the eye in the eyebrow, the eye being an infidel [or sinner] because it tempts the believer to misbehavior, and the eyebrow being a "prayer niche" because it is the point to which all the lovers turn to worship.)

55. Neshâtî

d. 1674

We are desire hidden in the love-crazed call
of the nightingale
We are blood hidden in the crimson heart
of the unbloomed rose

We are pouring pearl-tears over the thinness
of our lovesick bodies
We are hidden, like the divine strand
that pierces the jewel's heart

So what if we are famous for having no worldly fame?
We are hidden, like the heart, in the strange mystery
of life's riddle

The east wind is the only confidante
for our every condition
We are always hidden in the disheveled twist
of the beloved's curl

Like the rose, the color of our essence
is obviously bright
But we are hidden in the joy of the wine-cup's
subtle way

Sometimes we are like the reed pen that illuminates
the plaints of love
Sometimes like the lament hidden in the pen
as it writes

Oh Neshâtî, we are ever abandoning the visible
presence of our selves
We are hidden in the absolute brilliance
of the perfect mirror

56. **Neshâtî**

You're gone—I'm alone in the company
 of longing
I no longer want sweet talk with friends
 if you're not there

I dare not go to the garden without you
The laughing rose seems red as fire,
 the swaying cypress a pointed flame

Let me tear a cry from my breast,
 let me voice such pain
The wheel of the sky turns backward,
 along with the shining sun

The passing cup at the party is a whirlpool
 of sadness without you
A whirlpool of bright wine inside the turning bowl

What a shame! Poor Neshâtî is so sick
 with grief and pain
Both the skirt of companionship, and its collar,
 are torn by separation's thorn

57. Neshâtî

The sky's face has turned dark, don't believe
a cloud has come
In the garden, snow changed the raven
to a falcon of white

Oh what designs might the magician of cold
display?
Like a mirror, the page of the water
is bound in ice

Is it surprising, since the whole world is frozen,
north to south
That the pure and flaming wine of the party
wraps itself in ice?

What is this violence of cold?
What is this fear?
The world has dressed the glowing coal
in the grey of a squirrel coat

Oh Neşâtî, against the curse
of the winter wind
The candle of the world-illuminating sun
holds up the cloud as a veil

58. Nedîm

d. 1730

At the gathering of desire you made me a wine-cup
with your sugar smile
Oh saki, give me only half a cup of wine,
you've made me drunk enough

You crushed me under the hoof of a wild horse
that runs like fire
In those places flames rise up from my ashes
like cypress trees

Ah, east wind, you came to me with the scent
of my lover's hair
You made me love-bewildered like the hyacinth's
curl

With your beauteous grace my hair has been standing
like a jinn
With love you've made me mirror-colored from head
to foot

Don't make your crying Nedîm drunk and devastated
like that
Saki, give me only half a cup of wine, you've made
me drunk enough

59. Nedîm

When the east wind leaves that curl,
    it carries the scent of musk
And when it opens the knot of your gown,
    it carries the scent of rose

On that rose-petal lip, I would find the taste
    of sugar
On that rosebud mouth, I would discover
    the scent of wine

At what party did you stay up all night
    in conversation?
Your drunken narcissus-eye is still perfumed
    with sleep

Alas, we were unable to see her without her veil
A shame that my rival should smell that silver
    neck unveiled

My tormented flesh became ash in the searing
    heat of love
The grass that grows there smells of burning
    until the Judgment Day

The rose-charm of coquettishness brought rosewater
    to your brow
Oh rose, the small apple of your chin smelled sweet!

Oh Nedîm, are you again cutting open and revealing
    meaning?
The point of the sword of the pen smells of the blood
    of difficult choice

60. **Nedîm**

As the morning wind blows, you are disheveled,
 my heart
You are imprisoned in the curls of the beloved,
 my heart

In this time of the rose, we are both ashamed
Ashamed for having given up wine, my heart

Why are the tears like a flame within my eye?
Are you hidden in the fire of weeping, my heart?

Did I say, "Drink no wine"?
 Did I say, "Don't love the beloved"?
Why do you run from me, my heart?

Your behavior is a stranger to wisdom
 and good sense
You are a guest in the depths of my breast,
 my heart

Looking at you in wonder, the mirror melts
 to a silver pool
Oh God, what a harshly burning flame you are,
 my heart

Like the lanterns of the caravan along
 the pilgrims' road
You shine among the people of love, my heart

Within you, the sun of talent shows itself,
 you are the nest of divine light
You are the border of the morning of passion,
 my heart

Since you have offered the cup of love to Nedîm,
 don't take the cup away
Let him quench his thirst before you,
 my heart

61. Nedîm

Take yourself to the rose-garden, it's the season
of our wandering
Oh swaying cypress, give back the ruined spring
its reign
Pour down your dark curls, let your cheek
be dressed in sable
Oh swaying cypress, give back the ruined spring
its reign

Come rose-mouthed one, your nightingales
are calling
Come to the garden, that we might forget
the rose has gone
Come, before the meadow is ravaged
by winter
Oh swaying cypress, give back the ruined spring
its reign

Cast your black down onto that red cheek
This year, border your crimson shawl in mink
And if the tulip cups are lacking, bring wine cups
in their stead
Oh swaying cypress, give back the ruined spring
its reign

The world is a Paradise, it is the season
of plentiful fruit
Won't you make the fruit of union ours as well?
Secretly bless your lovers, give each of them
a kiss
Oh swaying cypress, give back the ruined spring
its reign

Oh my heart-brightening beauty, I heard
a line of verse
It was lovely, though I don't know what
it meant
Oh Nedîm, I suppose you spoke the line
knowingly . . . it is this
Oh swaying cypress, give back the ruined spring
its reign

Lover and beloved with cypresses and willow
From the *Hamse-i Hatifî*, Topkapı Palace Museum Library, Revan 1520 (fol. 2a)

62. Nedîm

Delicacy was drawn out like the finest wire
    and became your slender body
Wine poured from the bottle and became
    your crimson cheek

The scent of the rose was distilled,
    a perfumed bead upon your cheek
The thorn embroidered your handkerchief,
    your veil of shyness

Oh reed pen, your hollowed center is filled
    with magic and with spells
Your center, secret within you, can be named black,
    the locks of Hârût

Dark crusaders surrounded the temple
    of your face
They came to the altar of your brow,
    became the mole upon your cheek

That heretic asked—"Would you like
    to drink wine?"
The most difficult question she has asked you,
    God have mercy, oh heart!

Of what cup are you the drunkard?
    Whose love-bewildered one are you?
You have deceived yourself, my heart,
    you know not what has befallen you

Your lips will be wounded on the teeth
　　of the "s" of kiss
Thus is it impossible for you to let
　　your ruby mouth be kissed

Nedîm, you speak of a beloved not found
　　in this city
Perhaps she was some sweet illusion
　　with a faery's luring face

The letter sîn, *or the Arabic script "s"*
Note the "teeth" on the letter. Calligraphy by Ali Alparslan, from the private collection of Mehmet Kalpaklı

63. Koja Râgıb Pasha

1699–1763

Dark thought is revealed in the twists and curves
of the heart
Tarnish, in the pure essence of the mirror

You may attain your desires without untimely suffering
True rewards are revealed without unnecessary struggle

Beauty and ugliness are traces in the mirror
of human character
In all forms created by the wheel of fate
the sorcerer is revealed

The world-igniting lightning bolt of love
cannot be contained by modesty's veil
The one maddened by thirst reveals himself
without restraint

Where true beauty is manifest, none are deprived
of God's gifts
The vision is revealed in the trembling
of the mountain

The human soul is the chosen place for unveiling
the divine bride
The beloved reveals herself only to the one
she beckons

Oh Râgıb, these are the true rewards
for our acts in this world
If you question the victim of oppression,
the true tyrant shall be revealed

64. Râsih Bey

d. 1731

Don't lower your languid eyes, don't aim
 your pointed lashes
Don't fire black arrow after arrow
 into my wounded heart!

My heart is full of grief—oh happiness,
 do not come!
In one home you cannot welcome one guest
 upon another

That beauty scatters crushed diamonds
 over every wound she opens
I thank her for those favors that take
 my life away

While apart from the beloved, I wander
 the land of exile
The turning heavens have dealt me separation
 and its torment

They say we don't drink wine,
 they say we do not love her
Slander upon slander they have heaped
 on poor Râsih

65. Fıtnat Hanım

d. 1780

In a heart that bears the image
    of the life-giving lip
Lies the divine nurturer of the soul,
    speaker of colored words

That alluring one never glances at the one
    who would buy union
In her quarter, a thousand addicts of desire
    offer their souls in the palms of their hands

With all his wisdom, Plato was content
    to live in a cask
While Kays took his pleasure wandering
    the desert of madness

For tyranny and torment, there is love and faithfulness,
    for separation there is union
Oh my heart, for every sorrow in this world
    there is a cure

Oh Fıtnat, the Beloved has her way of treating
    the lover, she knows what to do
She offers faithfulness in one hand,
    absolute cruelty in the other

66. Esrâr Dede

1748–1796

In the ruins, in the tavern—
    what is built, endures
Outside—monuments, civilizations,
    lie collapsed, destroyed

Logic drowns in a whirlpool of distractions
And the pleasure of absolute freedom
    is found only in madness

Oh devout one, don't wander vainly through the mosque,
    hunting God's blessing
This divine gift is found only in the wine-house

Let the nightingale abandon its claims, in its heart
    there is no true sacrifice
The only trace of love found is in the burning
    destruction of the moth

I revealed my heart's agony, my truth,
    and that infidel smiled
"Now what's happened to Esrâr?" she said,
    "He's reciting crazy tales, these poems!"

67. Esrâr Dede

You left, but don't forget, my heart
has no other
You left, it's true, but don't forget
this wounded heart

Sometimes, when you wake in pleasure,
at your bed of midnight
Don't forget our togetherness, our sweet talk

In the bed of joy, as you fall into
a sugared sleep
Don't forget the eyes of the sleepless one,
drinking poison

I'll be patient with sorrow and the grief
of separation
But oh my beauty, don't forget
your promised words

You said you'd never make me cry,
never watch the streets with longing
Don't forget the vow you spoke again
and again

Oh my effendi, do me a favor,
this man cannot bear your separation
Don't forget Esrâr, sick at heart
for your love

The Indian Style

In India, during the fifteenth and sixteenth centuries, the great wealth of the Persian-speaking court of the Turkic Mughal rulers drew large numbers of Persian poets with the prospect of generous patronage. There the innovative artistry of such poets as Baba Figânî of Shiraz (d. 1519) was adopted and transmuted into a style that is strikingly distinctive. Called "the Indian style" (*sebk-i hindî*) by later scholars, this poetic mode began to spread back to Iran and the Persian-speaking courts of Central Asia in the sixteenth century. By the seventeenth century the works of such contemporary "Indian style" Persian poets as Sâ'ib and 'Urfî of Shiraz were widely read in Istanbul and an Ottoman version had taken firm root.

The character of the Indian style is a subject of much dispute and speculation by scholars of Persian literature. What it becomes when manifested in Ottoman Turkish literature, however, has scarcely been addressed. For example, in Persian poetry one of the supposedly "Indian" innovations was the inclusion of actual events and persons in lyric poems. But we see this in Ottoman poetry at least from Nejâtî (d. 1509) on, and poets of the sixteenth century (Nihâlî for example) had numerous *gazels* specifically mentioning attractive shopboys in the bazaar. For Ottoman poetry, it seems unlikely that this sort of "realism" is an "Indian" innovation at all.

Some other recognizably "Indian style" features begin to show up regularly in Ottoman poetry only during the seventeenth century. The conjuring up of images takes a more fantastical turn and the "almost-rule" that the image must revolve about congruous or related vocabulary—relations either by similarity (*mura'ât-i nazîr/tenâsüb*) or by opposition (*tezâd*)—is no longer quite so rigidly in force. The poets begin to build involved and exaggerated conceits depending on comparisons between incongruous points. This results in individual couplets that are highly complex and packed with images whose relations to one another are highly ambiguous. This in turn foregrounds the poetry's imaginative, speculative, and philosophical aspects.

The syntax of poetry also takes a turn toward increased ambiguity by favoring long strings of Persian genitive/adjectival compounds. The conceptual difficulty of this style of verse becomes a value to the poets and their audiences. For example, Sheyh Gâlib has a quatrain in which he praises the obscurity of his poems:

I am that poet rare and seldom seen, Gâlib,
There is no shame in failure to comprehend my conceits
Each is a unique pearl from Being's mysterious deep
And the diver of intellect has no luck in that mystery

The kind of thing that is so difficult about this kind of verse is exemplified, rather less confusingly than usual, in the phrase translated as "pearl from Being's mysterious deep." The actual form of the expression is something like "pearl of the hidden/unseen world of he/she/it-ness" where the 'of' can indicate either a genitive relation ("pearl of the deep") or an adjectival one ("coat of red"). So it is not really possible to tell if it is a pearl/jewel made of Divine essence or a pearl from the unseen world of Divine essence or a pearl of mysterious, unseen character, and so on. The possibilities do tend to boggle the mind and make translation extremely difficult. Nonetheless, this is also the most challenging and rewarding poetry to translate.

This confounding of rational intellect, which can be interpreted as a parallel to the abandonment of rationality sought by the mystics, becomes thematic in some (but not all) of the poetry of a long line of poets represented most prominently in this anthology by Nef'î, Nâ'ilî, Neshâtî, and Sheyh Gâlib.

68. Sheyh Gâlib

1757–1799

You are my effendi, if I have any respect in the world,
    it is because of you
If I am famed at all among the lovers,
    it is because of you

In simple words, you are the loving soul,
    the illumination of my life
If there is profit from the treasure of my life,
    it is because of you

The color of your beauty gives brilliance to all
    my thoughts
If the rose-garden of my imagining exists,
    it is because of you

During your reign, I've not suffered
    even the smallest pain
Oh my shining sun, if I cry out,
    it is because of you

I am the moth of separation, I annihilate myself in the brightness
    of your beauty, for you are the candle of union
If every evening I desire a kiss and warm embrace,
    it is because of you

I am a martyr for you, my breast is a tulip garden
    of love's burns
If my tomb has a lantern and my grave a candle,
    it is because of you

He who sees me crazy with love would suppose
    I was a whirlwind of the desert
I am the annihilation within annihilation,
    whatever I have, it is because of you

Why did you cast me out to wander when I was your jewel,
    your perfect pearl?
If there is dust on the mirror of my heart, if there is this longing,
    it is because of you

Oh Saki, you filled my cup with tears of blood,
    it glows scarlet like the dawn
On the morning after the wine-party, if I'm still drunk,
    it is because of you

Oh Mevlânâ, it is in you that Gâlib takes his deepest
    and holy refuge
If on my head there is a dervish crown of honor,
    it is, my beloved, because of you

69. Sheyh Gâlib

I won't abandon you, though you cause me
one hundred thousand sorrows—I love you
The pen of fate has thus written on my brow
I won't break my word, though the nine spheres
of heaven turn
May the earth and sky be witness to my vow—
I love you

The shackles on my heart are your cruel eyebrows
The cord that binds me, your black-doing curl
I am sick and my only hope for health
is in your languid eye
I have been stricken by an illness that has no cure—
I love you

Oh you with an eyebrow like a new moon,
my heart turns toward you
If I look at the *mihrab*, it's only from the corner
of my eye
Were I to turn away from the *râ* of your eyebrow,
it would be hypocrisy
This may be good, or it may be evil, I care not—
I love you

Longing for the black down of your cheek,
I become earth that has no dust
Were I to be completely destroyed, I would still speak
of your cheek and lip
Were I split down the middle, I would still not sever
myself from the sword of your glance
Oh beloved don't torture me in vain—
I love you

I am Gâlib the Mad, greetings to Ferhâd and Mejnûn!
I won't turn away from you, though I part ways
with this world
I am the moth to your candle, what use have I
of despair?
Let both stranger and friend know this truth—
I love you

The letter râ
Calligraphy by Ali Alparslan, from the private collection of Mehmet Kalpaklı

70. Sheyh Gâlib

To me, love is the flame—
the divine manifestation to Mansûr.
To me, every cross-beam of the gallows—
the burning bush of Sinai.

That rose-adorned cypress
is the essence of attraction
In a longing cry to heaven,
tender branches yearn upwards,
a tree of God's light.

It's become clear to me now—
the house of unity
stands in the neighborhood
of calamity
And its marker-stone
is the minaret of Mansûr
melting as he shouts,
"God is Great!"

I am a pearl
born of a fevered trembling
rolling perfectly
in exile.
To me,
mother-of-pearl sun,
dawn sun,
you are a morning in Nishapur—
earthshaking!

I am the one who knows well
the pathways of the invisible world.
I am the famed companion
of the *'ankâ*—
bird of the wilderness,
of frightfulness,
of terrible aloneness.

The shadow-green down of your lips
with the blood-tears on my lashes
soft, dark, red,
Are the image of a colored bird
in the sweet garden of faithfulness.

I do not twist my face in pain
fearing for worldly treasure,
tormented!
The sagas of kings are but a painted rose
nothing more
on a fragile Chinese cup,
made for the ruler's hand
not my own.

He who is drunk on love
pays no attention
to the pleasures
of the golden bowl, passing.
To me, the true alchemy
is that languid-eyed narcissus.

This ruined breast of mine, pierced
with a hundred arrows of separation
Is the living soundboard of the *santûr,*
my music forever a lament.

I am the traveler
wandering the path of love,
driven mad,
insane!

Oh Gâlip!
Like the droplet of dew
in the morning—pure, patient,
I cannot say the sun of God
is distant from me.

There is no sky
between us.
We are one.

71. Sünbülzâde Vehbî

d. 1809

Oh east wind, come, what news from that garden
  of roses?
What news from the nightingale of spring,
  who's now seen autumn days?

What news from that beguiling young cypress?
Oh flowing tears, see who's embracing her now

Oh my eye, the breeze came with dust upon its
  feet
What news from the dust of the path
  of my beloved?

The spy of my thought has gone to the land
  of her beauty
What news from the lady of the kingdom
  of pride?

Oh Vehbî, the messenger of the sigh will soon
  set out and return
What news from the beloved?
  What sweet messages of union?

72. Enderunlu Vâsıf

d. 1824

The gazelles have bound their hearts
to your eyelids black with kohl
And from your dark glance, witches read
a book of spells

Last night, drunk in the garden, they stole
the scent of your curl
The night's flowers perfumed the senses
of the people of love

Fate gives to the wealthy the coin
of people in need
So do small streams all run down
to the sea

Don't always use imitations in place
of what is real
Does your cheek want for rouge, or your eyebrow
beg for the painted line?

Oh Vâṣıf, this poem is a *gazel* adorned,
a parallel of Es'ad
It would only be right that all masters of language
give it praise

73. ‘İzzet Mollâ

1786–1829

Everyone knows this world will not be ruined
by sin
Destruction will come when flattery is spoken
in place of truth

He who wants the world destroyed because his own home
is in ruins
Doesn’t know, in others’ eyes, he will be
twice destroyed

Good deeds are the ladder that leads
to the castle of Heaven
Is it possible to reach this Paradise
if the ladder is in ruins?

We have reached a luckless spring
in this sad world
When the nightingale is silent, the pool is empty,
and the rose-garden is in ruins

The helpless nightingale cannot go out to meet
the spring
Its wing is broken, the season is winter,
its nest is all in ruins

Oh ‘İzzet, if there were even one pillar
remaining to this dome
This transitory world would not end in ruins

And if the key of rule were given to our
wise master,
Not one family in Ottoman lands
would fall in ruins

74. ʻİzzet Mollâ

I am a nightingale in the garden of grief,
    I'm not seeking a nest in this world
I've no interest in this rose-garden,
    this ancient cage

Oh my jinn, the glass of my eye is yours,
    and yours alone
If the houris came from Paradise,
    I would not turn my gaze upon them

The black of my eye has become dust
    on the path of hopeful waiting
If I see the god-light of her eye,
    I'll seek the world no more

What I'm truly seeking is that rose-cheek
    of hers
Not those rose-tears on my lashes,
    watered by my cries

The hell of my sighs rains abundance
    upon the garden of my soul
I've no need for this flood of tears,
    were it the river of Paradise

My heart is a garden of rose-wounds,
    your image banished by love
I no longer seek a place there
    for that swaying cypress

Oh ʻİzzet, the smoke of sighs has so blinded
    my eyes
I long for neither her blue eye
    nor the world's open sky

It is enough that the door of Mevlânâ's blessing
    not be closed to me
No palace gate is as dear to me, God knows

75. Yenishehirli 'Avnî

1827–1884

Don't think we came to ask for wealth
    and prestige
We came into the world to sigh for a beloved

Fate is a torture to us, in one hundred caravans
    we came to make complaint
We came to take refuge in the dust
    before the beloved's door

Burns of desire, a hundred eyes, cover us
    from head to foot
We came to look into the mirror
    of the beloved's beautiful face

Oh Hoja, if it's a sin to gaze at the face
    of an idol
We came to this fictitious world
    to commit a sin

Tell the enemy—don't become a thorn
    in this illusive garden
We came to ornament our turban
    with only a single rose

Just like Avnî, we came to the tavern
    of suffering
We came for wine, and to abandon
    our troubled hearts

"Lover and Beloved"

From an untitled *mecmua*, Topkapı Palace Museum Library, Revan 958 (fol. 29a)

Notes

Nesîmî

1. *Oh my idol*

Idol of the temple: The association of the beloved with an idol has a long history in the Islamic literatures. The pre-Islamic religions and cultures of the area were famously producers of representational art—from Byzantine iconography, to Greek and Roman statuary, to Chinese painting and Hindu temple carvings. All these representations of human beauty were considered idols by most Muslims. So the beloved, when she is worshiped by the lover, becomes an idol. Moreover, because sin and error and heresy are black, the beloved's face, marble-white with a black mole and black lovelock, is also a temple of idols.

The wheel of the skies: the *çarh* which represents the spheres of heaven that turn to change a person's fortune. See *The Cosmos and the Earth* following poem no. 19.

Ahmed-i Dâ'î

2. *The torture of the beloved*

Trouble-making brows: This introduces the notion of *fitne*, which involves disturbing the peace and harmony of the community by doing something (or having a quality) that causes trouble, unrest, riot, or misbehavior. The beloved causes such trouble in innumerable ways.

Sheyhî

3. *Your sun-face*

Both worlds: In the traditional cosmology, this material world, the world of being, coming-into-being, and passing-out-of-being, is only the last emanation of the true ground of being (God). Although there are a vast number of "worlds" or stages in this emanation, the "two worlds" are this world and the invisible, ideal world representing the prior emanations. For the mystics this "other world" is the world of true reality in which the essential, Divine unity of all existence is manifested.

The saz: The most common Turkish musical instrument. A lutelike stringed instrument with a small half-pear body and long thin neck, usually carrying four double courses of strings.

4. *It's the season of spring*

Wild tulip . . . narcissus: Here most likely a wild peony or poppy. See the notes for poem no. 33. The narcissus (*nergis*) is usually compared to an eye, sometimes a watchful eye, sometimes the sleepy eye of a party-goer on the morning-after, sometimes the languid eye of the beloved.

Jem: Also known by the longer name Jemshîd (Jem the Brilliant), this Persian ruler is related to the Avestan hero Yima (also "the brilliant") and, according to the tradition as it came to the Ottomans, he was the fourth king of ancient Iran. There are many legends surrounding Jemshîd, his heroic works, magical powers, and tragic fall from glory. The most important of these to Ottoman poetry are the story of his inventions of wine and the solar calendar, his magic wine-cup (also called his mirror) in which he could see all that passed in the world, his inception of the New Year (*Nevrûz*) celebration, and his famous palace. It is said that Jemshîd traveled to the East, near the place of the sun's rising, and there built a fabulous, bejeweled palace called the Throne of Jemshîd. And when, at the dawning of the day, he ascended the throne of his palace dressed in gem-studded robes of many colors the horizon was set ablaze with unimaginable magnificence. This the people of the world called "the New Day" or *nevrûz* in Persian and from then on the day when the sun enters Ares, about March 21, was considered to be the day on which the new solar year began.

Key, throwing open: The word for "conquer" (*feth*) is the same as the word for "to open." "Key" (*miftah*) comes from the same root. So here there is both a play on the double meaning of "conquer/open" (the figure called *tevriye* by the Turks) and a meaningful connection by root derivation (the figure called *iştikâk*).

In the spring: Spring is the time when the Istanbul elites—that is, any who were sensitive, emotional, spiritually wise, enlightened—would go out into the gardens and fields for parties with food and drink and flowers. The season would begin with the official festival at the Persian New Year (*Nevrûz*). (See *Jem* above).

Ahmet Pasha

5. *Ask about my wailing*

Bird of dawn: There is a time just before the sunrise when all the birds seem to sing and chatter at the same time as if to usher in the sun. This is known in Turkish as *kuşluk vakti* (the bird time), a term that confusingly also refers to the time between morning and noon (midmorning). The break of dawn is also the time when the gates to heaven stand open and prayers are especially effective. Thus the lover is still awake and still mourning aloud after a sleepless night, wailing his prayers in the hope of this time being heard. The nightingale is also known as the bird of dawn and is often identified with the poet. The word used for "prayer" here is *zemzeme* which means both "the muttered prayers of Zoroastrian priests" and "the cooing of a dove."

Wounded heart: In Turkish what most often aches or is wounded or is burned by the emotional consequences of passion is the liver and not the heart. Because it would be quite strange in English to say "my aching liver" or "my liver burns for you," we have most often (but not always) substituted "heart" for "liver."

Fire of my sighs/burning pen: In the usual metaphoric physiology of love, the inside, the heart/liver of the beloved, is set aflame by love. The liver is roasted (becomes a kebab) in the conflagration, the heart is singed and scarred by burns, the throat becomes like a chimney from which hot and smoky sighs emerge in a shower of sparks. Many, many related images occur in poems in this volume. Here the lover, bent over the letter he is composing to his beloved, emits such burning sighs that he sets the end of his reed pen aflame.

Cycle of the Moon: According to ancient belief an age of the world was forty nine thousand years divided into seven cycles of seven thousand years. Each cycle begins with a thousand years under the influence of one of the seven "wandering stars" (planets) of the ancients and is named after that planet. The planets in order according to the heavenly circle they belong to are: the Moon (first heaven), Mercury (second heaven, etc.), Venus, the Sun, Mars, Jupiter, Saturn. The cycles of the world begin, in reverse order, with the Cycle of Saturn (or the Cycle of Adam) and end with the Cycle of the Moon. In the last Cycle (that of the Moon) there will be all kinds of calamity and disruption in preparation for the end of the world and the last judgment. So here the poet says "ask the Cycle of the Moon. . . " in the sense "blame the Cycle of the Moon" with the understanding that "moon" also means the beloved (with her bright moon-face), and so, for the lover, the "Cycle of the Moon" is the age of his own life influenced by her subversive, trouble-making presence.

6. *Is there any heart*

Arrows of your glance: The beloved's glance is commonly compared to an arrow shot from the bow of the eyebrow to pierce and wound the heart of the lover. The eyelashes are the visible glance-arrows lined up to be shot. (Eyelashes are also compared to spears or javelins.)

A life spent without you: In the Turkish this line is marked by two repetitions. The word *'ömr* (life, life span) is repeated three times in the first hemistich and the word *cân* (life, soul, life-force) is repeated three times in the second (or four times if one includes the form *cânân* which means "beloved"). The result is more interesting and poetic in Turkish than a similar repetition might be in English.

Rose/nightingale: The image of the rose and the nightingale is one of the most common in Ottoman poetry. The basic story is that the nightingale comes to the garden to sing to the rose, with which it is in love. The rose blossoms receptively but is guarded by its thorn, which, like an angry protector, pierces the breast of the impassioned bird when it dares embrace its beloved. This is, they say, why some species of nightingales have a red mark on their breasts. From this story a vast number of ingenious conceits are spun. Often the nightingale represents the poet, because of its impassioned nature and sweet song. In this poem the poet/nightingale's red-marked breast is not pierced but branded by the fire of love.

Nejâtî

7. *Those glances rain down*

Tatar . . . magic stone: In the Persian dictionary *Burhân-i Kâti'* there is an entry for a *seng-e yede*: "a stone in Turkistan used for making rain." Thus the eye or its pupil is like both a dark-skinned and pagan Tatar and the (black) stone he uses to make rain.

When the black wind blows: Nejâtî is famous for incorporating Turkish proverbs in his poetry (the figure called *irsâl-i mesel*). Here the "black wind" is a wind heavily laden with moisture.

Jesus-breath: In Muslim lore Jesus shares many qualities with Hızır (see the article *Iskender/Alexander* following poem no. 10), especially the ability to bring the dead back to life. Because his mother was impregnated not by a father but by the "breath" of Gabriel, Jesus' miracles of resurrection are thought to have been done by his breathing on the dead person. Therefore, the "breath of Jesus" is used metaphorically to mean something that revives a dead or dying person.

When the south wind: Another proverb.

Becomes a pearl: The image seems obvious on the surface: raindrops or teardrops look like pearls. However, in an Ottoman context the tale is a bit more complex. According to literary myth pearls are formed when rain falls over the sea and oysters rise up from the depths, each opening to capture a raindrop in its shell. The droplets are then nourished in these mother-of-pearl cradles until they become pearls. (By the way, drops that fall into the mouth of a snake become its poison.)

8. *The heart is pleased*

The sun of the love-thief: The term in the text is simply "thief"; the translation here is interpretive. This is another proverb or proverb-like aphorism: "the sun [i.e., the luck] of the thief rises when the moon is dark," that is, utter darkness is good for thieves.

Using sand to cleanse: The Muslim is obliged to pray five times during the day and before each period of prayer there must be an ablution (ritual washing). When a Muslim has no access to water or enough water for washing, he or she may use sand instead. This is the inferior alternative.

Yâ hû: "Oh He!" This is a phrase used by dervishes in their ecstatic invocation of the Divine (*zikr*) and also in greeting one another or upon departing from a ceremony. "He" refers to the Divine.

Musk of China: Musk was brought to Anatolia from Eastern Turkistan on the borders of China often by the Tatars or Central Asian Turks. It came in the form of the dried (black) musk-sacs (scent glands) of the Asian deer sometimes called a Chinese gazelle. These musk-sacs were thought to be nodules that grew on the bellies of the deer/gazelle as a result of disease, infection, or injury. The nodules filled with a clot of blood and then began to itch. According to this notion, the musk collectors put out sharp stakes on which the deer would scratch themselves causing the nodules to fall off. The scent-gland was taken to be this blood-filled nodule. The fact that the word for China (*çîn*) is also the word for "twist, curl" makes this a plentiful source of conceits for the Ottoman poet. Here the musk declines to come to Anatolia, where it is not needed so long as the beloved's black and fragrant lock—into which one can read "China" (*çîn*)—is there (already).

9. *Those tulip-cheeked ones*

Tulip: See the notes for poems no. 4 and no. 33.

Bow ... arrows: The eyebrow is often seen as a bow which the glance (see the note for poem no. 6) uses to shoot eyelash-arrows into the heart of the lover.

Joseph: In Muslim culture, Joseph (Yûsuf) is the embodiment of masculine beauty. In the Quranic version of the Joseph story (Sura XII), when Joseph is sold into slavery in Egypt his master's wife is overcome by his beauty and tries to seduce him. When her desire becomes public knowledge and opens her to ridicule, she invites her women friends to her house and invites Joseph in while they are eating fruit. The women are so bedazzled by his beauty that they cut themselves with their fruit knives.

Sakis: The *sâḳî* (from the Arabic root *saḳâ*, "to pour") is the servant who pours wine at the typal party, often held in a garden where the gathering of good friends drink wine, eat delicate morsels of food, listen to music, recite poetry, and engage in conversation. This epicene young person is also a potential (or actual) beloved and is often addressed as such in the love lyrics. In the mystical poetry this beloved is the master, who pours out the intoxicating wine of Divine love, which causes the adept to let go of reason and turn to the unreasoning logic of the heart.

The water of life: See *Iskender/Alexander* following poem no. 10.

The rivers of Paradise: See the notes for poem no. 18.

10. *Spiraling, the sparks*

The sparks: See the notes for poem no. 5. Here the sparks of the burning sigh are assumed to have set the sun afire. This is the often used figure *hüsn-i ta'lîl* (beautifully fanciful reason for something).

Touch his feet to the ground: There is a double meaning here (the figure *tevriye*): "to touch the feet to the ground" has both the obvious meaning and the colloquial sense "to be very happy."

Damascus . . . Egypt: There are several interlocking double (or multiple) meanings here (*tevriye* again). The word translated as "Damascus" (*şâm*) also means "night" or "dark." (We represent this by calling Damascus "black," which is not in the original.) The word for "Egypt" (*mısır*) means "a city" or "the city of Cairo" or "Egypt." The historical conflict between Egypt and Syria (Damascus) was well known.

Like holy pilgrims: During the pilgrimage to Mecca, all pilgrims make the *tavaf* in which they circle seven times around the Kaaba. This is often compared to the lovers circling the beloved's house or neighborhood. Here the sun and moon circling around the earth (in the traditional cosmology) are seen as lovers circling the Kaaba of the beloved's door.

The mirrors, turning: There are many references to mirrors in Ottoman poetry (see for example, *Rûmî's Mirror* following poem no. 50) but this one is a bit more unusual. It seems to refer either to the spherical, many-faceted mirrors that some shop-keepers hung outside their shop doors (for decoration and so that those inside could see who is passing by) or to the round mirrors that were once hung in the great mosques.

Fresh new verse: Because the themes and stories and base metaphors of Ottoman poetry continue with little significant change over a long period, it is sometimes difficult for us to see what constitutes the fresh and new for an Ottoman poet. However, they were tremendously ingenious in creating new relations, comparisons, and conceits from the palette of elements they chose to restrict themselves to. This constant creativity is what the Ottomans know as originality.

Mihrî Hatun

11. *I opened my eyes*

My star of good luck . . . Jupiter: Good luck is always described as a "rising." Jupiter is both a lucky star and masculine; it is a judge (and hence a legal scholar) and a companion to the moon.

By his dress an infidel: Non-Muslims usually wore clothing different from that of Muslims and in some cases were required to do so. The usual difference referred to in the poetry is that the Christians wore belts with their robes.

The water of life: See *Iskender/Alexander* following poem no. 10. The reference here may also be to the Iskender with whom Mihrî was said to be in love (see her biography).

12. *At times, my longing*

The thorn of love: Here she compares herself to the nightingale, which, when impassioned by love, tries to embrace the rose and is killed by its thorn.

Rival: See the notes for poem no. 23. The rival here is compared to a pariah dog that haunts the graveyard.

13. *My heart burns*

This poem is a *nazîre* "parallel" to Nejâtî's "Spiraling, the sparks" (poem no. 10).

Lantern: Here the word for "lantern" *fener* must mean a kind of lantern that revolves. It is either the "magic lantern" that rotates a series of images in front of a light or the revolving lantern of a lighthouse. Bâkî, in his own parallel to Nejâtî and Mihrî (no. 36), chooses the magic lantern image. We have decided to use the lighthouse in our translation of this poem.

The sun and moon: In the Quranic story of Joseph, the archetypical beauty, the youth relates to his father a dream of which he says, (Sura XII:4) "I saw the eleven stars and the sun and the moon; I saw them prostrate themselves before me." This was interpreted to mean that in the future his parents and eleven brothers would bow to him. The brothers were so enraged by envy that they sold him into slavery.

My heart burned: The Turkish says "my heart became a kebab." Najaat did not find this rather common image serious and poetic enough in English and so wrote around it when she could.

Zeyneb Hatun

14. *Remove your veil*

The black down ... wrote a royal command: There is a play here (*tevriye*) on the word *hat*, which means both "cheek down" and "calligraphy/calligraphed official order."

The water of life: See İskender/Alexander following poem no. 10. The second line has the more literal sense: "Even if it takes a thousand years searching [like] Alexander with Hızır [at your side]."

Simply, bravely: This translates the word *merdâne* which is "manly" but means "brave and forthright [as men are]." We have given up the "manly," which would retain the irony of the fact that there is no word for the kind of bravery Zeyneb intends except one that refers solely to men. Also, this world was seen by many Ottoman men as a woman, because women were thought to be inexplicably full of complexities and deceits, interested in adornments and superficial beauties instead of essences. Men, in contrast, considered themselves to be *by nature* honest, ingenuous, straightforward, and focused on spiritual realities.

Revânî

15. *What do you say*

Oh Nâsih: Here we meet one of the usual characters in the Ottoman lyric party: the *nâsih*, who gives advice to the distraught lover. We will meet another character in the last line of this poem: the zealot or *zâhid*, who abstains from all pleasure in the hope of attaining Paradise and who warns others that they must do likewise. This person is one of a class of shallow moralists and religious literalists, who censure poets for their live-for-today behavior.

Pious one: See note above. This is the *sôfî*, another of the naively religious characters of the lyric. While fixing his gaze on Paradise he misses the beauties of this world, which are a sure sign of Divine presence.

Lâmi'î

16. *Yesterday I saw*

Bird of fortune: This is the *hümâ* (see *Fabulous Birds* following poem no. 29).

Zâtî

17. *Oh heavens, why do you cry*

Swaying cypress: The body of the beloved—tall, graceful, slender—is often compared to the cypress. The cypress is also an evergreen, unaffected by the change of seasons; it has no fruit to offer the lover, and, when the wind blows it sways, as does the beloved when he/she walks. In Ottoman miniature painting the cypress is often depicted being embraced by a flowering branch as a symbol for love. It is frequently planted as part of the border of a garden and so looks over the wall, as in Zâtî's image, like a beloved with a wandering eye.

Oh nightingale: See the notes for poem no. 6. Here the thorn is compared to the rival in love who threatens the life of the nightingale/poet.

Haunting as a jinn: One of the three classes of intelligent beings according to Muslim lore, the jinn (English "genie") are made of fire or vapor (of the other two classes, angels are made of light, and humans of clay). They are mentioned several times in the Quran. These invisible creatures (the female jinn are called *perî* or faeries) live lives similar in every way to the lives of humans. They have societies, are religious or not, and are subject to their own rulers. There are many stories about relations between human beings and jinn, usually having to do with harm done by the jinn to the humans and human attempts to compel the jinn to behave or give rewards. Among these stories are several about love affairs between humans and jinn (or *perîs*). Out of all this comes the image of the beloved as jinn and a host of conceits having to do with the mischievous, seditious, harmful, deceitful behavior of the jinn/beloved, her unworldly beauty, his body of flame, the magical bewitchment of the lover, etc. The demon lover of Western folklore is not too dissimilar an image. Here, however, the poet makes a play on the word *perîşân* which usually means "distraught, all broken up, disheveled," as it does in the first half-line. But when it is repeated in the second half-line as *yâr-ı perîşân* it is, we believe, to be read as if it were a compound *perî–şân* "one who acts like or has the reputation of being a [female] jinn." As was demonstrated in the introductory essay, Zâtî likes to do this sort of thing.

Hayretî

18. *We are not slaves*

Slaves: The phrase "we are slaves" is the *redîf* in this poem. In the Ottoman context where many of the elite and wealthy were actually slaves of the ruler, it is most often a source of pride to call oneself a slave. See also the story about this couplet in the biography of Hayretî.

The rivers of Paradise: In the original this is "the Kevser of the Paradises of Comfort." Kevser is the river, or pool that runs through Paradise. The word *kevser* means "abundance" and comes from an enigmatic short Sura (chapter) of the Quran (no. 108) entitled *Kevser*). The meaning of the Sura in translation would be something like, "1. We have given you as a gift, the Abundance. 2. So pray to your Lord and make sacrifice. 3. Truly he who wishes you evil, he will be cut off." In trying to make sense of this verse, the Kevser has been interpreted as a river or pool that refreshes the believers in Paradise. It is said to be as white as milk, sweet as honey, smooth as cream, cool as snow, and able to quench all thirst with a single sip. The Paradise(s) of Comfort is one of eight paradisial gardens; it is believed to be made of white silver.

Silken cloak ... dervish cap ... coarse robes: This is another point of difficult multiple meaning. The word *tâc* translated as "dervish cap" is also the word for "crown" and is commonly used for both or either. "Crown" goes well with *kabâ* when it means "silken robes" (as it does in Arabic), but the people other than the ruler who wear a *tâc* are the institutionalized dervishes and so it is most likely that the poet refers to giving up the symbols of respectable, higher class dervishes (the Mevlevîs, for example) and turning to the dress (a crude blanket) of those who have completely renounced the world. In this sense the relationship between words (*tenâsüb*) is maintained by the second (and unsought) sense of *kabâ* in Turkish, which is "coarse."

Figânî

19. *My sad heart is burnt*

Burnt black: The burning liver/heart is often compared to a roasting kebab (as it is here). It is important to remember that the fictional garden-party with wine and beloved is often represented as a picnic with delicious foods.

Blood-colored wine: In Ottoman poetry the grief-stricken lover usually cries until his tears are mixed with blood. The parallel between this mixing and the usual mixing of wine with water is the source of many metaphors.

The nine vaults ... throne of God: see The Cosmos and the Earth following poem no. 19.

The freezing gale: This is the *sarsar yeli* or the "wind [named] sarsar" that is mentioned twice in the Quran (XLI:16: "We sent against them a furious wind through days of disaster ... " and LXIX:6: "And the people of 'Âd, they were destroyed by a furious wind of great violence." The people of 'Âd were a powerful and materialistic race of great builders living in southern Arabia. According to legend they were visited by a prophet named Hûd, whose divine message they rejected (see Quran VII:65–72 and XXVI:123–140). As a result God sent down a terrible blast of wind that destroyed them and their works, leaving only a remnant that became the people of Thamûd, who later were to make the same error and suffer a similar fate.

20. *Your kiss does not satisfy*

Your body rises like the dead: There is a play here on the fact that the word for "body" *kâmet* is from the same root as the word for "the Resurrection" *kıyâmet*. So the beloved's body becomes something that reminds the poet—by etymology—of the Resurrection and hence of the promise that even though he should be killed by love there will be a rebirth in the afterlife. (Also, "the Resurrection" in the expression "for the Resurrection to break out" [*kıyâmet kopmak*] is more or less an equivalent to the English "for all Hell to break loose," which is what happens when one falls in love.)

That which makes me crazy: The Turkish has a "folded" parallel here between "crimson/flaming crazy," "black mourning clothes" and "black eyebrows," "reddish/chestnut eyes."

Fevrî

21. *The arrow of your glance*

The form of this poem is called *mürabba'* (quatrains). The rhyme scheme of this example is *a a a* A // *b b b* A etc., where A is a repeated line rhyming in *a*.

Arrow: The beloved's glance is commonly described as an arrow (or dart, knife, spear, or javelin) shot from her eyes by the bow of her eyebrow into the heart of the lover. He is thus wounded and bleeds bloody tears of woe. This is how one catches love, unsuspectingly shot from ambush by a seductive look. The eyelashes then are the arrows aimed at the heart or a row of spears that her glances will direct in an assault on the castle of the lover's breast.

Cheek, black down: see The Down on Your Cheek following poem no. 43.

The seven-layered heavens: see The Poetic Cosmos following poem no. 19.

Sigh: The burning heart/liver sends a smoky sigh (*âh*) up through the chimney of the throat, from which it rises in a shower of sparks to the sky. Here the smoke is cited as a fanciful explanation for why the sky is blue.

Both worlds: See the notes for poem no. 3.

For the sake of Muhammad: In the text the name used is actually Mustafâ, one of the names used to refer to Muhammad.

Hayâlî

22. *They do not know how to search*

World-Adorner: God, who is responsible for the beauties of this world.

Hey ascetic: See the notes for poem no. 15.

The arrow of desire: The image of the bent body as a bow strung by a stream of tears pouring to the ground also refers somewhat obliquely to the person who vainly hunts the pleasures of this world.

23. *We are among those*

Moths to the candle: See the notes for poem no. 68.

Orphans . . . begging: This refers to a particular kind of begging. Students in the theological schools (*medrese*) would have a three month break during which they would go into the countryside, where they would preach, give religious advice and instruction, and do readings from the Quran in exchange for money, food, and clothing. So what is being done here is begging by offering religious services in exchange for sustenance.

The dogs who guard your door: In the general story of the lover and beloved the beloved is surrounded by protectors and rivals. The usual protector is the *rakîb*, the watchful relative who guards the honor of the family by protecting the beloved from improper advances or gossip-causing attentions. This character is often referred to as a dog or guard-dog. (Here the lover claims that he is trying to be polite and proper in his attempts to approach the beloved by making friends with members of her family.)

Ascetic . . . drunken friends: This couplet contrasts two antagonists in the party-context: the ascetic (see the note for poem no. 15) and the drinker/partygoer (*rind*). The *rind* is that person who frequents the tavern and the party, who is always intoxicated and ready for a good time. He often represents the true mystic, who has neither concern for the proprieties of this world nor a simplistic hope for the pleasures of the next world and who wanders about intoxicated by love of the Divine. Thus the *rind* and the *zâhid* become typed as "dervish" and "antidervish." But this is not to ignore the fact that, according to contemporary biographers, many Ottoman poets, at one time in their lives at least, were actually addicted to wine, drugs, parties, and passionate affairs of the heart.

Oh my sultan: In Ottoman poetry the beloved is often referred to by some term meaning "ruler" or "monarch." This identification of beloved and ruler means that love for the ruler—which was a significant feature of the relation between the dependent elites and the sultan—is always a possible theme of a lyric poem, and certainly some of these poems were intended for the ruler and refer to him.

24. *When dawn hennas her hands*

Hennas: In Turkey and much of the Middle East, brides customarily dye their hands and the tips of their fingers reddish- orange with henna. Thus Hayâlî's image here is the equivalent of Homer's "rosy-fingered dawn."

New bride of the golden veil: The fourth veil or the fourth sphere of the heavens is the sphere of the sun (the golden sphere, see The Cosmos and the Earth following poem no. 19) and the rising of the sun is compared to the bride lifting her veil to her husband for the first time.

Jemshîd: See the notes for poem no. 4.

Let Venus: This couplet can only be partially translated. It depends in large part on knowing that Venus is the musician of the spheres (see *The Cosmos*) and here takes the rays of sunlight for lute strings so that she can play two of the set melodic modes of traditional Turkish music: the first, *Sünbüle* or "the Melody of (the Constellation) Virgo", and the second *Nevâ* or "the (Harmonious) Song." This is a good example of the figure called *tenâsüb*, where vocabulary belonging to the same general category is brought together. This use is especially brilliant as most of the terms belong both to the spheres of the sky and to music (and moreso if one considers that the word *nevâ* can be related by a false derivation to the word *nev'* which means "the helical rising or setting of a star," a fanciful consideration that its primary audience would not find all that strange in an Ottoman poem).

Mirrored in the magic of the glass: This is a reference to the cup of Jem(shîd) (see above) in which can be reflected whatever the holder wishes to see of what passes in the world. This image is carried further in the next couplet.

Like writing on the water: A well-known Arabic phrase is cited here *ke nakşin fi'l-mâ'* "like writing in water" which means "transitory, impermanent." However, in this case, the drinker staring closely and intently into the wine (as though his eyes were floating bubbles on its surface) has a momentary vision of the beloved of both the physical (seen) world and the invisible world of ideal forms (which gives the sense that she embodies the ideal form of beauty).

Brilliance of the face: There is an untranslatable play on an idiom here. The compound *âb-i rû* (water of the face) which is translated "brilliance of the face" actually means "the beauty or glory that comes from doing the right thing well." So the poet says, "wine is the water . . ." which keeps both parts of the metaphor in the class of drinkable things, which relationship is important to the skillfulness of the line. Also in the second hemistich the round, full bowl is compared to the *çeşm-i çirâg* or the "lantern-eye" of the poet, which creates a relationship to the "face" of the first hemistich.

Fuzûlî

25. *Oh God, don't let anyone*

Merciless idols: See the notes for poem no. 1.

Arrowhead: This is the arrowhead of the arrow of the beloved's glance. See the notes for poem no. 6.

This tavern . . . brought to ruin: There is the hint of a play here on the fact that the tavern is often represented by the metaphoric term "ruins" (*harâbât*). The source of this association is the new Islamic city built on the outskirts of the older, ruined city of an ancient civilization. Since wine was not allowed in the Muslim city and no Muslim could make wine, the wine-maker was the "magian," a fire-worshiper, pagan, Zoroastrian, or Christian monk who set himself up to sell his wine on the outskirts of the city, in the "ruins." And in this ruins the ancient magian plies his trade with the help of his beautiful pagan boy who steals the hearts of the drinkers. In Istanbul, during Ottoman times, the wine-selling suburb was Galata, where the Christian and Jewish communities were located and where were found the taverns in which Ottoman pleasure-seekers drank their wine. For Fuzûlî (who never lived in Istanbul) and generally for the mystics, the tavern is the treasure-house of love, the heart wherein the intoxicating wine of passion is served to the lover.

26. *If my heart were a wild bird*

Jinn: See the notes for poem no. 17. Also the word "jinn" is here a translation of *perî* (a female jinn). Jinn is an anglicization of *cinn* which is the root from which the name Mejnûn comes. (Hence *mejnûn* means "possessed or maddened by jinn.") And so we are brought to recall Mejnûn (see the article *Leylâ and Mejnûn* ... following poem no. 23) who was so mad as he wandered in the wilds that birds nested in his tangled hair. (This is how Ottoman poets thought!)

The wick of your spirit: This couplet contains a very involved conceit. The wick of the spirit is that thread of spiritual attachment (*rişte*) that binds the lover to the beloved. This soul-thread runs through all of his physical being and all his actions. And its concrete form is the attachment of the lover to the thread of the beloved's hair. So the mystical lover here has become so entangled in his physical attraction to the actual beloved that the spiritual thread has begun to resemble the clumped and twisted flower-stalks of the hyacinth, a common symbol for the hair of the beloved (which is tousled and twisted too). Moreover, this spiritual thread running through the physical being of the lover is like a candle wick in which the many individual threads are twisted together to form a larger thread. Only as the spiritual thread burns (and melts away the physical self/wax) does the wick (the spiritual thread) untwist itself and reveal its true attachment to the Ultimate Beloved.

27. *For long years*

For long years ... vagrants: The translation of this couplet is quite interpretive and foregrounds the less obvious sense of its inherent ambiguities, one of which is repeated throughout the poem in the *redîf* word *beklerüz* "we wait, we stand guard/protect, we wait for or expect or hope for." The first hemistich has the more literal sense "For ever so many years we have stood guard over the neighborhood/town/street of blame." The sense of blame here is that ordinary people look on the spiritually aware as persons who do not behave according to generally accepted values. The aware do not seem to be *settled* in this world, and the poet felt that this idea was best expressed by the censure implied by the notion (enshrined in our legal codes) of vagrancy.

Sultan of the spiritually wise: The phrase *sultan-i 'irfân* is more literally the "Ruler of mystical or occult knowledge." Mystical or gnostic knowledge is knowledge of the truth of the other (nonphysical) world, which is represented here as analogue of this world with its own soldiers, waiting for their ruler to lead them as patiently and silently as the Ottoman elite troops were known to do. European observers in the sixteenth century marveled at the ability of the Sultan's Janissary guard, as many as three thousand strong, to remain absolutely silent and immobile for hours on end. This kind of obedient waiting—in attendance or on guard—is certainly the ruling theme of this poem.

Waiting for God to befriend us: This is another interpretive phrase that depends on the ambiguity of the word *vilâyet*, which can mean "province, dominion" or "mystical union with God, a relationship of friendship or love." So there is an obvious reading "We are soldiers of the sultan of gnostic knowledge standing guard over a province [i.e., the province of blame]." And there is a second, less ordinary reading: "We are the soldiers ... waiting and hoping for the Sultan [God] to grant us his friendship [mystical union]." This kind of translation is difficult for scholars but seems to convey the more interesting (and least accessible) of the possible senses of the couplet.

The contented Phoenix ... Kâf mountain: This is the *'ankâ* (see Fabulous Birds) following poem no. 29 and its nesting place on the world's highest peak. As an example of the complexity of mystical readings, Prof.essor Tarlan (1985) points out that the letters of *'ankâ* (*ayin, nûn, kâf*) when read backward are the root letters of *kanâ'ât* "contentment" (i.e., not needing anything of this world, having overcome desire). This is the figure called "anagram" (*kalb*), wherein words are related anagramatically.

Treasure of the secrets of love: The vocabulary here recalls the Sacred Tradition (something Muhammad reported that God said to him) "I was a hidden treasure and desired to be known." This is the secret of creation and the reason why human beings were created with the ability to know: that they might know God as manifested in His creation.

The stones of the wall: The phrase *sûret-i divâr* was translated by Walsh and Tarlan as "pictures on the wall," which is most likely what the original means. See, for example, Nev'î's couplet (*Dîvân*, no. 278:1.b.) "Oh heart,

[when] you hope for sweet words from the beauties / You long for the pictures on the wall [*sûret-i divâr*] to speak, oh heart." Nonetheless, we translate it as if it were "like the wall" (which it could be) and so read "still as the [garden] wall," a minor and acceptable liberty, we think, and in keeping with the rest of the couplet. The image is of a lover immobilized by love, his eyes wide and staring.

The path of isolation: This refers to *tecrîd* or the mystic's stripping away of all ties to worldly things, the stage of abstracting the self from this world.

Ferhâd and Mejnûn: The two great self-sacrificed lovers of the narrative romances. See The Story of Leylâ and Mejnûn following poem no. 23 and Hüsrev, Shîrîn and Ferhâd following poem no. 28.

28. *The pointed reproach of the enemy*

Iron skin: The reproach of the enemy/rival is a common theme. The beloved is protected by her family, and the lover is accused of causing a public scandal by making his love known, which casts doubt on the morality of the beloved and the vigilance of her family. These accusations are likened here and elsewhere to stones and arrows, which in this case have struck so often that their iron arrowheads form a second skin which protects the lover from further barbs.

Light of my eye ... My worldly vision: This is a difficult couplet for several reasons. The phrase we have translated 'worldly vision" is *dîde-i rûşen* (bright vision), which in Turkish mystical parlance comes to mean "the inner, omniscient vision of the adept"—is exactly the opposite of our interpretation here. It is our reading that Fuzûlî, who is not a late-Ottoman mystic, intends a contrast between "light of my eye" *gözüm nûru* and hence "divine light of my eye") and "bright vision" by which he intends the vision which sees things of this world. This corresponds to Tarlan's (1985) reading.

The rose-garden of many delights: This is another problem passage. In Ottoman Turkish the word *nezzâre* usually means "onlookers, spectators," so the phrase *nezzâre-i gülşen* would seem to mean something like "those who visit the garden to look at it or watch the people in it." In this passage, however, we interpret the garden as a contrast to the cypress. The cypress is single, shaped like the letter *elif* and so is also the number "1" and is thus the symbol of Divine unity. We also read *nezzâre* not as "spectators" but as "seeing things, observing things" in the way it is often used in Persian. So the line would mean something like, "When I have Divine unity to observe [in the form of the cypress] what do I need with this-worldly multiplicity [the many sights of the garden]." We must remember that Fuzûlî is writing in a milieu far more Persian and Azerî than Ottoman.

The warm ashes of the hamam: The *hamam* or Turkish bath was an important institution in Turkish cities. The ashes from the great fires that warmed these baths were carefully collected to avoid the kind of conflagration that often caused great damage in cities constructed mostly of wood. In the ash-heaps (called *külhân*) homeless ruffians and vagabonds would sleep at night, kept from the chill by the still-warm ashes. These toughs, who often protected the neighborhood from disruptive intruders, were called "Lords of the Ash-heap" (*külhan beys*). They were the lowest of powers and as far from the throne of power as one could get.

Nisâyî

29. *We are the Mejnûn*

This poem is in the five-line stanza form called *muhammes* (fiver). It rhymes *a a a a a // b b b b a // c c c c a.*

Mejnûn: See The Story of Leylâ and Mejnûn following poem no. 24.

Oh zâhid: See the notes for poem no. 15.

Phoenix ... summit: The Phoenix here is the *'ankâ* and the "summit" is mount Kâf, see Fabulous Birds following poem no. 29.

Vâmık ... Ferhâd: For Ferhâd, see Hüsrev, Shîrîn, and Ferhâd following poem no. 28. Vamık is another of the famous lovers of the romantic narrative poems, son of the king of China and famed for his great beauty. Through an exchange of pictures and many adventures he falls in love with 'Azrâ, daughter of the Ruler of Turan. The two are kept parted by a variety of circumstances, but in the end they persevere staunchly in their love and against all odds are happily married.

We are the Hüsrev: This stanza is an example of the extended use of related vocabulary from one thematic source (the figure *tenâsüb*). Here the theme is the story of Hüsrev and Shîrîn (see the article following poem no. 28.)

Nev'î

30. *We don't need the cup of pleasure*

Jemshîd: See the notes for poem no. 4.

The borders were full of verse: In traditional Ottoman manuscripts, notes, commentary, and relevant verses were written in the margins of a text instead of at the bottom (footnotes) as is our present custom.

That Bîsütûn: Ferhâd (see Hüsrev, Shîrîn, and Ferhâd following poem no. 28) was able to perform the impossible task of cutting a road through Mount Bîsütûn in order to win his love but, according to the poet, could not cut through the obstacle of his own physical existence to reach union with the Divine.

31. *Help me, oh sapling*

This poem is in the form called *muhammes* (fiver/five-line stanzas). This particular example has the rhyme scheme *a a a* A A // *b b b* A A, etc., where the A A is a repeated couplet rhyming in *a*.

All my life: More literally, everything I have in my span of life in this world.

Cherished moon in the sky: The Turkish actually says "moon in the sky/heaven of preciousness/dearness." Our reworking seems more poetic and more true to the actual sense of the original.

Don't provoke my sighs: The sense of the Turkish here (*alma âhumla yaşum*) is related to the saying *alma mazlumun ahını, çıkar aheste aheste* (Don't provoke the sighs of the oppressed, they will come back to you/be a curse to you slowly over time).

Lower your ear like a bending rose: This is an image more familiar to the Ottoman reader than it would be to us. The rose is an ear that when heavy with blossom or dew or rain bends toward the ground, often listening for the approach or news of the beloved.

Written on my brow: There is a popular belief expressed in Turkish by the compound *alın yazısı* "writing on the brow" according to which the lines on a person's brow are lines of writing from the eternally existing inscription of the universe describing that person's individual destiny.

Bâkî

32. *That tyrant*

It is important to remember that Ottoman poems were not circulated in printed editions. Poems were copied by hand, and each copy was different in small or large ways from every other copy. In the case of this poem which has appeared in the major modern editions of Bâkî's work and under his name in a number of anthologies, it has recently been suggested (Küçük 1987) that it may not be a poem of Bâkî's at all. The major arguments for doubting its authorship point out that the poem does not appear in many of the manuscripts and that it does appear in a slightly different form in the collected poems of a poet called Mânî, a name which written in the Arabic script looks a lot like Bâkî. We have decided to keep the poem under Bâkî's name—where it has resided for many years—without intending to suggest that we are convinced that it is *not* Mânî's. Mânî was an intellectual and talented poet of Sultan Süleymân's time. He worked as a *kâdî* (judge) and as a professor in theological school.

Five Line Stanzas: The form of this poem is called *tahmîs* (making a five-line stanza) in Turkish. It begins with a poem in couplets by one poet—in this case by Fuzûlî—which is expanded by the second poet (Bâkî/Mânî) from couplets to five line stanzas in the following manner. The original poem's rhythm is used for all lines (here ⌣ – – – four times) and the rhyme, which in the first poem is *a a* // *b a* // *c a* etc., becomes *a a a a a* // *b b b b a* . . . . And the last two lines of every stanza are the poem by Fuzûlî. It is noteworthy that the original poem by Fuzûlî also has an internal rhyme as a nonrequired additional adornment in all but the first couplet. Thus, considering the internal rhyme, the rhyme-scheme of the Fuzûlî poem is *a a* // *b b b a* // *c c c a*, etc. When Bâkî/Mânî expands the poem he also maintains the internal rhyme so that a stanza actually rhymes *b b b b b b b a*. (The *b* is the added internal rhyme.) To do all this and end up with a beautiful poem is a masterful accomplishment and part of the competitive character of this kind of poetry.

Resurrection: The sense here—which might be missed—is that there will be a final judgment when the beloved will be called to answer for her crimes against the lover.

The heavens are set aflame: See the notes for poem no. 5.

That laughing rose looks: Here the rose pays attention to the imploring nightingale, but the manifestation of her attention is only to give him more torment.

Ash: The ash-heap of the *hamam* (Turkish bath) is a common image (see Fuzûlî, "The pointed reproach of the enemy"). In such ash-heaps the vagabonds of the city slept on cold winter nights. There is also a play on words that cannot be seen in English: the word for ash (*kül*) looks exactly the same as the word for rose (*gül*) in the Arabic script.

Pearls from my eyes: See the notes for poem no. 7.

Run dark with blood: this is a typical Ottoman poetic comparison. Here the idea is that the lovers tears are dark with blood because it is spring and he is impassioned by the rose; all water that flows in the spring rushes by in a flood and is dark and murky with sediment. Conversely, there also is a fanciful explanation for the murkiness of water in the spring: because all earth is weeping blood for love of the rose.

Sugar: The reference here is to the parrot, which according to one poetic myth learns to speak by eating sugar. Thus the poet, in tasting of the beloved's (sweet) lip, learns to speak sweet (poetic) words in describing it.

Brought to his knees: Actually the Turkish is *bî-ser ü pâ* (without head or foot), which generally means "powerless, destitute." We wanted to use an idiom that retains the figurative character of the original.

Black passion: In the traditional physiology of bodily humors, this mad passion is the product and producer of black (liver) bile. (And hence the relation between the liver and love: see Ahmed Pasha, "Ask about my wailing").

33. *Oh beloved, since the origin*

Shah of love: In the poetry of the Ottoman elites the beloved is often referred to as ruler or monarch (*şâh, sultân*). Thus the power that the beloved holds over the abject lover/slave-of-love is always identified with the power of the ruler over his closest subjects. Thus too, the appropriate relation between ruler and subject comes to be expressed as one of intense and passionate (and self-sacrificing) love. For this reason, some lyric poems are really mini-odes (*kasides*) that praise the ruler or some other power-holder and ask for something, usually a job or cash. This poem could easily be one such. (For more on this see Andrews 1985.)

Poppies: The word for "poppies" here is *lâle*, which is usually translated as "tulip." However, in the sixteenth century in the Ottoman Empire what we know as tulips did not exist and the *lâle* seems to have been at times a kind of peony (*şakayik*) and at times a sort of wild poppy later called the *lâle-i nu'mân* to distinguish it from true tulips. Here the burns of love are compared to the poppy, the charred center and red/inflamed surrounding area being like the red petals and black center of the poppy.

Cup, cupbearer: The translation here is a compromise and vain attempt to hint at the poet's play on the ambiguity of the word *câmî* which can mean "he who holds the cup, cup-bearer" and is also the name of the famous Persian poet Jâmî (d. 1492). Thus when he says, "I am the jâmî [*câmî*] of the age," he intends both "I am the Jâmî [the greatest poet] of the age" and "I am the [best] cup-bearer [the greatest producer of the wine of poetry] of the age." The poet plays with ambiguity often, and this makes some of his best poetry impossible to translate without abandoning much of what made it amusing.

34. *The fountain of my spirit*

Water of life, fountain of youth: Both of these refer to the water of eternal life that plays an important role in the Alexander legend (see İskender/Alexander following poem no. 10).

A drink: The word for "a drink, sip, gulp" (*cur'a*) also refers to the sediment left by the wine in the bottom of the cup. It is something not valued and thrown away on the ground. Thus the line also indicates that the least and most worthless drop of moisture from her lip would be coveted by the most powerful fountain.

The world-sea: In the traditional, mythic geography the main mass of land is surrounded by an all-encompassing sea, called dry-lipped here because of its dry and sandy beaches.

Leylâ, Mejnûn: See The Story of Lelylâ and Mejnûn following poem no. 24.

35. *If only the bud would open*

Scatter turquoise: It was customary at feasts and special ceremonies for valuables, usually coins, to be scattered as a gift to the onlookers.

Saki: See Nejâtî: *Those tulip-cheeked ones* . . . .

Love's burn within: As above (Bâkî, "Oh beloved, since the origin) the black center of the poppy is compared to the love-burn on the lover's heart. (See also Sheyh Gâlib, "You are my effendi").

See the rose: This is actually "let us see the rose."

Near . . . along the bank: There is a play on words here involving *kenâr*, which means "the edge of something." In this couplet it means "the bank of the stream" and in the compound *der-kenâr*, "next to/near to" the beloved as well.

36. *Sparks from my heart*

This poem is a parallel (*nazîre*) to Nejâtî's famous "Spiraling, the sparks". It has the same rhythm, themes, and rhyme-scheme and is intended to show how Bâkî can create a better, more original poem using the same formal materials.

Magic lantern: The "lantern of images" or "magic lantern" had pictures painted on the glass of the lantern, which became large as life when projected onto a wall. This lantern is often used as a trope for the sphere of the sky, which reflects the images of the "real" or ideal world onto this "illusory" world.

The ferris-wheel weeping: In the sixteenth century during the great festivals (*bayram*), amusement parks were set up and one of the popular entertainments would be a large ferris-wheel. As it rotated on an axle, this wheel would creak loudly, which is the sound compared here to the lover's weeping as he watches his beloved taking a ride.

The jeweler's wheel: This is literally "the jeweler or engraver of the wheel [of the heavens]." It equates the wheel of heaven with the jeweler's wheel and then conflates the wheel and the jeweler. We have unpacked the metaphor and metonymy a bit so that they make sense in English.

These pearls, these jewels: Bâkî's images strung on threads of poetic form.

37. *Your rebellious glance*

A flock of cranes: Migrating cranes, crying mournfully, were, in popular mythology, said to be the souls of the dead ascending to Paradise.

The water-seller: Wherever people gathered, the water seller, with a huge, ornate metal water-jug on his back, would work the crowd selling fresh water by the cupful.

Hands clasped: Standing with the hands clasped is a sign of respect and humility. (See also Nâbî, "In the garden of time and destiny").

Yahyâ Bey

38. *Come wander through the city*

Wander through the city: This translates the phrase *ayak seyri* incompletely. *Ayak* means both "foot" and "cup" and *seyr* is "wandering around." So the phrase could mean either "going around the city [to watch the beloveds there or to go from tavern to tavern]" or "passing the cup around" (this is *tevriye* "multiple meaning" again). Even though the most likely primary meaning here is the passing of the cup, we have retained the idea of going around the city to look at its beautiful inhabitants because Yahyâ has used the phrase in that sense elsewhere and the sense of the drinking bout was not lost in the translated couplet.

Learn how to burn from the moth: The moth flying about the candle and finally burning itself up in the flame is a favorite image of the Ottoman poets. See the notes for poem no. 68.

39. *Poetry holds the written veil*

Like Joseph: Joseph represents the ideal of male beauty (see Nejâtî "Those tulip-cheeked ones") and also the ideal of modesty and purity. According to the popular tale, although he was a slave, loved passionately by Züleyha, the wife of the Grand Vizier of Egypt and the most beautiful woman in the world, he clung to his religion, his modesty, and purity. That is to say, he did not display or use his beauty in such a way as to cause trouble. Thus the second line refers to poetry speaking through a veil concealing passions that might inflame the uninitiated or ideas that might lead them astray.

The shattered mountain of Moses: In the Turkish, the phrase is only "the Sinai of Moses," but an Ottoman reader would immediately think of the story based on the Quran (VII:143), in which Moses comes to the place God has appointed and asks to see God, who says that Moses would not endure the manifestation. God says that He will show Himself to the mountain and if it can endure He will then show himself to Moses. The mountain shakes itself to dust; Moses faints and recovers, repentant and confirmed in his belief.

The realm of essence: This translates *âlem-i ma'nâ*, which is a world or emanation prior to the physical world. In it exist the true meanings of this-worldly objects. The word *ma'nâ*, which has the sense of both "meaning" and "essential meaning," is used often and has been translated by us in various ways depending on context. The "voice of the unseen world" *lisân-i gayb* speaks the language of this true meaning.

Rûhî

40. *Curse the thorns of fate*

We have cheated a little with this poem. It looks like one of the other short lyrics but it is actually a stanza from a much longer poem. The poetic form is called *terkîb-bend* or *terkîb-i bend* (compounded stanza), in which each stanza is formally a *gazel* (short monorhyming lyric) and an added rhyming couplet with its own rhyme. Rûhî's *Terkîb-bend* is a famous and quite long (seventeen stanza) critique of the foibles of his age. It is such a forceful example of the kind of social criticism that we will see later in Nâbî and others that we could not pass it up.

The wasteland of death: This is literally "the wasteland of annihilation or nonexistence." As we interpret it, this line refers to the fact that this world is a wasteland of which death is the ultimate fact. Thus the poet curses the commerce of this world and the one who tries to tell you how to live in it.

Whirling trances: This interpretively translates a phrase that says something like "curse their bewilderment" and means "curse their trance-like states of ecstasy."

Fixed stars: In the traditional astronomy the planets were "moving stars" and what we call "stars" were the "fixed stars."

Sheyhülislâm Yahyâ

41. *Saki, offer the cup*

Call it a ruin: The ruins are also the place where wine is sold, a tavern.

The secret truth: It is always important to remember that for the Ottoman poet the metaphors of the party, wine, love, passion, and intoxication have well understood meanings as part of the vocabulary of mysticism. It is the ever-present possibility of a coherent mystical reading that allows the rake or drunkard and the Supreme Justice of Islamic Law (Şeyhülislâm) to write amazingly similar verses. This is the secret: that what the poet is writing about, in some cases, is the emotional, charismatic dimension of a relation to the Divine.

42. *Let the hypocrites*

Mosque ... tavern: As mentioned above, there is a constantly maintained irony in much Ottoman poetry, wherein doctors of religious law seem to be valuing the tavern over the mosque. The tavern, however, represents the inward, spiritual experience of religion available only to a spiritual elite, while the mosque stands for observance of religion's outward forms, which are available to anyone.

Jem: See the notes for poem no. 4.

43. *Is there no heart*

Black stone into ruby: The ruby as it comes from the mine is merely a black stone until it is left out in the sun which turns it into a red jewel. (See The Cosmos and the Earth following poem no. 19.)

Nef'î

44. *That black drunken eye*

Party of Jemshîd: Because Jem/Jemshîd is the inventor of wine (see the note for poem no. 4), the wine party is often given this name. Here there is a strikingly stark contrast between the drunkard, so close to passing out that his turban almost touches the ground, and Jemshîd, one of most splendid legendary monarchs.

Prays to the beloved while drunk: Muslims are forbidden to perform their prayers when drunk because they cannot properly attend to the meaning of what they are doing, which is why alcohol is prohibited.

Rostam: Rostam (or Rüstem) is the greatest warrior-hero of the Persian *Shâhnâme* (Book of Kings) by Firdevsî. He was immensely powerful, so huge that his feet sunk into the earth when he walked, and ever-victorious in war.

45. *Those who painted my portrait*

Drunkard: This character, the drunkard (*rind* or *mest*), stands in contrast to the ascetic (*zâhid*), whom we see in the following couplet.

The darkness of her cheek-down: Another play on the two meanings of the word for "cheek-down" (*hat*): "down" and "writing." Here the shadow on the white of her eye is imagined to be writing (or the writing of the reflection of her dark down) on the white page of her eye. (See The Down on Your Cheek following poem no. 43.)

Mejnûn have written it in vain: See The Story of Leylâ and Mejnûn following poem no. 23. The phrase translated as "they have written it in vain" is an idiom that is literally something like "they have written it in[to] the wilderness" (*yabana yazmışlar*). This creates a play on the fact that Mejnûn fled in his madness to the wilderness.

46. *The heart is both the cup and the wine*

The world of eternal signs: This translates the phrase *'âlem-i ma'nâ* "the world of meaning," wherein the true essences of things—that which grounds or is the essence of the meaning of things in this world—exist eternally and without change.

Celebrates alone: The *bezm-i hass* is a private party where the lover entertains the beloved alone and not in the usual company of friends.

Sheyhülislâm Bahâyî

47. *Oh cry, what are you doing*

When she wakes: There is a saying popular among the Ottomans, "Discord (*fitne*) is sleeping, cursed be he who wakes it [her]." The term *fitne* means a general social or individual trouble or discord or temptation to evil-doing or to antisocial behavior—anything that disturbs the well-being of the community. In the last age, the "Cycle of the Moon," a general discord will break out all over the world (see Ahmed Pasha, "Ask about my wailing"). The beloved and her beauties are often mentioned by the poets as the source and even the ultimate source of *fitne*.

Trap of her curl: The curl is often compared to a snare for birds. It is like a ring of cord or wire with the black seed of the mole inside it for bait.

Born with the madness: That is, if the doctor continuously tries to treat or cure those whose disease is inborn and hence natural to them, he actually does them damage.

You've caused havoc: Muslim women cover their hair in order to protect them and the community from the arousal of dangerous desires in men.

Thus the hair is seen as a potential source of trouble, *fitne*. The beloved releasing her hair or letting fall a lock is often described as the hair scattering *fitne*. Here the wind is to blame for releasing the hair and spreading *fitne* (here "havoc").

Behzad: (Bihzâd), was a famous miniature painter in the court of Hüseyin Baykara in Herat (1469–1506). He was also befriended by the giant of Chaghatay Turkic poets, Mîr 'Alî Shîr Nevâyî.

Troubling charm: That is, how are you going to paint the *fitne* concealed in these beautiful features of her face?

Nâbî

48. *When we watch the spinning of the sky*

Boy of the garden ... on the turban of the rival: When an Ottoman gentleman relaxed in the garden he would often pluck a flower and put it in the folds of his turban. Here the rival is not a protector so much as a rival in love. The "boy of the garden" is more literally "the charming boy of the rose-garden" (i.e., the fairest flower, the rose). One must remember that the conventions of Ottoman literature often require or allow a masculine beloved and homoerotic imagery no matter what the actual proclivities of the poet might be. It is also necessary to remember that here the beloved (flower) longs for autumn because he (or she or it) is a this-worldly beloved who is bound to the cycle of birth and decay.

Scented candle: This is the *micmer*, a large perfumed candle that was commonly burned at parties.

49. *In the garden of time and destiny*

Exploding sigh: In the Turkish it is "the shattering cannonball of the sigh."

Hands folded: Standing with hands folded was the formal way for an Ottoman to show humility and respect. (See the notes for poem no. 37.)

50. *At the gathering of joy*

Jesus: See the notes for poem no. 7. Jesus brings the dead to life. (For this poem, see also Andrews 1985, 26–35).

Nâ'ilî

51. *We are the snake*

The snake ... the ant: The snake refers to the magic of Moses that changed Aaron's staff into a snake. To the Muslim mystics Moses is the symbol of the Perfect Man who has cleansed his spirit until he perfectly reflects the Divine and its power. (See Rûmî's Mirror following poem no. 50.) The ant refers to the story of the ant and Solomon (Süleymân) in which the ant lord warns his people that they must flee Solomon's oncoming army or be crushed. Solomon, who can speak the languages of jinn and animals, converses with the ant and asks why he would think that a Prophet of God would crush an ant. To this the ant replies that he thought Solomon's glory would confuse the ants and they would forget their prayers. Solomon usually represents the most powerful of human beings and the ant the weakest of creatures.

Mirror ... proud gaze: See *Rûmî's Mirror*. The phrase here is literally "self-adorning gaze." The gaze of this-worldly intellect takes in only the surface of things and hence only perceives the adornment and not the essence. This is because it is bound to the self and the pride of self in its own lucidity.

Mejnûn, Leylâ: See The Story of Leylâ and Mejnûn following poem no. 23.

Were it diamonds: This is a complex reference. The diamonds represent a very expensive cure, but a cure—crushed diamonds—that would keep a wound open and painful forever.

Brand of madness ... black center of the heart: In this image the heart is compared to one of the brands of love (see the note for poem no. 68) with a black (charred) center surrounded by a red inflammation. The black spot is thought to exist as the core of the heart of every rational being with the power of speech. It is the source of black bile, one of the four humors of the body, and is the center of spiritual existence and understanding as well as the source of passion.

Our health is an addict: The sense here is that sickness is the lovers' normal (and hence healthy) state. So the physician's cure actually makes them unhealthy (or abnormal) by making them well.

Changing wand: This is actually the "deceitful or deceiver's ball" of the sleight-of-hand artist, magician, juggler, or trickster of the heavens.

This world is like the ball that the prestidigitator uses to take the audience's (thousand watching) eyes off what is really happening. And this world is the magician too, using its physical appearance (the ball) to confuse the unaware. Also, the sorcerer or caster-of-spells uses a mirror in the shape of a ball to conjure with. So does the Divine use the reflection of its own beauties in the mirror of human beauty to enchant the lover and turn him to desiring spiritual union with the ultimately real.

Visible in our words: Others know what the words usually mean but their real truth (and our real reality) is hidden to all but those who are mystically aware.

52. *My tears became desire*

Bewildered gazelles: Mejnûn in his maddened state wandered the desert in the company of shy and usually unapprochable gazelles who realized that he was harmless in his madness (see The Story of Leylâ and Mejnûn following poem no. 24). The gazelle is often compared to the beloved because of its large brown eyes. Here the eyes are large with surprise.

The slender elif *in the* âh: (See the illustration following poem no. 52.) The *elif* is the slender upright stroke that is the first letter of the word *âh* which means "sigh." It is often compared to a cypress tree, as is the body of the beloved.

From the rising of your verses: The word that has been translated in the sense "rising" here is *tal'at*, which usually means "appearance, face." It is from a root that in other forms means "the appearance or rising of a star or other heavenly body." Thus, in context and given the Ottoman tendency to group like notions (according to *tenâsüb*), "rising" seems particularly apt and gives the sense of the poem as a bright star rising.

53. *Since the thunderbolt of disaster*

The Kaaba of love: At the sanctuary of the Kaaba in Mecca, pilgrims do a series of ritual circles about the holy place as lovers circumambulate the home of the beloved.

The veil of meaning: This is more literally the veil of innocence or shyness or modesty. This veil is commonly the screen or curtain set up around the ruler's tent to keep his privacy. It would be richly colored, as is the skirt stained with blood. Thus, what we truly mean is disguised by our outward appearance (as lovers with skirts stained by the blood we weep) and our powerful truth is like the sultan, modestly concealed behind the tent-curtain.

54. *What witch are you*

Who sets traps: It was forbidden to hunt or trap in the sanctuaries of Mecca and Medina. In this case the gazelle, which it would be a crime to hunt in the sanctuary, becomes the illegal hunter by turning Kaaba into a trap for those inclined to worship. The gazelle is here and elsewhere a metaphor for the beloved because of its graceful body, large brown eyes, and shy demeanor. The beloved entraps the lover into worshiping her and substituting her house or neighborhood for the Kaaba (because the lover walks round and round them as worshipers do at the Kaaba). Of course, the beloved of the Kaaba is the Divine, which entraps the pilgrim who is following only the outward forms of religion into an inward, emotional spirituality.

Hulagu: Hulagu was the grandson of Genghiz Khan and warlord of the Mongols when the Tatar soldiers invaded the central Middle East and sacked Baghdad in the mid-thirteenth century. The Mongols gained a reputation as invincible warriors and cruel conquerors, who ruthlessly sacked cities that refused to surrender and massacred their inhabitants.

Hızır, Jesus, Alexander: For Hızır and Alexander (İskender) see İskender/Alexander following poem no. 10. For Jesus see the note for poem no. 7. Both Hızır and Jesus are known for bringing the dead to life. In this couplet both of the most famous raisers-of-the-dead are willing to die for a taste of the beloved's moist lip, and for it Alexander would give up the search for the Fountain of Eternal Life.

Oh my love, my sun: This couplet has a complex internal sense, in the fashion of the *sebk-i hindî* (see the article following poem no. 67), that is not apparent from the translation (nor could it be made apparent in English). The theme of Jesus is carried on by a very oblique reference to the legend that when Jesus, most holy for having given up things of this world even including marriage and family, was taken up into heaven, he was required to completely divest himself (*tecrîd*) of all worldly things. As he ascended through the nine spheres/heavens he was stopped in the fourth—the sphere of the sun—because he had unwittingly brought a needle with him. So he remains in that heaven and has not yet risen to the

Heaven of the Throne of God (see The Cosmos and the Earth following poem no. 19). The word used here for sun (*mihr*) also means "love" and is a common source of the play on double meaning the Ottomans called *tevriye*. So the beloved is linked to the sun, to Jesus, and from there to the wild rose, which is unique, alone (not with other flowers in a garden), and white (like the sun and Jesus in his rejection of worldly adornment) rather than red (like the beloved's cheek).

Her mouth: In the Ottoman mythology of attractiveness, the beloved's mouth is supposed to be vanishingly small. Here it has been compared to the tip of her curl or, in the original, the tip of a hair (i.e., a hair's breadth) and the beloved is furious because this describes it as far larger than it really is.

Neshâtî

55. *We are desire*

This poem is a parallel (*nazîre*) to Nâ'ilî's "We are the snake" (poem no. 51). The practice of writing poems in the same rhythm, rhyme, and thematic environment as a poem by another poet was very common among the Ottomans. It could be flattery (see Poetic Parallels following poem no. 54) or competition and usually was a combination of both. Nâ'ilî and especially Neshâtî were practitioners of the Indian style (*sebk-i hindî*: see the article following poem no. 67), which delights in complex compounds and strange juxtapositions that make it very difficult (but rewarding) to comprehend and equally difficult to translate.

The divine strand: The *rişte-i cân* or "thread of the soul" is that delicate bond that ever links lover and beloved and makes everything the lover does a part of that relation. For the mystic it is the link to the Divine unity of all existence. This thread is often compared to the thread that links the pearls in a necklace.

So what if we are famous: The contradiction "we are famous for having no fame" is set up here as a model for the situation of the heart (the site of Divine experience) caught up in the riddle or enigma (*mu'ammâ*), recognizing itself only when manifested in a mundane and transitory carnal self. Our fame is for leaving no trace in this world, for having nothing to do with it.

The color of our essence: We had a hard time with this translation. The Ottoman *rengînî-i ma'nâ* means something like "the colorfulness of meaning or the inner, spiritual truth [i.e., the essential, Divine spirit that shines out of a person who has been purified of worldly attachments to the external or formal]"— obviously impossible to convey in a single half-line. The notion here is that you can see us shining (or perceive, in some way, our inner state, which is the meaning or Divine essence of which our selves are but the signs), but you recognize it as something else because it is inseparably embodied in us just as joy is implicit in but not a quality of the wine.

The lament hidden in the pen: This is a lovely Indian style image. The lament, on one hand, is the ability of the pen to write out the lament of the lover, yet it is also the squeaking or moaning sound that a reed pen makes as it is pushed (remember that in Arabic script one writes from right to left and so pushes the pen) across the page.

The perfect mirror: Here is the mirror of the purified self as in Rûmî's Mirror following poem no. 50. When the "rust" of this world has been polished away, the recognizable, material self is no longer visible; what is visible is the true, eternal essence that cannot be seen by those who see only the surface.

56. *You're gone—I'm alone*

The wheel of the sky: The *çarh* or revolving spheres of the heavens. See The Cosmos and the Earth following poem no. 19.

57. *The sky's face has turned dark*

Here we have another seasonal poem, here a *şitayye* or winter poem, which most likely celebrates the especially violent winter of 1622, when the Bosphorus was said to have been covered with ice.

Wraps itself in ice: This refers to the wine being in crystal or glass bowls or goblets.

The grey of a squirrel coat: Actually Ottoman squirrels were probably brownish. The image here is of an ember covered by a coating of ash, which reminds the poet of the squirrel coats that people of his day wore in the cold. Grey seemed to represent squirrels and ash to English-speakers better than brown.

Nedîm

58. *At the gathering of desire*

Standing like a jinn: Certain enchanters were able to construct magic circles in which a jinn or (as in this case) a *perî* could be entrapped. This image apparently refers to the hair standing (obediently) on end, enchanted like a *perî* by the beloved's charms.

Mirror colored: Combines the mystical mirror (i.e., loss of self; see Rûmî's Mirror following poem no. 50) and the notion of the jinn living in mirrors (see the note for poem no. 74).

59. *When the east wind*

Narcissus-eye: The eye of the morning-after the drinking party. See the notes for poem no. 4.

60. *As the morning wind blows*

In this time of the rose: See the notes for poem no. 4.

Like the lanterns of the caravan: During the Month of Pilgrimage, huge caravans would set out from Istanbul and the surrounding areas to make the difficult and dangerous journey to Mecca—a trip through bandit-infested wild lands that one could make safely only in a large and well-armed company. The long line of lovers waiting for a glimpse of the beloved is compared to one of these caravans camped for the night, with the love-illuminated bodies of the lovers resembling the pilgrims' lights strung out along the road.

61. *Take yourself to the rose-garden*

This poem is of the type called *şarkı* (song). Although the form is similar to the *mürabba'* (poem in four-line stanzas), it is not one of the standard high-culture Perso-Ottoman forms but is adapted from the Turkish popular tradition. The subject matter, while still on the theme of love, is usually lightly handled with local and contemporary references. This type of poem was commonly set to music. The rhyme-scheme of the four-line stanzas in this poem is *a* A *a* A // *b b b* A // *c c c* A, etc.; as in the translation, the second and fourth lines of the opening stanza and all the other fourth lines (A) are repeated exactly.

Black down: See The Down on Your Cheek following poem no. 43.

62. *Delicacy was drawn out*

Your hollowed center . . . locks of Hârût: This is another line impossible to translate, which we translated anyway. Remember that the reed pen of traditional Arabic script calligraphy was cut from a hollow reed. The center is filled with soft pith (called *nâl*), which, when the reed is dried, becomes a twisted fibrous substance that soaks up the ink and becomes black like curly dark hairs. Hârût is one of a pair of angels (the other is Mârût) mentioned in the Quran (Sura II:102). The accepted explanations of this verse include a number of stories. The short version of one is this: One day the angels, appalled at the sinfulness of humans, went to God and said, "Our Lord, human beings are steeped in sin, how can you endure it?" And God replied, "If you were in their place you would do the same. You only say this because you were born without lust and carnal desire." "Not so!" said the angels. God then allowed them to pick two from among them to go down and live like humans, and the angels chose the two best of their company, who were sent down to Babylon, where they set about advising the people on matters of religion. One day a woman named Zühre (Venus) came to them for advice and they were both immediately smitten by lust. They both desired this woman uncontrollably and she agreed to grant their desires if they would drink wine, murder her husband, and bow down before idols. In their passion, this they did. God then confronted them with their guilt and demanded that they choose between a heavenly or earthly punishment. Because the things of heaven are eternal, they chose a punishment of the earth and were cast into a fiery pit in Babylon, where they thirsted ever and were burnt black by the flames. And from that pit, black Hârût taught spells and magic to human beings. So the witchcraft of the black lovelock is fancifully personified in Hârût.

Dark crusaders: This phrase represents the term *firengistân*, which more accurately (and less poetically) means "the land of the Franks" by which is meant "Christian Europeans." The Christians are twice dark: in the darkness of error for having failed to heed the message of Muhammad and accustomed (in the case of monks and priests especially) to dress in dark clothing. Here the black down on the beloved's face is compared to a band of Christian soldiers, who when they are gathered together in a tight group become the mole on her cheek.

That heretic: Actually "heretic's idol," representing the non-Muslims who can drink wine (and tempt the Muslim to do so too).

The teeth of the "s" of kiss: The letter *sîn* or "s" in the Arabic script has little upraised spikes called "teeth" by calligraphers and the word for "kiss" (*bûse*) contains a *sîn*; therefore, a "kiss" has sharp "teeth."

Koja Râgıb Pasha

63. *Dark thought is revealed*

Râgıb Pasha's poetry is often described as "philosophical," which describes his preoccupation with abstract, mystical concepts and lesser attention to concrete images. His style makes this poem, and much of his poetry, quite difficult to understand and to translate. The poem is, however, typical of both Râgib and a more general kind of Ottoman poetry, so we have included it despite its problems and provided a few more notes than usual.

Dark thought . . . twists and curves . . . tarnish: The original has "thought" not "dark thought." However, these are obscure, hidden thoughts that reveal the "twists and curves" of one's inner self. The "twists and curves/curls" relate the heart to the very common image of the "twists and curls" of the beloved's locks, which are said to be the outward manifestation of a complex inward deviousness related to the multiplicities of this much-desired physical world. This attraction to the deluding and devious world is the tarnish that stains the mirror of the spiritual self (see Rûmî's Mirror following poem no. 50).

Untimely suffering . . . unnecessary struggle: We learn from living in this world that we must struggle to get what we desire of the things of this world. And there is a spirituality which assumes that what we desire of the other world can be attained in the same manner. So the ascetic, the zealot, torments himself or deprives herself or struggles to do without or to perform prodigious tasks of devotion and all of this is to no avail. This situation is compared by Rûmî (see the article following poem no. 50) to the vast efforts of the Chinese artists to paint the perfect picture when all that was really needed was to remove the tarnish that prevented true, ideal beauty from being reflected.

The sorcerer: This is a difficult couplet. It seems to depend on the notion that human beings were created in order to embody (and thus reflect) the attributes of God. So fate—the turning of the wheel of the heavens—gives physical beauty or ugliness to people randomly but true beauty or ugliness resides in the degree of accuracy or distortion with which a person's character reflects the Divine. Also, the sorcerer/magician is identified with the beloved and hence with the Divine Beloved. The sorcerer employs a mirror (in the form of a ball) to cast spells enchanting the lover, which is the analog for God arousing a desire for union by revealing the Divine Attributes in the mirror of human spiritual and physical beauty. (See also Nâ'ilî, poem no. 51.)

Where true beauty: In the physical world many lovers long in vain for the favors of their beloveds. In the spiritual realm, the mass of unfulfilled lovers *could* see that the beauty which is the object of their love is actually the beauty of the Divine— and the Divine is able to fulfill the desire of all its lovers. So the love-induced trembling of the true lovers is compared to the mountain shaking as God manifests to it. (See Yahyâ, poem no. 39.)

The divine bride: Although the Divine is revealed in its creation, it is also hidden by the veil of physical existence. As the bride only unveils before her husband, so do the true beauty and meaning of the created world reveal themselves only to a chosen (mystically aware) few.

Râsih Bey

64. *Don't lower your languid eyes*

Black arrow: The couplet is a perfect expression of the glance shooting eyelash-arrows into the heart of the lover motif. The "black" is not in the Turkish but was added to intensify the relation to eyelashes (which would be obvious to an Ottoman).

In one home: Another example of the quoting of proverbs (*irsâl-i mesel*).

Crushed diamonds: This is a reference to a form of torture in which crushed glass is put on a wound to keep it open and painful (see also Nâ'ilî, " We are the snake"). Here, instead of glass, precious diamonds are used.

Fıtnat Hanım

64. *In a heart*

Divine nurturer of the soul: This represents a difficult to translate concept expressed in the phrase *ma'nî-i rûh-perverî*, which can mean "the [Divine] essence of spiritual nurture" or even "a spirit-nurturing dream," where *ma'nî* means "dream" or "the unconscious vision of the world of essential meanings." This is to say that the beloved's lip (life-giving because it resembles the fountain of eternal life, see İskender/Alexander following poem no. 10) is held as the image of its essential meaning in the heart, from which it speaks eloquently in the poet's words (words being meaning's outward form).

Plato: Plato is the symbol of the ultimate in this-worldly wisdom and learning. (See the Plato character in İskender/Alexander.) However, in this case the poet seems to have confused Plato with another famous philospher, Diogenes *Diyûcen*, who at one point retired from the world and lived in a large barrel or cask with only a sack, a staff, and a bowl as possessions. Here he, in the guise of Plato, represents renunciation of the world and the intellect that attempts to understand it.

Kays: This is the family name of Mejnûn (see the article following poem no. 24).

Esrâr Dede

65. *In the ruins*

Ruins ... monuments: The ruins/tavern (see Fuzûlî, "Oh God don't let anyone") for the mystic is the heart; the dervish lodge and the "monuments, etc.," which translate *âsâr-i 'imâret* "works of improvement by building" are juxtaposed here with the sense that the tavern is the heart, meaning, or spiritual essence and the good works constructed by the powerful are the body, transitory and corrupt.

Whirlpool of distractions: The Turkish says "whirlpool of comprehension, conscious understanding." We interpret that to mean attempts to understand this world intellectually, by the aid of reason, which creates a whirlpool of speculation that sucks a person down and away from true meaning—hence the "distractions."

Devout one: Another character in the poetic drama. The devout believer (*sûfî*) who sees only the surface and not the inner meaning of religion.

Nightingale: Here the nightingale (who is always an analogue for the poet), pierced by the beloved rose's thorn and singing his painful woe, is unfavorably compared to the moth (the dervish), who simply burns himself up for love.

67. *You left, but don't forget*

My heart has no other: Translates a phrase (*dil-i nâçâr*) that has the sense "helpless heart/heart with no remedy" but means "a heart that cannot be cured by anyone other than you."

Sheyh Gâlib

68. *You are my effendi*

Effendi: "Lord, master." Gâlib refers in this poem, as in many of his poems, to his spiritual master, Mevlânâ Jelâleddîn Rûmî (1207–1273). (See Rûmî's Mirror following poem no. 50.)

Moth: The moth and candle theme is one of the commonplaces of Ottoman (and Persian) poetry. The issue here is not the newness of the imagery but the uniqueness of the beauty and delicacy with which it is done. So are old images constantly renewed. In this case the moth's annihilation in the flame is compared to the annihilation sought by the dervish—an annihilation of self in the fire of love for his master.

Love's burns: The lover and the dervish lover (the sufi) would often show the intensity of their love by burning themselves with a smoldering roll of material about the size of a cigarette. The burn is often depicted as a tulip (or wild poppy) with a black (charred) anther surrounded by red (inflamed) petals.

Perfect pearl: the original is *gevher-i ġalṭân*, which means "round, rolling pearl" (*gevher* means "jewel, the precious essence of a thing" as well as "pearl"). A round pearl so round that it will roll without spinning or curving to a stop is "perfectly" round and hence very precious.

Dust on the mirror of my heart: See, Rûmî's Mirror following poem no. 50.

Saki: See the notes for poem no. 9.

Deepest and holy refuge: The word used here is *ilticâ*, which means "taking refuge." The "deepest and holy" is a translator's gloss intended to convey that *ilticâ* also means "taking refuge in or seeking to be protected by a person." In the case of a refugee who is a dervish and a protector who is his spiritual master, the refuge is spiritual, inward, and ultimately oriented toward the Divine.

Dervish crown: Many of the dervish orders had a particular identifying headgear. The Mevlevî dervishes (the order founded by Rûmî, popularly known as Mevlânâ) wore a special conical hat they called the *elif tacı* or "the [letter] *elif*-hat or crown." (For the letter *elif*, see the illustration following poem no. 52.)

69. *I won't abandon you*

The form of this poem is the *mürabba'/şarkı* (four-line stanzas). It rhymes *a a b a // c c c a // d d d a*, etc.

The pen of fate: The *alın yazısı* "writing on the brow" is a common Turkish expression. The furrows on the brow are seen as Arabic script writing that describe a person's fate.

The nine spheres: See The Cosmos and the Earth following poem no. 19.

The cord that binds me: This is the *rişte*, the thread that binds the lover and beloved together, conceived of here as the beloved's lovelock. See the notes for poem no. 26.

Mihrab: The *mihrâb* is the niche in the wall of a mosque that tells the worshiper the direction of Mecca, the direction he or she must face to pray. This lover is drawn to face the beloved and not Mecca.

The râ *of your eyebrow*: The letter *râ* in the Arabic script is curved like an eyebrow. Both the *râ* and the eyebrow are curved and nichelike, reminding the poet of the *mihrâb*. *Râ* is also the first letter in the word for "hypocrisy."

The black down: See The Down on Your Cheek following poem no. 43.

The sword of your glance: The lover's glance, which is usually an arrow, here becomes a sword that gets at the lover's heart by splitting him open.

Ferhâd and Mejnun: The famous self-sacrificed lovers of the narrative romances. See Hüsrev, Shîrîn and Ferhâd following poem no. 28 and The Story of Leylâ and Mejnûn following poem no. 24.

Moth to your candle: See the notes for poem no. 68.

70. *To me, love is the flame*

This is a tremendously complex and difficult poem, a perfect example of the late-Ottoman marriage of the Indian style and a highly developed mystical poetry tradition. One could write a short book explaining it in detail. But it was too good to pass up, so we translated it anyway in a very interpretive version. To give some idea of what is involved we will provide a rather more extensive than usual exegesis of some of its couplets.

Mansûr: The famous sufi martyr who lived in Irak from 857 to 922. He is most often known as Mansûr al-Hallâj (Mansûr the Wool-carder) and about his person a host of legends have grown up. In its shortest version the tale goes something like this: Mansûr turned to mysticism early in his life and in his time consorted with some of the greatest masters of the age. At one point, while in a state of mystical ecstasy, he uttered the famous Arabic phrase *ene'l-Hakk* (I am the Truth/God). This was taken as blasphemy by more literalist religious authorities, and Mansûr was viewed with suspicion until he was finally arrested. Accused of abetting revolutionary activities that were taking place at the time, he was sentenced to be executed and was subsequently killed by being whipped, cut to pieces, and hung on a gallows. The latter became the popular image of the "gallows of Mansûr," which is referred to often in Ottoman poetry as the place of final torment for those who die for love.

Divine manifestation ... burning bush: The term *tecellî* has the sense "manifestation or self-disclosure of the Divine." The epitome of this manifestation is the appearance of God to Moses on Mount Sinai and, disguised, in the burning bush, but for the mystic, God manifests in every human being. The manifestation to Mansûr, therefore, is the internal recognition of Divine essence expressed in the "I am God" outcry.

That rose-adorned cypress: This brief couplet contains a rather long poem's worth of imagery that the translation can only suggest by some obscurity of its own. There is a "rose-selling cypress" (a cypress that looks like a beloved selling roses) or a cypress adorned with roses (as was done for celebrations) that is described as being a "manifestation [again] of attractiveness" or "a manifestation like the bride unveiling herself for the first time to her husband on their wedding night." The cypress or "swaying cypress" is a common trope for the beloved (see Zâtî, "Oh heavens, why do you cry"), and the beloved represents the Divine—its perfect unity here hidden in the multiplicity represented by the roses. And because of this beloved (or because of her manifestation) the lover sighs and the smoke with sparks pouring from his burning heart looks like a *nahl*, which is itself an artificial tree made of branches and flowers especially for festivals. To the lover (dervish) this tree seems to be a tree of Divine light, which is the form of the manifestation of God to Moses on Sinai.

Marker stone ... minaret of Mansûr: The marker stone is used as the identifying marker of a house in Ottoman times. However, as a popular story goes, when the martyr Mansûr was being taken to the place of his execution, he heard a *muezzin* calling the faithful to prayer. When the *muezzin* cried out, "God is great" (*Allahu ekber*), he turned to his guards and said, "If he said that with his whole heart and soul, the minaret would melt beneath his feet." The guards, accusers, and executioners scoffed at this claim, whereupon Mansûr climbed a huge stone standing by the path and from the depths of his being shouted, "God is great!" And the stone beneath him melted away. This stone, for the dervish, is the marker stone of the dwelling of Divine Unity.

I am a pearl: In mystical terms, the true essence of a human being is an exiled portion of the Divine unity, a perfect pearl/jewel that the Divine created in order that it might be known. Thus the fevered trembling of the lover (here God) for His creation (which is the Divine as an object of love, distinct from the Divine as the ultimate subject of love) is what creates the universe. The "love" (*mihr*) is a "sun" (also *mihr*) rising pink on the horizon—like the pink of mother-of-pearl in which the "perfect pearl" is nurtured—but this is a sunrise, a pearl-birth, that is accompanied by the fevered trembling of creation, a sunrise in Nishapur (present Neyshâbûr in north-eastern Iran), a city famed for its frequent and violent earthquakes. It is also relevant that eathquakes at sea were said to cause oysters to open and send pearls floating to the surface.

I am the one who knows well: The poet/dervish here highlights his familiarity with the unseen world (the world of essential meanings) by making the *'ankâ* (see Fabulous Birds) his companion. To the mystics the *'ankâ*, which is always alone, without physical form, ever flying above this world, is a symbol of the unseen world, so for it to take the poet as its companion would be the ultimate sign of the poet's spiritual wisdom.

The shadow-green down: Out of the lover's red tears and the dark-greenish down about the beloved's lip like the greenery—and Hızır, the green man (see İskender/Alexander following poem no. 10—about the fountain of eternal life), the poet creates a parrot in the eternal garden of "faithfulness" (*vefâ*), which is the faithful promise of God's assistance to the devoted spiritual lover.

The sagas of kings: This is actually "the story/adventure of Jem" (see the note for poem no. 4), who stands for the most glorious of monarchs.

The true alchemy: The mystic has no use for worldly treasure (the golden bowl) but all is turned to gold for him though love of the Divine.

Soundboard of the santûr: The *santûr* is a stringed instrument played by striking the strings with tiny hammers (loosely resembling the hammered dulcimer but with many more strings). The soundboard, therefore, is pierced by many tiny vertical pegs that anchor the strings.

The droplet of dew: When the sun rises the droplet of dew (often a pearl of dew!) evaporates and returns to the sphere of vapor. So does the dervish wait patiently for the sun of the Divine (or, in the case of the Mevlevîs, Rûmî's master Shems-i Tabriz "the Sun of Tabriz" as stand-in for the Divine) to dissolve him back into the essential unity.

Sünbülzâde Vehbî

71. *Oh east wind, come*

East wind: The breeze that blows from where the beloved lives is thought of as a messenger bringing news of her (her scent, the dust of her street, etc.).

Lady of the kingdom of pride: This is actually "the *hüsrev* [ruler] of the kingdom of pride." Here as elsewhere we have made the beloved feminine in order to correct for the fact that it was not proper (or usual) for an Ottoman poet to address or describe a female beloved.

Enderunlu Vâsıf

72. *The gazelles have bound their hearts*

Gazelles: Usually gazelles are a trope for the beloveds because of their grace, shyness, and especially their large, beautiful brown eyes. Here the gazelles themselves are captivated by the eyes of this beloved.

The night's flowers: The flower that stole the curl's scent here was the wallflower. This illustrates a general problem for translators, since wallflowers have a common and inescapable connotation in English that is entirely inappropriate to the Ottoman poem. So an "exact" translation would be wildly wrong. Our solution was an oblique reference to the Ottoman word for the wallflower, *şeb-bû* (night-scent).

A parallel of Es'ad: This is a parallel poem (see Poetic Parallels) after a poem most likely by a poet named Es'ad, who was the son of Hasan Efendi, the *müfti* (issuer of legal decrees) of Ayash. He left a small *dîvân* and died in 1850.

ʻİzzet Mollâ

73. *Everyone knows*

When the nightingale is silent: Spring with its garden, the pool, and the nightingale is the centuries-old trope for the time of maximum joy, relaxation, merriment. This spring has changed within a couplet to resemble winter, which, for the Ottoman, is a symbol of utmost despair.

This transitory world: The material world is commonly referred to as the world of "being and location" (i.e., becoming and being in place, *kevn ü mekân*) or the world of "being and decay" (*kevn ü fesâd*).

Wise master: This is Mevlânâ Jelâleddîn Rûmî, the ultimate spiritual master of the Mevlevîs.

Ottoman lands: The lands of Rûm (*diyâr-ı Rûm*).

74. *I am a nightingale*

Oh my jinn : A reasonable surface translation of the Ottoman would be "the glass of my eye is yours." The sense of this might depend on knowing (as Turks do) that the jinn *cinn* (see the note for poem no. 17) live in mirrors; so, because the beloved is always reflected in the lover's eye, she is like a jinn living in the mirror of his eye. We took the liberty here of reading the word *şîşe* (glass) in its other usual meaning "small round bottle" (which is certainly intentionally related to the "eye" image). This makes the line correspond more to the familiar notion that the genie can be caught in a bottle and, more particularly, to the story that Solomon used his famous seal to put the *peris* in a bottle.

The houris: The beloveds of Paradise, the most beautiful of all creatures.

The black of my eye: The pupil of the eye is often compared to a seed or gall-nut that is crushed to dust with a mortar and pestle—for spice like a peppercorn or for making ink.

Those rose-tears on my lashes: The image here is that the eyelashes have drops of bloody red teardrops on them and so are like roses brought to blooming by the abundant rain of tears.

Rains abundance: This is a difficult image for us, but not for an Ottoman. The hot hell of sighs causes burns to the heart/soul/inner-self that are inflamed, red like blossoms, and abundant enough to seem like a flourishing garden. If the garden grows this well from burning then what need is there of any sort of watering?

Mevlânâ: Rûmî.

Yenishehirli 'Avnî

75. *Don't think we came to ask*

Burns of desire: The burns that the lover inflicts on himself in his passion are here compared to eyes. (See the notes for poem no. 68.)

Hoja: Generally means "teacher"; it is a term usually of respect but here it means a religious person in the category of *sôfû/sûfî* or *zâhid* who admonishes the lover and fails to see the mystical significance of his love.

This fictitious world: Translates the *'âlem-i îjâd* or the world of created things—thus it is a "made-up" (unreal) world.

A single rose: It was a long-standing custom among the Ottoman elites for the truly sensitive person to pluck one spring rose to decorate his turban.

The Poets

Nesîmî

Nesîmî comes, as much legend as not, out of the mist clouding the earliest days of Turkish poetry in Anatolia. He is an Ottoman poet only insofar as he had contacts with the Ottomans during his lifetime and was considered by the Ottomans as a direct ancestor of their art. In this anthology he stands for a group of the earliest Anatolian poets who will, as a class, be somewhat underrepresented. His given name was 'İmâdüddîn and he is said to be from Tabriz, or from Shiraz, or from Diyarbekir, or from a province named Nesîm near Aleppo. The latter origin would explain his pen name, but no such province has been found to exist and it is just as likely that the pen name actually derives from the Arabic word *nesîm* (a soft breeze).

The sources make it seem likely that he was a Turcoman, but he was also given the title *seyyid*, which indicates that he could trace his descent back to the Prophet. In any case, he was certainly a dervish and a mystical poet of some renown. In the early years of the fifteenth century he became an enthusiastic adherent of Sheyh Fazlullâh the Hurûfî. The Hurûfîs were mystics who believed that the secret, true, and inner meaning of the Quran could be derived from a rereading based on an understanding of a mysterious letter-symbolism. According to them, the letters of the Arabic alphabet stood not only for numbers (which were one source of interpretation) but for parts of the body, which in turn had hidden meanings, and so on. This reading grounded a spirituality of the unity of all being, which celebrated the world—the *real* world—as a manifestation of Divine qualities, thereby linking the individual with the Divine Truth of all existence.

As popular as this mystery was with the nomadic tribes and villagers of the periphery, it was anathema to the religious authorities of the various town and city centers. At one point, Nesîmî, who like many of the great dervish-poets of his day must have traveled from village to village and tribe to tribe, seems to have found himself in Aleppo. Here some local religious authorities took exception to his pronouncing the oneness of all existence more or less as the earlier martyr Mansûr (see the notes for poem no. 70) had put it: "I am the Truth" (Truth being one of the names of God, according to which the statement means, "I am God"). A religious judgment was issued ordering the poet's execution; as the story goes, Nesîmî was skinned alive on the gates of the city sometime around the year 1404.

Out of this gruesome execution and the fame of Nesîmî's poetry a number of legends grew. In some, the poet mocks his tormenters with extemporized verses even as he is being tortured; in another the poet-mystic gathers up his discarded skin, throws it over his shoulders, and departs for the invisible world. Stories about his exploits prior to his death also proliferate as he takes on a form of popular sainthood not unusual for provincial dervish masters.

When he died, Nesîmî left behind not only the stuff of many legends but collections of poetry in both Turkish and Persian.

Ahmed-i Dâ'î

We know very little for sure about Ahmed-i Dâ'î (Ahmed the Missionary). It appears he was born during the latter part of the fourteenth century in the princedom of Germiyan in west central Anatolia. By this time Germiyan was no longer the power it had been in the past and was inclined to seek amicable relations with its ambitious Ottoman neighbor to the north. The court of the dynasty in Kütahya was nonetheless a center for cultural activity. Ahmed-i Dâ'î was a contemporary of Ahmedî, the famous composer of verse narratives in rhyming couplets (*mesnevî*), and of Sheyhî (see below). Although he began his career in the court of the princes of Germiyan, after the major disruption caused by the invasion of Timur (Tamurlane) he sought patronage in the courts of the Ottoman princes, Süleymân and Mehmed, at a time when the Ottomans were but one of several competing Anatolian dynasties. He was later tutor to Prince Murâd (II) and dedicated works to a number of Ottoman officials.

Like many premodern intellectuals, Ahmed-i Dâ'î was a master of many fields of knowledge from law to medicine, to literature and linguistics, to history and natural sciences. He wrote at least seventeen major works that we know of and collections of poetry in both Turkish and Persian. In addition he is thought to have been an excellent calligrapher.

Though we know little of his early years, of the latter years of his life we know almost nothing. We think that he died either in 1417 or sometime after 1421. He is said to be buried in Bursa, the first Ottoman capital; however, his grave-site is not known.

Sheyhî

Like Ahmed-i Dâ'î and the famous epic poet Ahmedî, Sheyhî lived in the province of Germiyan during the period surrounding Timur's invasion of Anatolia. At that time, the court of the Princes of Germiyan in Kütahya was a major center for learning and literature. Sheyhî was most likely from a prominent family of the Germiyan Türkmen clan. He was born in Kütahya, probably between 1371 and 1376.

Most of the sources for Sheyhî's life were written more than one hundred years after his death and hence are often contradictory and rely more on anecdotes than on information we can check against other sources. It is believed that he received an excellent education in his hometown; some sources report that he later went to Iran to complete his education. There he, like Ahmed-i Dâ'î, studied literature, sufism (mysticism), and medicine, a combination that was common at the time.

It is said that Sheyhî practiced medicine and also treated diseases of the eye. 'Âshık Chelebî tells an amusing story about his ophthalmological career. It seems that Sheyhî himself was afflicted with constant conjunctivitis and poor vision. As the story goes:

> *At one time he advertised in his shop that there was a remedy for every disease and a cure for every ill, and for conjunctivitis and weak vision to some he sold eye-healing* kohl *salve and to others eye-strengthening* sürme *salve. As people were grabbing them up as eye-ointments, a witty person asked him for an* akche *(silver piece) worth of* kohl *and Sheyhî wrapped the* akche *of* kohl *in a piece of paper. The fellow then asked for another* akche *of* kohl, *bought it and handed it to Sheyhî, saying, "Learned doctor and physician, as a favor, take this and use it to treat your own eyes!"*

Another anecdote about Sheyhî's skills as a physician fancifully accounts for his connection with the Ottomans. When Timur conquered Anatolia by defeating the Ottomans under Bâyezîd I in 1402, he left behind what he hoped was a divided territory that could not produce another major power. The Prince of Karaman was given control of much of central Anatolia, and various Ottoman princes were given charge of territories in Anatolia and the European provinces. A crucial period of Sheyhî's life was lived in the atmosphere of uncertainty and conflict that marked this era which lasted until 1413 when Ottoman territories were reunited under Prince Mehmed, who would become Sultan Mehmed I. For long periods the poet lived in Kütahya in the court of the Germiyanid

Prince Ya'kub II, but at one point he and Ahmedî found themselves for a time at the court of the Ottoman Prince Süleymân in Edirne, where they engaged in some memorable poetry contests. Our story, however, concerns Sheyhî's meeting Sultan Mehmed I. According to the biographers 'Âshık and Hasan, the Sultan had been ill for some time with a disease that only grew worse and did not respond to medical care. They sought everywhere for a skilled physician and finally (in 'Âshık's words):

They discovered Sheyhî and brought him into the presence of the Sultan. When he had taken the Sultan's pulse and looked at a bottle of his urine, he said "The cause of this illness is this: the various dense humors have become mingled. The remedy for the disease is an extreme joy that would be a source of cheerfulness and a cause of respite for the spirits."

At this point a messenger arrives, announcing the capture of an impregnable castle that controlled an area Mehmed had much desired to take. The Sultan is overjoyed, his disease immediately begins to lessen, and he soon is entirely cured.

There is a sequel to this story in which the poet/physician is showered with gifts and favors by the grateful Sultan. Among the gifts was a fief (*timâr*), the village of Dokuzlar, which was turned over to Sheyhî's keeping (and tax collecting). On his way to his new fief, Sheyhî was met on the road by the former fief-holders, who plundered his goods and set about to murder him and his companions. The miserable, abused poet finally returned half-dead to the Sultan's court, where he wrote his famous *Book of the Ass*, ridiculing these envious opponents. The ridicule had its effect. In the end the chagrined enemies restored Sheyhî's goods and chattels to him and begged his forgiveness.

Some of the sources seem eager to make of Sheyhî a mystic of the type that abounded in Anatolia at the time. The biographer Latîfî reports that he met with Nesîmî (see above); others have him receiving his pen name from Hajî Bayrâm Velî, a famous sufi master. However, there is little evidence that the calling of a dervish was central either in his life or in his poetry.

Sheyhî's true fame derives from his poetry. The biographers of the sixteenth century, who see themselves and their peers as the end point of cultural progress, consider Sheyhî the master-poet of the first step in the glorious journey of Western Turkish high-culture poetry. In addition to a wonderful collection of lyric poems, he wrote a famous adaptation of the Persian master Nizâmî's verse romance *Hüsrev ü Shîrîn* (see the article following poem no. 28) presented to Sultan Mehmed's successor, Murâd II. A less dramatic but more plausible story says that the satirical *Book of the Ass* was written in response to envious criticisms of his *Hüsrev ü Shîrîn*.

Little is known of the last years of Sheyhî's life. He wrote an elegy on the death of his patron, the Germiyanid Prince Ya'kûb Bey, who died in 1429. The poet is believed to have died rather soon thereafter. The date of his death is sometime around 1431; he is said to have been sixty years old at the time.

Ahmed Pasha

Ahmed Pasha is considered by many to be the first great Ottoman poet. Although there were several talented poets before him who wrote in the Western Turkic dialect that would later be referred to as the Ottoman dialect, he is associated with the culture of the Ottoman state at a crucial initial stage of its ascent to world prominence and was the poet considered by the Ottoman poets themselves to be the true founder of their tradition.

Ahmed Pasha was born in either Edirne (Adrianople) or Bursa sometime in the early years of the fifteenth century. His father was one Veliyüddîn, who served as chief military judge during the reign of Sultan Murâd II (1413–1421). Ahmed was well educated and in the course of his career served as a professor, local judge, and chief military judge to Sultan Mehmed II (1451–1481). His intelligence and wit attracted the attention of the Sultan, who following the conquest of Istanbul (in 1453) had gathered about him a brilliant circle of intellectuals, artists, and poets. Ahmed's popularity at court rose rapidly; he was promoted to the offices of Special Tutor (*lâlâ*) to the Sultan and subsequently to the office of Vizier—one of the highest positions in the land.

After a time, he fell precipitously from favor. There are several stories that purport to describe his fall. The two most common versions are as follows. The first version is by a sixteenth century biographer of poets, Latîfî:

Concerning the late aforementioned, it was widely known and commented upon that he was exceedingly a boy-chaser and love-addict, that out of the clamor and ardor of his spirit he was drunk with passion and hand-in-glove with love. On account of this condition, he greatly loathed women and the pursuit of women and scrupulously avoided both their companionship and their very company. He was the prince of princes in the world of abandoning mundane relationships and never imagined or conceived of wedding or kissing or embracing a woman. It has been heard that his lordship Mehmed Han one day disciplined one of his imperial pages—a slender, cypress-bodied boy—by putting him in chains, thus harvesting the seed of irritation and punishment in the field of rage and anger. When the Pasha saw that bondsman bound in those bonds there issued forth from him, one after the other, in a flash of inspiration, the following lines:

Let the earth burn, for that candle which feeds on sugar
Lies weeping, his feet bound in iron chains

His lip is a sweet from Shiraz, which were it sold
Would cost all Egypt, Bukhara, and Samarkand

When these verses reached the ear of his lordship Sultan Mehmed, he had the abovementioned Pasha imprisoned in the Seven Towers.

The second version is from another sixteenth century biographer, 'Âshık Chelebî:

While he served in the post of minister, a few troublemakers, jealous to the depth of their souls, made up a story, based on hearsay, to arouse suspicion, in which it was said that the Pasha had fallen in love with one of the royal pages in the Imperial Harem and with unmitigated lust was befriending that silver-skinned lovely intending to have his way with him. As a test, Sultan Mehmed had the page stripped naked and sent to the steambaths at the same time as Ahmed Pasha. They shaved the lovelocks from the page and sent him to the Pasha with a cool drink. Extemporaneously, Ahmed Pasha spoke the following couplet and thereby revealed what was hidden in his heart:

That Idol has given up his lovelocks, but not his heathen ways
He has cut off his Christian belt, but not become a Muslim

The Monarch first of all ordered the Pasha's execution but later imprisoned him in the Gate-keeper's Quarters. While in the Gatekeeper's Quarters he sent his "Mercy" panegyric to the Monarch, and Sultan Mehmed, in a display of manly virtue, appointed him as administrator of the Endowment of Orhân in Bursa at a salary of thirty silver pieces.

We do know that Ahmed Pasha was imprisoned, exiled from court, and appointed to positions in Bursa for the rest of his days. His final appointment, under Mehmed the Conqueror's successor, Bâyezîd II, was as governor of the Province of Bursa. He died in Bursa in the year 1496.

Nejâtî

We have no idea when exactly the poet Nejâtî was born, although it must have been sometime in the middle of the fifteenth century; nor do we know where he might have come from. Some of the stories about him indicate that he may have been a slave taken as a youth in war. His pen name, which means "He Who Takes Refuge," and his given name in some sources 'Isâ (Jesus) (Nûh [Noah], in other sources) hints that he was a convert to Islam. One of the tales says he is the adopted son (possible for an Ottoman slave) of an elderly widow of Edirne, who sees to his education; another story makes him the slave of a poet named Sâ'ilî, who does the same. The biographer Latîfî claims that he got his start in Kastamonu, but 'Âshık Chelebî points out that Latîfî traces everyone he can back to his own hometown. It is possible that Nejâtî was raised in Edirne and later lived in Kastamonu.

Nejâtî apparently never had a complete theological school education, but he obviously mastered the knowledge necessary to become an accomplished poet and enter the scribal bureaucracy. How he got to Istanbul and attracted the attention of important patrons is also a mystery. Kınalızâde Hasan many years later relates a story supposedly told by Nejâtî's son, which says that the poets of the time used to gather in conversation about the famous Ahmed Pasha (see above). One day a caravan arrived from Kastamonu and reported that a poet named Nûh with the pen name Nejâtî had appeared in that city and had won fame with two *gazels* that ended with the *redîf* (repetition after the rhyme) *döne döne* (turning and turning). (For a translation of one of them, see poem no. 10.) And Ahmed Pasha, it seems, approved of the poems, which would have made it possible for Nejâtî's work to receive a reading at court.

However it happened, Nejâtî did manage to make his way to Istanbul and to present poems to Sultan Mehmed II (the Conqueror of Istanbul). 'Âshık Chelebî tells an interesting story about how the poet attracted the attention of the Sultan.

. . . one day the late Necâtî composed his gazel *with the opening line ' What can we do, the sigh of early morn makes no mark on you // Oh my beloved friend, would that God might grant you justice" and he inserted it in [the folds of] the turban of one of the late Sultan Mehmed's companions who was named Chyurgi [Yurgi/Jyurgi?]. When he went in to the Sultan's gathering, Sultan Mehmed began playing chess with him. During the game, he [the Sultan]*

noticed the paper in his turban; when he took it out and read it, he made him [Necâtî] a dîvân secretary at a salary of 17 akche [silver pieces] a day.

This appointment took place in 1481, and Sultan Mehmed died soon after. Under his successor, Bâyezîd II, Nejâtî was given the position of Council Secretary to Prince 'Abdullâh when he went to the province of Karaman to serve as Governor. After a brief governorship, 'Abdullâh too died; Nejâtî was again without a position, apparently living off the rewards given for his poems. In the next phase of his life he was, however, to enjoy the patronage of the famous Mü'eyyedzâde 'Abdürrahmân Chelebî, whose life Bâyezîd had saved from a sentence of death during his father's reign (see the entry for Mihrî below).

In 1504 Nejâtî accompanied another Prince to the provinces. Prince Mahmûd was a mature intellectual and poet, many of whose retainers were also noted poets. This was a step up, and the time in Saruhan Province was a good one for the poet. By this time he was justly famed and in the succeeding generation would be considered the poet who brought Ottoman poetry to a level at which it could compete successfully with Persian poetry. His lyrics with their brilliant images and clever citations of popular proverbs certainly stand out in comparison to those of his predecessors. He collected his poems into a volume dedicated to Mü'eyyedzâde, did some translating, composed works of various kinds, and increased his fame. After just three years, this Prince too met an untimely end.

Nejâtî seems to have been devastated. He took no more official positions and retired to a house in Istanbul, where he lived off a pension granted by the ruler and surrounded himself with the company of close friends, including his pupil, the first Ottoman biographer of poets, Sehî. In the year following Prince Mahmûd's death (March 1509), according to 'Âshık, the aging and ailing poet gathered all his dearest friends about him and gave them a *gazel*, saying, "This is my farewell to you and to poetry." He then begged forgiveness of God and the indulgence of his companions and closed his eyes forever.

Mihrî Hatun

Mihrî Hatun (Ms./Lady Mihrî), whose name and pen name were the same (Mihrî means both "Sunlike" and "Loving") lived in the town of Amasya in north central Anatolia during the latter years of the fifteenth and early years of the sixteenth centuries. She is said to have been the descendant of a Halvetî dervish master named Pîr İlyâs and the daughter of a local judge (*kadî*) who, according to Latîfî, wrote poetry under the pen name Belâyî (Afflicted by Calamity). In archival records of royal gifts to Mihrî, her father's name is given as Mevlânâ Hasan of Amasya.

In that day it was considered important, for religious and social reasons, that women lead very private lives. Therefore we know nothing about Mihrî's life except as it involves her strikingly unusual career as a poet. And even her public poet-life is difficult for Ottoman biographers to talk about. They accord her some respect as a poet—which they could hardly avoid. Latîfî describes her with grudging double negatives: "In the art of poetry she is not without rank and dignity and in the essentials of wisdom she is not of little worth". But they seem to have no idea of how to talk about her since the world of poetry and the narrative describing it were exclusively male. So Mihrî is made into an honorary male—with reference to the Turkish saying, "If the male lion is a lion, is not the lioness a lion too?" She is said to have been of a passionate nature and to have fallen in love several times, which her poetry is then presumed to reflect.

According to the tales, her earliest love is said to have been for the later famous Chief Military Justice, poet, and patron of the arts Mü'eyyedzâde 'Abdürrahmân Chelebî, who was born in Amasya. The love story is told without much elaboration and seems to hang in large part on a humorously ambiguous couplet addressed to Mü'eyyedzâde by his pen name, Hâtemî (the Seal-holder?):

> Oh Hâtemî you came to Mihrî falsely as a lover
> And yet, by God, Mihrî loves you better than any boy

Mihrî is known to have had some sort of relation to the conversational and literary circle of Prince Ahmed, son of Bâyezîd II, while he was serving as Governor of Amasya between 1481 and 1513. It is told that she conceived a passion for one of this circle, a young man named İskender Chelebî, the son of Sinân Pasha, and wrote several *gazels* (including one translated in this anthology) supposedly addressed to him. She also has a famous exchange of poems with a poet named Güvâhî (the Witness/Proof), who is also cast as a beloved.

The biographers are quick to point out, however, that despite these loves Mihrî—whom some describe as quite beautiful—remained pure, virginal, and honorable to the end of her life. To exemplify this virtue in the face of an uncommonly public posture, Latîfî says that at one time the poets and wits of Ahmed's court made fun of her relation to İskender Chelebî, to which she responded with a couplet referring cleverly to the famous story of the legendary İskender and his search for the fountain of eternal life (see the article following poem no. 10):

> The sweet-water of my ruby lip sent many Alexanders
> In search of water and sent them back still thirsting

Mihrî's poetic idol appears to have been Nejâtî, to whose poetry she wrote many parallels. The biographers tell that Nejâtî was testy about these rather competitive attempts and take a short piece of his to be a rebuke of Mihrî.

> Oh you who would parallel my verses
> Beware stepping off the path of decency
>
> Don't say my poems in rhyme and rhythm
> Are just the same as Nejâtî's
>
> There being five letters in both words
> Are "skill" and "error" the same?

If we take the Register of Royal Gifts from the court of Bâyezîd II published by Professor Erunsal (1981) as an example, Nejâtî certainly had grounds for his testiness. The famed Nejâtî is recorded as having few such gifts (officially granted in return for poems or other literary works), while Mihrî is regularly mentioned and receives monetary gifts quite a bit larger than those of most other poets, including her idol. Unfortunately, we do not yet have a reasonable account of the position of poets in Ottoman society that would explain how and why a woman would be permitted to take, and even be rewarded officially for taking, a public role in an artistic profession considered highly dubious or sensitive because of its sexual implications.

Mihrî Hatun died in Amasya sometime after 1512, when the last official record of her name appears. She is said to have been buried in the cemetery attached to the dervish lodge of her ancestor, Pîr Ilyâs.

Zeyneb Hatun

Zeyneb Hatun (Madam Zeyneb) was born in Anatolia, either in Kastamonu, according to Latîfî, or in Amasya, in 'Âshık Chelebî's account, sometime in the first part of the fifteenth century. As is the case with all of the woman poets, precious little is known of her life. Latîfî says of her that:

. . . her inborn intellectual charm amazed the ordinary people of the world and astounded the discerning of the age. Her father saw ability in her nature and brilliance in her intellect and educated her in all manner of sciences and all sorts of arts, teaching her from the poem-collections of the Persians and the odes of the Arabs. After she had done with gathering wisdom and acquiring ability, according to the [Persian] saying "When all the conceits [that go into poetry] have been gathered, then being a poet is easy," thus equipped with a natural poetic incisiveness she composed a collection of poems in Persian and Turkish dedicated to Sultan Mehmed [II].

It appears that she, in time, may have become friends with Mihrî (see above), with whom she is said to have exchanged poems and conversation. As unusual as her opportunity to receive an education and apply her outstanding abilities may have been, the latter part of her life returns her to the public obscurity of most high-born women of her day. Unlike Mihrî, who never married and continued to lead a somewhat public life (that is, not a life in public but a life where people outside the immediate family know what you are doing) Zeyneb married a Amasya magistrate named İshâk (Iss-hock) Fehmî Efendi. Either by her choice or at her husband's insistence, as the biographer 'Âshık indicates, she gave up writing poetry and all conversation with other men. From this time on there is no other report of her except the unattested rumor that she died in the period 1473–1474.

Revânî

Revânî was born Shüjâ' in the city of Edirne. Although he would become a very well-known poet and public figure, nothing is known about his early life, including the date of his birth. He first comes to the attention of biographers during the reign of Sultan Bâyezîd II (1481–1512) as the central figure in an amusing anecdote. As the story goes, Sultan Bâyezîd (in some versions, Sultan Selîm I) made it his pious duty to send money to the poor of Mecca during the season of pilgrimage, a custom that had been practiced irregularly since the time of his father. One year Revânî was made Guardian of the Purse, leader of the official Procession of the Purse, which took the Sultan's largesse to the holy city. Apparently there was a general suspicion and widespread rumors that Revânî had helped himself to some of the money he was charged with delivering. When the rumors reached the Sultan's ears, Revânî was dismissed from his post, his stipend was cut off, and the chagrined poet departed for Trabzon to become a member of the court of Prince Selîm, who was serving a term there as Provincial Governor. His disgrace was the talk of the town, and when he developed a condition that reddened his eyes, one of the poets circulated the following verses, which depend for their cleverness on understanding that the word for "true or right" means "someone's deserved share" (hence the "Kaaba's right" is the purse sent to Mecca) and is also one of the Names of God:

Is this the way to be a Muslim, oh Revânî?
When you got to the Kaaba you forgot the Right.
Who cares if you come up short in your faith
You just made an advance in your worldly things.
Now your eye has filled up with blood
And in the end the Kaaba's Right [God/the money] won't cure you.

From 'Âshık we learn that Revânî was with Selîm when the prince returned to Istanbul after his father's death to receive the oath of obedience from the troops. This assured Selîm's succession to the throne and, according to 'Âshık, Mü'eyyedzâde reported to him that:

Revânî was there right beside me on a horse and saw the whole thing. He was so thrilled and overjoyed that he took off his turban and sent it flying through the air. Afterward he spoke to me saying that each and every high and noble person had now been raised to the heavens like the sun and droplets from the cloud of the abundant gifts of God had rained down upon the garden of all their hopes, and thus did he effusively sing the praises of the late Sultan Selîm.

The reign of Sultan Selîm (1512–1520) was a good time for Revânî. He was part of a group of like-minded drinkers and pleasure-seekers that included Zâtî and several other well-known poets. Stories about him abound. At one point he greatly displeased Selîm who took almost everything he had but was forgiven, as it is told, on account of a clever poem. There is also a story in two versions about a *Winter Kasîde* with the *redîf* "snow" that he originally wrote for Bâyezîd and apparently reworked for Sultan Selîm. As the historian Mustafâ 'Âlî of Gallipoli tells it, Revânî had accompanied the Sultan on his victorious campaign to Egypt:

On the way to Egypt, Revânî recited a kasîde *with the* redîf *"snow" and when that Sovereign Possessed of Purity said, "Why should you do a poem like this in a hot land that has no idea what snow is?" the poet Süjûdî took the opportunity to compose the following:*

You've filled the world with chilly words
Let snow fall on your head, oh Revânî

To which Revânî replied, with pointed reference to the pen name Süjûdî (Who Prostrates Himself in Prayer) and his extreme youth (or drinking habits):

There's no place on earth you haven't fallen on your face
And that is why they all call you the Prostrate One (i.e., Süjûdî)

In Latîfî's version the Sultan's reply is "What kind of a thing to be praised is snow that you should intentionally make a description with such cold words and present it to me as a kasîde?" The implication is that the Sultan felt he was being described as a cold, unfeeling person.

During Selîm's time and into the reign of his son, Süleymân, Revânî, despite his reputation for fiscal irresponsibility, held the post of Overseer of Pious Endowments for the hot-springs of Bursa and the great mosque of Aya Sophia. During this time he had a mosque built bearing his name in the district of Kırk Cheshme, with attached rooms and dwelling places for the needy. According to Hasan Chelebî and 'Âshık, Sultan Selîm passed through the district at one time and, seeing the mosque, asked whose it was. When they told him it belonged to Revânî, the Overseer of Aya Sophia, he quipped, "In truth, it is crystal clear that Aya Sophia is the greatest of all mosques. But it is not improbable that he (Revânî) will cause several mosques like it to appear every year."

When Revânî died in 1524, he left behind a substantial collection of good poems and an unusual verse essay on drinking and parties (*'Ishretnâme*). He was buried in Istanbul in front of the mosque he had built.

Lâmi'î

Lâmi'î was born in Bursa in 1472 to a family with a long and distinguished lineage. His full name is Sheyh Mahmûd bin Osmân bin 'Alî bin en-Nakkâsh bin İlyâs Lâmi'î Chelebî (The Elder Mahmûd, son of Osmân, son of 'Alî son of the Embellishment Artist, son of İlyâs). His father, Osmân, was manager of the treasury under Sultan Bâyezîd and his great grandfather, 'Alî Pasha the Embellishment Artist, had been brought to

Samarkand by Tîmûr (Tamurlaine), where he learned the artist's craft that he later applied with great success to some of the most famous architectural monuments of the fifteenth century.

Lâmi'î studied under some of the most famous scholars of his day and received a complete theological school education. However, while he was still quite young he was attracted to mysticism and the circle of the great Nakshbendî sheyh, Emîr Ahmed Buhârî. Sheyh Buhârî had come to Istanbul from Persia (the town of Buhârâ) with the famous Sheyh İlâhî, whom he succeeded as head of the Istanbul lodge of the Nakshbendî order. At the time when Lâmi'î joined the order, the lodge was rapidly becoming a spiritual center for the artists and intellectuals of the capital.

Lâmi'î's attachment to his Sheyh seems to have been deep and sincere, lasting beyond the death of his master in 1516. His collected poems (*dîvân*) contains a number of lyrics dedicated to the Sheyh, including the following lines cited by one of his recent biographers:

> Let me, like a hound, lie abject at your door
> This is glory enough for me, alas, I need no more
> I am but a tiny ant, come to learn the tongue of birds
> By Solomon's court and magnificence I set no store
>
> (The reference in the last couplet is tangentially to the story of Solomon and the ant and the [mystical] power of Solomon to speak the languages of all living creatures [see the notes for poem no. 51].)

Lâmi'î married while still quite young and had several children, of whom three sons and a daughter survived into adulthood. Despite a formidable education, he did not follow the usual career path of theological school graduates, instead preferring to lead the life of a scholar, poet, and mystic. He was a prolific author and is most famous for his many translations of major Persian narrative poems into Turkish. Latîfî, who is quite critical of his talent, praises him for having as many great works as there are hours in the day—which underestimates his productivity by almost one-half. In any case, his work was highly regarded by three sultans (Bâyezîd II, Selîm I, Süleymân), who granted him gifts and stipends adequate to live a comfortable life. The biographer 'Âshık Chelebî tells the following anecdote about the latter years of his life:

Near the end of his life, while he was keeping himself busy with learning and worship, heart at ease, free of concern, composed of mind, and in comfortable circumstances, he wrote a gazel *at the urging of some of his friends about a notorious young man called Tatar Memi* [Memi is a nickname for Mehmed], *of which the first couplet is:*

> *His brows a bow, arrows his lashes, his glance a dagger*
> *In all the world is there a heart-thief like Memi the Tatar*

The heart-thief's lovers and admirers—especially the chief of his lovers known by the name İslî 'Abdî—were incensed and tormented the late Lâmi'î with wild satires and vehement insults and wounded him with the stone of public reproach.

Not long after, in 1532, as he approached his sixtieth year, Lâmi'î died in the city of Bursa.

Zâtî

Zâtî was born in Balıkesir in west-central Anatolia approximately on a line between Istanbul and Izmir. His father was a poor bootmaker, and it is said that Zâtî too worked for a time as a bootmaker in his hometown. There is some confusion about his actual name. Some sources say it was Satılmısh (which means "Sold") and report that he was called by the nickname Sati from which he created a similar sounding pen name. However, 'Âshık reports, on the authority of the poet himself, that his name was 'İvaż and that number values of the letters of his name added up to his birthdate 876 of the Hijra or 1471 c.e. (the letter *'ayin* = 70, the letter *vâv* = 6, the letter *żâd* = 800). Whatever his real name, it is under the pen name Zâtî that he would become one of the most famous Ottoman poets and the subject of numerous tales and anecdotes.

There is no evidence that Zâtî ever had the kind of higher education typical of the best poets. Several of the biographers marvel that someone with so little education could produce such wonderful verses. 'Âlî calls his poetry *'ârizî* which means more or less "accidental," that is, "produced without a background in the craft." This, he says, makes the name Zâtî ("personal/original") especially appropriate.

Kınalızâde gives a first-person account of Zâtî's career supposedly related to the biographer's father by the poet himself. In this tale, the poet recounts that, finding no outlet for his talents in his hometown, he came to Istanbul during the reign of Sultan Bâyezîd II (1481–1512) and made the acquaintance of the poets and wits of the city. He submitted poems to the Sultan and the Vizier 'Alî Pasha and became the recipient of their gifts and favors. Because he was plagued by a deafness that made the usual secretarial positions impossible for him, the Vizier offered him a *tevliyet* (the administratorship of a pious foundation), but the poet, confident in his abilities, felt that he could live much better on the royal stipend given to poets coupled with the generous gifts of his patrons, who also included the Military Magistrate Müeyyedzâde, the Inscriptor of the Royal Signature Tâjîzâde, and the Minister of Finance Pîrî Pasha. So he turned the offer down, as he did similar offers at other times, preferring to stay in Istanbul in the company of his close friends, with whom he was accustomed to spend pleasant hours in amorous pursuits, drinking, and pleasant conversation.

But near the end of Bâyezîd's reign, in troubled times, Zâtî's great patron 'Alî Pasha died in battle and other powerful supporters lost their positions. So the poet was reduced to opening a shop, where he wrote poems for cash and eked out a living as the kind of fortuneteller who does readings from marks in sand and as a writer of amulets and talismans.

When Selîm I (1512–1520) ascended the throne, Zâtî submitted an accession ode which won him back a modest yearly stipend. However, according to the poet, Selîm was so often out of the city on campaigns of conquest that neither he nor members of his court were available to provide adequate patronage. Nonetheless, for many years Zâtî's shop was a haven for poets and he served as mentor for many young poets, including Bâkî, somewhat later. The biographers report that no aspiring poet would dare submit a poem without first having it read by Zâtî. They also report that Zâtî made it a habit to borrow verses he liked, either by directly including them in his poems or by slightly altering them. When confronted by the unwilling lenders, he would point out that they had no reputation at all and their verses would be forgotten, except for those that appeared in Zâtî's poems.

By the time of Süleymân's accession, Zâtî was recognized as one of the greatest Ottoman poets. He was the center of a circle that included such well-known poets as Keshfî, Kandî (see the entry for Hayâlî), Basîrî, and Kadrî. Under the patronage of the new Sultan and his court, Zâtî again flourished for a time. Eventually, however, he ran into trouble with the Sultan's Grand Vizier and confidant, İbrâhîm Pasha (see the entry for Figânî) who was himself a great patron of the arts. The first source of difficulty was the affair of his friend Keshfî's brother Hasbî, who had been arrested for some crime or another, was tortured briefly, and sentenced to ten years in prison by İbrâhîm. Zâtî says that he gathered the local poets to protest the sentence to İbrâhîm and urge that he pardon the poet, who by this time had changed his pen name from Hasbî ("Confident in God or Honorable") to Habsî ("Imprisoned").

Again, when Hayâlî, in a fit of pique, stoned the candy shop of Kandî (see the entry for Hayâlî), Zâtî urged the poets to protest. Apparently there were those at court—Hayâlî among them—who then told İbrâhîm that Zâtî had inspired the poetic community to satirize the Grand Vizier. Finally, Zâtî wrote a celebratory ode on the occasion of the Pasha's marriage, and when İbrâhîm had finished reading it, the Vizier recited a line from an ode of Hayâlî's and said, "You ought to write poetry like this." The line, referring to a well-known Persian poet, was

> The dust thrown up by the steed of my well-formed nature
> Kemâl in Isfahan would use as salve for his eyes

When Zâtî responded that this was not how the line went, the Pasha asked, "Then how does it go?" "Like this," said Zâtî:

> The dust thrown up by the steed of Zâtî's natural ability
> Kemâl in Isfahan . . .

İbrâhîm attempted to dismiss the whole thing by pointing out that poets are always jealously accusing each other of theft, to which an incensed Zâtî replied that the verses in question could be found in an ode he had submitted upon the accession of Sultan Süleyman and that a copy of the ode could be found in the archives of the Royal Harem. This kind of backtalk did not please the Pasha at all and was the occasion, in the poet's words, of a coolness growing up between them.

So Zâtî continued to work at his shop, scrambling for cash and presents, the center of a lively poetic circle, deaf, they say, when it came to criticism but quite able to pick up words of praise. When Zâtî was near the end of his life, palsied and troubled by heart palpitations, his dear friend Kadrî became Military Magistrate of Anatolia and managed to secure the administratorship of a pious foundation for the poet. Shortly thereafter, in 1546, Zâtî died leaving behind him a huge collection of poems, some 1,600 *gazels* and more than 400 *kasîdes*, a book of witticisms, some prose works, and a romantic narrative in rhyming couplets.

Hayretî

Hayretî (the Bewildered), like Hayâlî, was from the town of Vardar Yenichesi in Macedonia near to Salonika—a small town, its environs settled by Turkic peoples since Byzantine times that for some reason produced an unusual number of poets. We do not know the date of his birth, which must have been in the second half of the fifteenth century. His everyday name was Mehmed, and he seems to have been a professional soldier attached to the Yahyâlı corps of the Akınjı (Raider) branch of the Sipahîs (the feudal cavalry). The Akınjı were skilled horsemen, swordsmen, and archers whose role was to carry out raids on enemy territory, disrupting life in areas scheduled for invasion and occupation by the regular army.

At some point during the early years of the reign of Sultan Süleymân, Hayretî came to Istanbul and began to submit poems to the noted patrons of the age. 'Âshık Chelebî tells an interesting story about a *kasîde* presented to the Grand Vizier İbrâhîm Pasha. It appears that this *kasîde* impressed the Grand Vizier very much, and he thought to take Hayretî under his protection. However, before doing so he asked Hayâlî what he thought. In 'Âshık's words,

One day he [İbrâhîm] said to Hayâlî, "Do you know your fellow townsman Hayretî?" And Hayâlî responded, "I know him, he has no care for fame or position, neither for service to rulers nor attendance on viziers; he lives in disdain of worldly things. He dwells in his own climate, disheveled, destitute, and bewildered. Yet recently he composed a gazel and it has an exceptional opening couplet [matla'] to which I have been incapable of writing a parallel [nazîre]." When the late Pasha asked, "What is it?" he recited this couplet:

We are not slaves of Süleymân, nor the captives
  of Selîm
No one knows us, we are slaves of the shah
  of generosity

And although that mighty knight on the chessboard of viziership had wanted to send his horse into the battlefield of favors and remove the veil from the cheek of Hayretî's hopes, this [response] immediately made a diagonal assault like the queen, set the pawns of trouble to moving, and checkmated him by driving him into an impasse. [Hayâlî] did an immature thing and with chilly words poured cold water into the boiling cauldron of the Pasha's generosity and cooled it down.

Obviously the Pasha would look with suspicion on a potential adherent who did not care about serving the mighty and who was a known Shiite writing verses that seemed to reject service to the Ottoman Sultans

(Süleymân and Selîm) and claim devotion to some unnamed shah (which could as well have been the Safavid Shah İsmâ'îl, with whom the Ottomans were at war). The point of the story is that Hayâlî put an end to Hayretî's hopes for a career in the capital. In the end İbrâhîm granted him a partial fief in the European provinces, as a result of which he attached himself to the lords of the Akınjıs and made a living off their gifts and awards.

From his poetry it seems that Hayretî was most likely a dervish with Shiite leanings, perhaps a Bektashî dervish, as were many of the soldiery. His brother was the famous Yûsuf-i Sîne-châk (Joseph of the Rent Breast or the Broken-hearted), a noted poet and scholar of mysticism, who began his career as a Gülshenî dervish and then became an important Mevlevî master. During Hayretî's years in the provinces, it was apparently this brother who kept him in touch with literary circles and encouraged his poetry.

He is known to have built a dervish retreat in Yeniche and was buried there after his death in 1535. The historian 'Âlî tells us that the local people used to tell fortunes by randomly opening his collected poems and pointing out a line, as the Iranians often do with the *dîvân* of Hâfız.

Figânî

We don't know much about Figânî's origins. He was likely from Trabzon on the Black Sea coast, and his name was probably Ramazan. He was born sometime in the first years of the sixteenth century and, as a young man, came to Istanbul, where he took up the usual course of study in theology, law, and rhetoric. He was a brilliant learner—the way it is described he must have had a photographic memory; everything he learned or read he remembered exactly. His quick wit and prodigious memory did not, however, make him a successful scholar. Early on he became enamored of poetry and even though he apparently studied to be a medical doctor for a time, it is said, because several Persian poets had been doctors, he soon gave himself entirely over to the life of a poet.

Figânî did work occasionally as a secretary in the office that recorded grants of taxing privileges for certain properties and commodities, but the greater part of his life seems to have been devoted to parties with drugs and alcohol and the pursuit of attractive beloveds. His income from work was insufficient for his needs, and he supplemented his salary with gifts from grateful patrons of his poetry. Nonetheless, he seems often to have been impoverished and much aggrieved by this, to the extent that he changed his pen name from Hüseynî (honoring Hüseyin, the martyred son of ʿAlî) to Figânî (he who wails and cries).

Although he was quite young, Figânî was rather successful as a poet and was patronized by some of the greats of the day. His crowning achievement was the submission of a *kasîde* (ode of praise) to Sultan Süleymân on the occasion of the circumcisions of the princes Mustafâ, Mehmed, and Selîm in the summer of 1530. This particular circumcision ceremony was especially lavish: the festivities lasted for weeks as the Sultan competed in a display of wealth and munificence with his boyhood friend and present Grand Vizier İbrâhîm Pasha who had put on a magnificent and much talked-about wedding ceremony a few years before. Figânî's *Sûriyye* (Circumcision Ode) was accepted by the court critics and was read aloud in the presence of the Ruler during the entertainments—a stunning success that confirmed his youthful fame. Although the poet's star continued to rise, his success brought him enemies. His patronage by the powerful Minister of Finance İskender Chelebî made him the target of criticism by the circle of İbrâhîm Pasha, the Grand Vizier.

İbrâhîm Pasha was one of the great slaves of the Empire. Born a Greek near Parga, he had been somehow captured and brought to Istanbul where, because of his handsomeness and talent, he was selected to be trained in the elite palace school for royal pages. As one of the best of the best, he was chosen to be the private page of the then-Prince Süleymân. The two grew to manhood together and seem to have become close friends. In any case, when Süleymân ascended to the throne, İbrâhîm shared in his glory and power. He was immediately appointed as the Sultan's Chief Chamberlain, and a palatial residence was constructed for him on the Hippodrome Square just outside the Topkapı Palace. Shortly thereafter, İbrâhîm was made Grand Vizier and chief lord of the European provinces. He was a charming, talented man, victorious general, and brilliant diplomat, entrusted by the Sultan with a degree of power and control only a bit less than the monarch's own. He was a generous and unstinting patron of the arts. According to the biographer Latîfî during his time poetry was cherished, and recognized poets received regular stipends from the royal treasury, a practice that ceased after his death.

But the higher one rises the more powerful and numerous one's enemies. Although İbrâhîm had long since converted to Islam, he maintained ties to his Christian roots, even bringing his parents from Greece to live with him in Istanbul. Rumors abounded in Istanbul: that he was not a good Muslim, that he favored Christians or secretly aided European causes, that he had beguiled the Sultan and usurped his powers. And in this climate Figânî's fame was to turn into a disastrous notoriety. The story goes like this: Upon the Pasha's victorious return from the great campaign in Hungary in 1526, he had three bronze statues of Apollo, Hercules, and Diana brought from Buda and set up on marble pedestals in front of his palace. To the local people, who already called him Frenk İbrâhîm (İbrâhîm the European), this seemed, perhaps at the instigation of İbrâhîm's enemies, like a flouting of the Islamic prohibition against the worship of idols. As things heated up, the following Persian couplet attributed, some say falsely, to Figânî began to circulate:

Into this world two Abrahams appeared
One idols broke, the other idols reared

According to 'Âshık Chelebî, one night about this time a group of friends including Figânî had gathered in the mansion of Kara Bâlîzâde. While everyone else was enjoying food and drink and witty conversation, poor Figânî sat still and sad. When his host asked him how he could be so glum on a fine spring evening by the Bosphorus at sunset, the poet replied that he had had a disturbing dream. He had climbed a minaret on the dock, gave the call to prayer, and then awoke in terror. His friend and patron tried to calm him by saying that he would go to İskender Chelebî and get the poet a job on the dock.

Three days later the Police Magistrate of Istanbul came to Figânî's dwelling in Tahtakale and arrested him. He was first flogged, then paraded about the town bound to a donkey, and finally taken to the docks and hung. It was spring of 1532, and the poet would have been still in his twenties.

As a postscript, İbrâhîm Pasha, under whose orders the wretched Figânî was executed, continued to rise in power, finally concluding his feud with the young poet's one-time patron, İskender Chelebî, by arranging his death. However, in March of 1536, without warning, the deaf mutes (who were the palace executioners) came to İbrâhîm Pasha's private room in the Harem and, on the orders of his beloved friend the Sultan, took his life by strangling him with a cord, as was the custom for executions at court.

Fevrî

Of the poet Fevrî's origins we know nothing: neither the place of his birth nor the date, neither the name he was born under nor the name of his family. All that can be said is that sometime during the reign of Sultan Süleymân I he was captured in the raiding that usually preceded a summer of military campaigns in Eastern Europe. Some say that he was an Albanian and some that he was a Croat. We do know that like many others he became an Ottoman by first becoming a slave.

The young Fevrî was sold finally to a man named Pulad, perhaps himself a slave, who was the steward of Ferhâd Pasha's household. He received an education thanks to Pulad and about this time converted to Islam. As the biographer 'Âshık Chelebî, who would later be his friend, tells it:

. . . while he was still in the time of childhood, which is the era of heedlessness, and in the season of youth, which are the days of ignorance, he was guided to success by the grace of God, and by the direction of the rightly directed he was turned toward the Throne of Truth. The compendium of knowledge and spiritual insight and vision and works, his Lordship the Greatest of Masters, that is, the recipient of the light of Divine counsel and the inspiration of God, the [sufi] Master Muhiyuddîn 'Arabî [ibn 'Arabî] came to him in a dream and, gladdening him with the good news, guided him toward the security of Islam. And, as is natural, because the joy of Islam and the Faith were implanted in the unbroken purity of his nature and perfect certitude was preserved in his unmarred native wit, he came to the shore of belief from the whirlpool of the House of War's [Europe's] blasphemy and out of the dark gorge of error emerged into the open plain of the Faith's illumination.

Upon his conversion, Fevrî took the Muslim name Ahmed and the family name ibn 'Abdullâh (Son of the Servant of God), which was generic to slaves. When Pulad died Ahmed became the slave of his brother, who, recognizing his intelligence and value, gave him as a gift to the Lord of Lords of Anatolia Lutfî Pasha, hoping for favors in return. The pen name Fevrî, which means "the hasty one," was granted apropos of his ability to dash off a poem on the spur of the moment. One such poem, a *kasîde* (poem of praise) to Lutfî Pasha with the *redîf* (repeated word) *sûsen* (iris), resulted in his being freed from slavery—a rather common and religiously enjoined act on the part of Muslim slave-owners.

Fevrî, now a free man in a system where slaves and former slaves held some of the highest and most powerful positions in the land, had no trouble finding patrons and continuing his education under some of the Empire's most notable theology professors. He eventually became an assistant professor (*mülâzim*) himself. He was also quite well known as a poet. A *kasîde* in Arabic to Ebusu'ûd Efendi, the top legal authority in the Empire, was well received and resulted in his appointment to the rank of full professor (*müderris*). One *kasîde* on the occasion of his accompanying Sultan Süleymân on campaign to Nahchivan was said to have been rewarded by one hundred gold pieces and another on the same topic to have gained him a gold piece for every couplet.

Over the years Fevrî rose in prestige, his final and highest appointment being jointly the judgeship of Damascus and a professorship in the Theological School of Süleymân. In the year 1570, while performing his judicial duties in Damascus, Fevrî died and was buried in that city.

Hayâlî

Hayâlî, whose name was Mehmed, came from the European part of the Ottoman Empire, the town of Vardar Yenichesi. We do not know exactly when he was born, only that it was sometime during the reign of Bâyezîd II (1481-1512). His education, although substantial, seems to have been informal. However, the crucial event in his life occurred when he was still a youth—by Ottoman custom when he had not yet sprouted a beard and still had the dark peach-fuzz of a boy (or as the biographer 'Âshık, who was later to be his friend, put it: When ... "the reflection of his eyebrow was still cast upon the mirror of his cheek and the tiny ants of down still swarmed about his sweet lip ..."). To Yeniche at this time came the Kalenderî dervish adept Baba 'Alî Mest-i 'Ajem (Father 'Alî the Drunkard of Persia) and his band of disciples. Young Mehmed was intensely attracted to one of the disciples—in one of his verses he says:

In his face I saw rays of the divine light
    of Prophethood
Impassioned by the bright face of an Enlightened one
    I became an 'Alevî

(There is a typically untranslatable Ottoman word-play in the second line: 'Alevî commonly means a Shiite or a mystic with Shiite sympathies, who believes that Muhammad's son-in-law 'Alî and his descendants inherited the charismatic leadership of Islam, but it can also derive from the Turkish usage *'alev*, which means "flame": hence the line could end "I became one inflamed.")

In any case, Hayâlî, who seems to have been without a father to prevent him, left home to travel with the dervish band as it wended its way back toward Istanbul. In his time with the dervishes, he was said to have been unofficially adopted by Baba 'Alî, who continued his education in the arts of poetry and the spirit of sufism.

Sometime after the group arrived in Istanbul, the city's Chief Judge, Sarıgürz Nureddîn Efendi (Nureddîn the Yellow Mace), noticed the handsome, bright young man with a band of rather scruffy dervishes (the Kalenderî dervishes were notoriously inclined to defy all conventions of dress, grooming, and polite behavior). The judge found this relation to be inappropriate and taking Hayâlî from the dervishes turned him over to the City Police Chief Uzun 'Alî ('Alî the Tall). This new surrogate-father 'Alî saw to the continuation of Hayâlî's education in a more traditional manner. The young man, who was extremely intelligent, soon made a reputation for himself as a poet, adopted the apt pen name Hayâlî (the Imaginative), and gradually began to attract the attention of powerful patrons.

In time Hayâlî found himself in the circle of the Minister of Finance (*defterdâr*) İskender Chelebî, who in turn introduced him to the Grand Vizier İbrâhîm Pasha. Through İbrâhîm Pasha, Hayâlî came to the attention of Sultan Süleymân. The Sultan was pleased by the handsome young man and showed him great favor, bestowing many gifts on him and eventually granting him a yearly salary and then the income from major fiefs. In the highly competitive atmosphere of the court, this favoritism and Hayâlî's self-serving behavior brought upon him the envy and enmity—expressed in harsh lampoons—of many of his fellow poets, especially Zâtî and (Tashlıjalı) Yahyâ Bey (see the entries for these two poets).

The historian 'Âlî of Gelibolu, tells an amusing story about Hayâlî and this sort of poetic infighting. There was, it seems, a poet called Kandî (the Candyman, or Sweet), who was noted for composing chronograms (poems whose letter-values add up to a given date). He was an expert candy maker and used to set up a candy shop wherever he happened to live. As 'Âlî tells it:

After a time he came to Istanbul, opened a shop in the precinct of the Sultan Bâyezîd Mosque, and decorated it with all sorts of sugar ornaments and many glass bottles. At the same time the late Hayâlî was a young sapling finding nourishment in the garden of İbrâhîm Pasha's favor. So that he could be given a military salary he was enrolled in one of the sipâhî *corps and he took off the golden dervish collar. Kandî immediately came up with the following chronogram:*

Oh Hayâlî, your dervish collar won't ever come off

The rest of the poets who envied him made this verse quite famous and there came a time when it was repeated as a rumor to Hayâlî. He drank up one or two bottles of wine and loaded his skirts with rocks. Reciting a verse he just composed,

He is a truly crazed lover who in the bazaar of passion
Smashes these nine crystal domes with the stone of transcendence

he bombarded Kandî's shop with stones. He broke all the bottles and scattered its adornments and decorations. Kandî himself fled and only with difficulty escaped injury. The next day he appeared at the counsel meeting and in the glory of the presence of the Vizier he made his complaint. But Hayâlî was never questioned about it and in the end Kandî was given a few silver pieces as a gift. After that he had no desire to open any more shops.

Following the executions of his patrons İskender Chelebî and İbrâhîm Pasha (see the entry for Figânî), Hayâlî seems to have remained in the good graces of the Sultan, but the turn of events appears to have unnerved him. The new Grand Vizier, Rüstem Pasha, was no friend of poets and life was not quite as easy. For some time Hayâlî begged for a post outside of Istanbul and finally was granted the governorship of a provincial district, an important position which entitled him to the title *Bey*, for which reason he is most often spoken of as Hayâlî Bey.

Hayâlî never married and for that reason was also known by the familiar name Bekâr (Bachelor) Memi (a nickname for Mehmed). He did not return from the provinces and died in Edirne in the year 1557.

Fuzûlî

Fuzûlî exemplifies the unexpectedly problematic nature of calling someone an Ottoman poet. He was born in Iraq, most likely in the town of Kerbela in the province of Baghdad, sometime during the last quarter of the fifteenth century. His name was Mehmed (Muhammad), son of Süleymân. We know little else about his early life.

As he grew up he must have received an excellent education. It is likely that he came from an educated family, there being various reports that his father was at one time counsel in canon law (*müftî*) in the town of Hilla.

He was a talented poet and has collections (*dîvâns*) in Arabic, Persian, and Turkish. He could be called an Arabic poet, a Persian poet, and a Turkish poet, although such distinctions had little significance in his time. His Turkish also represents more the formal style of the Azerî Turkish dialect than the West Turkish of the Ottomans—another distinction not made in his time. He composed poems for various rulers of Baghdad: Elvend Bey of the White Sheep Dynasty, the Safavid Shah İsmâ'îl, and finally the Ottoman Sultan Süleymân the Magnificent and his entourage.

He was a unique person, an incisive scholar with a brilliant mind, a Shiite with a profound mystical sensibility, and a poet with a very unusual pen name. In the introduction to his Persian poems, he tells a highly self-revelatory story about the adoption of this pen name.

. . . In the early days when I was just beginning to write poetry, every few days I would set my heart on a particular pen name and then after a time change it for another because someone showed up who shared the same name. In the end it became clear to me that the poets who preceded me had stolen pen names from each other more than they did ideas. I imagined that if I adopted a shared pen name it would, in matters of attributing poems [to one poet or another], be a shame for me if I were overmastered [by someone with the same name] and a shame for him if I were to come out the master. So with the intention of removing any such surface connection, I made my pen name "Fuzûlî" [the Improper, Impertinent, or the Multiskilled]. Thus I took refuge in a zone of safety [or of pen name] from those who participate in malicious mischief, for I knew that this title would not be acceptable to anyone else and that fear of sharing a name could trouble me no more.

In fact, a pen name thus happened to appear that in so many ways conformed to my desire and a name came to pass that matched my claims to fame. First insofar as I wanted myself to be unique in my time, and this meaning is obviously bound to this name, the skirt of my individuality thus has escaped the hand of sharing's bonds. Also, by the grace of my own efforts, I was possessed of all the arts and sciences and found a pen name that also implies this sense since in the dictionary fuzûl *is given as a plural of* fazl *[learning] and has the same rhythm as* 'ulûm *[sciences] and* funûn *[arts]. Moreover, in common usage* fuzûlî *is pejorative [and means] "improper and impertinent," and what "impropriety and impertinence" is worse, in my case, than the fact that I, in spite of my lack of conversation with learned men of great worth, the total absence of nourishment by famed and merciful rulers, and my horror of traveling to far lands and great cities, should in intellectual disputes extend the hand of my opposition to the collar of the various rulings of learned judges and in matters of religion should lay claim to the right to disagree with doctors of canon law. Similarly, in these arts of poetry, I view myself as superior to the master of any single art in disputations about beauty of expression and conflicts concerning delicacy of phrase, even though this way of behaving is both a sign of the perfection of Fuzûlî and a mark of the rout of the officious.*

Fuzûlî was indeed a unique and powerful poet in Turkish and is generally considered one of the greatest Ottoman poets, even though he was neither an Ottoman subject nor wrote for Ottoman patrons until he was in his fifties. When Sultan Süleymân conquered Iraq in 1534, Fuzûlî seems to have eagerly welcomed him and his retinue which included the famous İbrâhîm Pasha (see the entry for Figânî) with the hope that finally he would be "nourished" by the mighty ruler of his dreams. He presented odes of praise, met and conversed with the poets Hayâlî and Tashlıjalı Yahyâ Bey, who had come with the army, and was promised a stipend of the sort that was generally granted to noted poets and scholars.

But the glories of the Sultan's progress soon faded. The promised stipend apparently became mired in bureaucratic red tape and, although he enjoyed his most productive literary period under the Ottomans, he never experienced great material success and spent most of his life as an attendant at the Shiite Shrine of 'Alî (Muhammad's son-in-law) in Najaf. In the year 1556 he died during an epidemic of the plague and was buried in his hometown, the shiite holy city of Kerbela, where 'Alî's son Hüseyin was martyred.

Nisâyî

Women are few among the recognized Ottoman poets, although many more are recognized than among the Persians or Arabs, and woman poets of the Sultan's harem are not recognized at all. Nisâyî does not appear in any of the usual sources and had been unknown until Professor Çavuşoğlu (1978) discovered a few poems by her in an informal sixteenth century anthology of poetry (*mejmû'a*).

Thus, what we know of Nisâyî we know from these few poems. Two are elegies (*mersiye*) on the death of Sultan Süleymân's son Prince Mustafâ, who was executed by his father's order. At that time the harem had begun to play an important and somewhat visible role in affairs of state. Süleymân's favorite, the Russian, Hürrem—Roxelana to Europeans—had supplanted Gülbahâr Hatun in the Sultan's eyes and had engineered the downfall of Gülbahâr's ally, İbrâhîm Pasha (see the entry for Figânî). Hürrem was promoting the cause of her son Selîm, while Gülbahâr and İbrâhîm took the side of Prince Mustafâ. When Mustafâ was executed for disloyalty to his father, this was considered to be a result of the sinister manipulations of the Hürrem camp. Nisâyî's elegies, with their bitter and accusatory tone, indicate that she was most likely a supporter of Gülbahâr. In fact, in one of the elegies she puts the general suspicion quite bluntly:

> He let the words of a Russian witch enter his ear
> Deceived by wiles and tricks he bent to hear that spiteful hag

Professor Çavuşoğlu also points out that one quatrain in the second elegy indicates that Nisâyî knew Sultan Süleymân as a young man and must have been advanced in age at the time of the Prince's death (1553). The pertinent lines are

> When you were a young man, you made your business justice and equity
> You made each and every one glad in heart and circumstance
> So why in your maturity have you now turned to tyranny and injustice?

The poem translated for this anthology seems to hint that she was an older woman at the time of writing, withdrawn from active affairs, independent—as her assertive chiding of the Sultan also shows—and disinclined to put much stock in the things of this world.

We know nothing of Nisâyî but what we guess in this manner. Her birth and her death are unremarked, as was the case for most women of the time. Her poetry alone stands as her epitaph.

Nev'î

Yahyâ, the son of Pîr 'Alî, the son of Nasûh, who took the pen name Nev'î ('the Varied/The One of Many Skills'), achieved his greatest fame as a scholar. He was born in 1533 in the European part of the Empire in a town called Malgara. At first educated by his father, when he reached the age of ten he began to study under Karamanîzâde Mehmed Efendi at the same time as did the future historian Sa'deddîn and the master-poet Bâkî, who would remain his lifetime friend.

Nev'î was an excellent student and born scholar. Upon finishing his education his rise through the various ranks of the intellectual (*'ulemâ*) establishment was rapid. He began as professor of a (theological) school in Gallipoli (in 1565-1566). By 1583 he was professor of the prestigious school in Istanbul endowed by Sultan Süleymân's daughter, Sultan Mihrümâh. Further promotions culminated in appointment to the chief judgeship of Baghdad, an appointment which he ended up refusing when the Sultan (Murâd III) asked him to serve as tutor to his son Prince Mustafâ. Subsequently he became tutor to the royal Princes Bâyezîd, 'Osmân, and 'Abdullâh as well.

Nev'î must have been the perfect royal tutor. The breadth of his learning was awesome. He wrote a popular and highly respected encyclopedia of the twelve branches of knowledge in addition to at least thirty major essays on matters of theology. He was also said by all his biographers to have been one of the sweetest and kindest of men, a pleasant conversationalist, a good friend and generous host.

His poetry is rather harshly dealt with by E. J. W. Gibb and his followers for being too "scholarly" and apparently not romantic enough for Victorian tastes. Nonetheless, much of it seems quite charming to us and was well thought of by contemporary critics.

In 1595 Nev'î's days as a tutor came to a sudden and sad end. The Sultan (Murâd) died, and as was the custom from the time of Mehmed the Conqueror the new Sultan, Ahmed, had all his nineteen brothers put to death immediately. Nev'î was broken-hearted. He composed a lovely elegy on the loss of his Sultan and his beloved pupils and retired completely from public life.

Nev'î lived comfortably for the next four years on a pension granted by the new Sultan and then passed away in June 1599.

Bâkî

Mahmûd 'Abdülbâkî, famed by the pen name Bâkî, was born in 1526, just six years into the reign of Süleymân the Lawgiver ("the Magnificent" to Europeans). His father was a poor *mu'ezzin* (caller-to-prayer) at the Mosque of Mehmed the Conqueror. As a child he was apprenticed either to a saddlemaker (*sarach*), as most of the stories go, or to a person who cared for the candles and lamps in a mosque (*sirâj*), as more recent scholarship quite plausibly suggests. But Bâkî was an exceptionally bright and eager student in the local Quran school and somehow found supporters who obtained him a place as a theological school (*medrese*) student.

Although he was not from a well-connected family, Bâkî made powerful and successful friends who ensured that his great intelligence and literary talents would come to the attention of important people. While still in his teens he was recognized as a promising poet and even had as his mentor the famed and prolific Zâtî.

After years of study, Bâkî received an appointment in the theological school system and rose through its various degrees to a full-professorship (*müderrislik*). During this period, in the early 1560s, he attracted the attention of Sultan Süleymân and became a member of his intellectual and conversational circle (see Poetic Parallels following poem no. 54). This was a tremendous honor and confirmed Bâkî as the acknowledged supreme poet of the age.

In addition to his fame as a poet, Bâkî was appointed by Süleymân and his successors to some of the highest positions available to members of the learned class including, the military judgeships of the Eastern (Anatolian) and Western (Rumelian/European) provinces. The only major hiatus in his career occurred during the early years of the reign of Süleymân's grandson, Murâd III. The biographer Kınalızâde Hasan Chelebî tells the story of this event:

When Sultan Murâd [III] took the royal throne some spiteful persons manifesting the saying "There is a disease in their hearts," masters of envy confirming the words, "About their necks they have ropes of strong cord" made malicious reports about the aforementioned [Bâkî], causing him to be dismissed from his position at the Süleymâniye Theological School and turning the ocean of many droplets that was his mind sad and troubled. The reason was this: first, a poet named Nâmî, who should be remembered as he deserves—if the Lord Most Powerful so wills—wrote the following gazel.

Better our own grain and water than this world's luxuries
Better than the stranger's mansion our own nook in a ruin

Better than a proud and restless lord on the high seat of wealth
Is our sleep-stained drunkard in the party of selflessness

Better than him without zeal, though like the Huma-bird on glory's summit,
Oh Nâmî, is our moth which burns its pinion in the candle of love

The spiteful ones, like the devil, made up deceitful and lying tales and altered the name of Nâmî by changing the dots to make it read Bâkî. Because the late Sultan Selîm of angelic morals had said [of himself]:

I am that one sound [*selîm*] of nature who inclines to ruddy wine

they said "what is meant by the drunkard in this poem [of Bâkî] is the aforementioned [Sultan Selîm]." And they also said to his Lordship, Refuge of the Caliphate, "He prefers your father to you and explicitly mentions that you lack zeal," thereby perpetrating this vile deed and unseemly affair, this sinful shrewdness and diseased troublemaking, and thus they committed injustice and slander against the abovementioned [Bâkî].

The truth did out and the offending verses were found in an old anthology. Bâkî was vindicated and restored to high office and some degree of royal favor, which lasted with the usual ups and downs until the end of his long life. Nonetheless, this little incident shows how important a verse and a subtle (if seditious) reading could be in the intrigue-filled atmosphere of the Ottoman court.

Bâkî, considered by many to be the best of all Ottoman poets, died in 1600, wasted by illness and embittered by his failure to obtain the highest judicial position in the land. It is said that the irascible old poet, former high judge and companion of sultans and viziers, collapsed and died in a fit of temper at the clumsiness of a serving girl.

Yahyâ Bey

Yahyâ Bey was brought into the service of the Ottomans through the *devshirme*, the levy of young men taken from the non-Muslim inhabitants of the European provinces. From his own works we learn that he was an Albanian of the noble Dukagin family, which was said to have descended from a Norman crusader named Duc Jean. He says that he came from a place abounding in stones, so he is also known by the place-name Tashlıjalı (from the Rocky Place or from the town Stoneland). We don't know exactly when he was born, but it must have been sometime near the end of the fifteenth century, since he was old enough to have taken up active service as a janissary and fight for Sultan Selîm in the battle of Chaldıran (1514) and the campaign in Egypt (1516–1517).

As a promising *devshirme* youth he would have first been taken into the corps of 'Ajemî Oğlans (The Foreign Boys). These young men were destined for service to the Palace. First they were sent into the provinces, where they served for a time under local lords, learning Turkish and how to live according to Muslim custom. They were then brought back and educated in special schools that instructed them in culture, the arts, and religion. Finally they would graduate into a Janissary corps serving either the Inner Palace (the residence of the Sultan) or the Outer Service (including the highest administrative positions in the land).

Upon graduating from the 'Ajemî Oğlans, Yahyâ, who must have distinguished himself as a poetic talent, was taken under the wing of an important secretary of the Janissary corps and given leeway to mingle with the leading artists and poets of the day. He claims to have studied with the famed legal scholar, poet, and historian Kemâlpâshâzâde (Son of Kemâl Pasha) and is known to have presented poems to both İbrâhîm Pasha and his rival İskender Chelebî (see the entries for Figânî and Hayâlî). Despite his copious poetic production—he has a large *dîvân* (collected poems) and a group of five long narrative verse-romances—much of his early life was spent on military campaigns from Vienna to Tabriz.

The story is told of Yahyâ that one day during the reign of Süleymân he attended the conversational circle of Kemâlpâshâzâde, where a large group of intellectuals and poets were in attendance, including two great military judges, the Minister of Finance (İskender Chelebî) and several poets, among them Hayâlî Bey. At one point Yahyâ Bey arose, resplendent in his full Janissary garb and headdress, and read a *kasîde* (ode of praise) to Kemâlpâshâzâde, who liked it so well that he had him read it again. When Yahyâ had finished, the host turned to the poet İshâk (pronounced "iss-hock") and commented on the appropriateness of the word *mihr* (sun/love) in the opening couplet, which goes something like:

With his excellence that perfect love [sun] is a high point in Rûm
As though he were the point of a mole on the cheek of the moon-faces

İshâk Chelebî made a few observations and was interrupted by the Finance Minister, İskender Chelebî, who said, "Indeed my Sultan, your noble name is Ahmed and Ahmed's [i.e., Muhammed's] nickname is *Shems* [sun], and *mihr* [sun] is synonymous with *shems*." Thus he cleverly pointed out that the compound *mihr-i kemâl* (perfect love/sun) contains the host's family name "Kemâl" and his given names Ahmed and Shemseddîn (Sun of the Faith).

The attention paid to his verses by such great and learned men was quite flattering to Yahyâ and greatly enhanced his stature. It seems that Hayâlî begrudged him his glory and came up with a few criticisms of the poem, which the others—to Hayâlî's intense displeasure—explained away. From about this time on Hayâlî and Yahyâ had little good to say of each other. There are a number of stories about this rivalry, which seems to stand as an emblem of a more general rivalry between the *sipâhîs*, fief-holding, free, Muslim, Turkish elite families supported by the intellectual establishment and the Janissary (slave) elites who were beginning to dominate the power bases of the Empire.

So, when Hayâlî was enjoying his halcyon period of closeness to Sultan Süleymân, Yahyâ, who was ferocious in pursuing his own interests, rankled. In a *kasîde* on the occasion of the second campaign to Iraq (1548), he included the following verses:

Had there been granted to me the honors shown to Hayâlî
God knows, I'd have made original verses like white magic

What a calamity that while he is as far beneath me as my shadow
Some flaming dervish should take a place above me like the sun

I am the sword of bravery, he an impotent mystic
I am a soldier on the day of war, and he dares only strip naked
[i.e., run around half-naked like a dervish]

The Grand Vizier Rüstem Pasha, who did not like poets and especially did not like Hayâlî, found this to his liking and granted Yahyâ five lucrative estate trusteeships. This good fortune did not last long, however. In 1553 Prince Mustafâ, who was very popular with the army, fell victim to palace intrigues (see the entry for Nisâyî) and was executed on his father's orders. Yahyâ was among those who wrote elegies that blamed the Sultan for having made a mistake (as did Nisâyî). When his protector Rüstem Pasha was dismissed from the grand vizierate for a time in 1555, Yahyâ's enemies—Hayâlî chief among them—pointed out to Rüstem how Yahyâ had questioned the wisdom of the Sultan and, by extension, of his Grand Vizier. On Rüstem's return to power he was dismissed from his trusteeships, and his conduct as trustee was subjected to a searching investigation. Even though he emerged without stain from the investigations, his trusteeships were not returned and he was exiled to a fief in Izvornik with a decent salary.

Nonetheless, he submitted all manner of poetry to the Sultan and his Viziers pleading for the return of his trusteeships, to no avail. When Rüstem Pasha died without restoring Yahyâ to his former position, the poet wrote a lengthy satire blaming him for all the ills that had befallen the Empire during his viziership. In the end he seems to have departed in great bitterness to the European frontier, where he served for a time with the Yahyâlı corps of raiders (*akıncı*: see the entry for Hayretî). At least we know that he was with them at the siege of Szigetvar (1565) where he presented his last *kasîde* to his great hero, Sultan Süleymân. In fact this poem never reached its addressee. The Sultan had died while attending the siege, a matter that was kept from the troops by the Sultan's highest advisors in order to prevent the premature end of the campaign and a rush back to Istanbul to participate in the seating of the new Sultan.

Following Süleymân's death and the accession of his son Selîm II, Yahyâ presented a few poems to viziers requesting positions for his children in the Janissary corps or other sources of income, but there are no poems either to Selîm or to his successor, Murâd III. It seems that at the end of his life, discouraged in his attempts to recover some measure of his old material success, Yahyâ gave himself over entirely to mysticism and retired from the affairs of this world. He died sometime around the year 1582, having lived more than ninety years.

Rûhî

Rûhî, whose name was Osmân, is known as Rûhî of Baghdad, after the city in which he was born sometime in the latter half of the sixteenth century. His father was a Turk from Anatolia who came to Baghdad as one of the retinue of Ayâs Pasha, who had been appointed by Sultan Süleymân to govern the recently conquered province. Rûhî's mother was a native of Baghdad.

The poet must have had an excellent education and is said to have been noted, in his youth, for his poetic aptitude and for frequenting the company of poets, scholars, and dervishes. On the matter of his career and later life there is a wide but not unbridgeable divergence of reports. He obviously had strong connections to dervish groups. Several biographers indicate that he became a Mevlevî dervish, and Esrâr Dede includes him in his biographical work on Mevlevî poets. From this Gibb and many later scholars infer that Rûhî's rather peripatetic career was spent in pursuit of mystical and Mevlevî ends.

Professor Gölpınarlı, however, makes a compelling argument for the conclusion that Rûhî was actually a soldier of the feudal militia (*sipâhî*) whose wanderings were a result of the various military campaigns in which he participated. The professor also concludes, with the help of indications from his poetry, that Rûhî was most likely a Hurûfî in the tradition of Nesîmî (see above) which would be more in keeping with the role and social class of a soldier than an affiliation with the more scholarly and upper-crust Mevlevîs. It is quite possible, however, that Rûhî attached himself to the Mevlevîs later in life and so is included in the history of the distinguished poets of that order.

In keeping with Gölpınarlı's surmise, Rûhî's poetry is rather simple and Turkish in its language, as would befit a less elevated mysticism and more soldierly audiences. However, his great fame today rests on his *terkîb-i bend*, a poem in seventeen *gazel*-length stanzas in which mystical resignation alternates with a biting critique of his age. The poem translated in this anthology is actually one stanza from this lengthy work, a stanza that manifests his critical stance at its plainest.

Rûhî's Mevlevî biography has him spending time in Istanbul at the famous retreat in Galata, from where he traveled to Konya and the Shrine of Rûmî and thence to Damascus, where he died in the year 1605.

Sheyhülislâm Yahyâ

Yahyâ Efendî, known as Sheyhülislâm Yahyâ (Chief Minister of Islamic Law Yahyâ) to distinguish him from Yahyâ the Janissary, is an example of the finest products of the Istanbul intellectual and religious elite culture. He was born in 1552, eldest son of Sheyhülislâm Bayrâmzâde Zekerîyâ of Ankara. Educated at first by his father, Yahyâ went on to study with some of the most famous religious scholars of the age.

While still in his early thirties he became a professor at some of the most prestigious theological schools in Istanbul and by 1595 was appointed Chief Magistrate (*kâdî*) of Aleppo which was followed in close succession by similar positions in major centers of the Empire. Beginning in 1603, he returned to Istanbul where he was Chief Magistrate of that city and then was promoted in turn to the positions of Chief Military Magistrate (*kâdî-'asker*) for Anatolia and the European Provinces. Then, in 1622, he was appointed for the first time as Sheyhülislâm, the highest and most powerful religious/legal post in the Empire.

This steady and spectacular rise through the intellectual hierarchy was accomplished in highly troubled times when relatively weak rulers were pulled this way and that by constant struggles for power between the palace, its slave-army, and the feudal elites. Where most of the survivors in high office seem to have been masters of manipulation and corruption, Yahyâ was noted as an honest and decent person, a pleasant conversational companion with a merry disposition.

His first tenure as Sheyhülislâm was rather brief. He apparently admonished the Grand Vizier 'Alî Pasha for his tolerance of the corrupting system of selling government positions to the highest bidder, and the Vizier responded by engineering Yahyâ's dismissal by the order of the very young and still tentative ruler Murâd IV. Nonetheless, Yahyâ was returned to the position a few years later and served in that role as a central support for the far-reaching reforms and stunning successes of Murâd's later sultanate. Only briefly, in a period of extreme political turmoil, was the Sultan forced to accede to the demands of powerful adversaries and dismiss Yahyâ. It is reported that he said to the jurist/poet, "These people have dismissed you but I have not dismissed you. Go to your farms and busy yourself praying for us. When the ruler again rules you will also be Chief Minister of Islamic Law as you once were." In 1633 Yahyâ was returned to his old position, in which he served until the year of his death, when Murâd's credulous son and successor, İbrâhîm, dismissed him while under the malevolent influence of a rascal named Hüseyin Efendi who earned the name Jinji Hoja (Master of the Jinn) by pretending to have influence over the spirits of the unseen world.

It is said that Yahyâ was so widely popular that upon his death in 1644 a huge crowd turned out at the place of his funeral ceremony and accompanied his coffin through the streets to its burial place.

In our day it seems somewhat strange that a famed scholar holding a position that combined the power and dignity of an archbishop and a supreme court justice could also be a renowned composer of love-lyrics, praised by such great—and worldly and competitive—poets as Nef'î (see below). A line such as Yahyâ's

> Let the hypocrites practice their way in
>   the mosque
> And you come to the tavern, where there is
>   neither hypocrite nor hypocrisy

could be misread by the ignorant, as in the anecdote about a preacher who cited the line and averred that "whosoever from among the Community of Muhammad should recite this couplet, he will become an infidel. For this line is a blatant blasphemy!" But among the elites, who amused themselves with tales of such simple ignorance, the relation between love, the tavern, and the highest reaches of spiritual ecstasy was universally understood, and both the rake and the saint could find common ground on the shifting, lovely surface of lyrical indeterminacy. Thus Yahyâ can be known as a great theologian, jurist, companion to rulers, and as the accomplished singer of songs of love and wine and the gardens of spring.

Nef'î

'Ömer Efendi, who was to become one of the most famed poets of the Ottoman Empire was born in the village of Hasankale in northeastern Anatolia in the vicinity of Erzurum. Of his early life in the provinces almost nothing is known. He seems to have come from an educated family of provincial elites and certainly received an excellent education himself. Indications are that he was born around the year 1572.

The story is that 'Ömer Efendi's father abandoned the family in the provinces and went to be the party-companion (*nedîm*) of the Khan of the Crimea. This appears to have left the poet and his family destitute. Professor Karahan points to one of his famous satires in which he says:

> While my father lived happily as companion to the Khan
> I was left without sight of either lentil or soup-stock

and

> He is no father, this dark disaster I've suffered

How and why Nef'î ended up in Istanbul we do not know for sure. While in Erzurum he met the Grand Vizier of the Giray Khans of the Crimea and might have gone at his suggestion. It is also possible that the historian Mustafâ 'Âlî of Gallipoli, who spent some time as an official in Erzurum, brought him to the capital when he returned. 'Âlî indeed tells of urging the young poet to change his pen name from Zarrî (he who is associated with loss, born-to-lose) to Nef'î (the Useful), most likely because the latter name would make him appear to be a person more beneficial to a patron.

In any case, during the reign of Ahmed I (1603–1617) Nef'î made his way to Istanbul, where he soon entered into a career of bureaucratic appointments and lavish favors in large part resulting from his growing fame as a writer of poems of praise (*kasîdes*). He wrote hugely successful poems for many of the greats of his day and enjoyed the attention of two Sultans, Ahmed and Murâd IV, remaining relatively silent during the brief and troubled reigns of Mustafâ I and 'Osmân II (1617-1618, 1618-1622). Although the fame of his *kasîdes* has overshadowed all his other poetry, Gibb's negative judgement about his lyrics is surely in error and resembles his erroneous dismissal of the lyric poems of Sheyh Gâlib (see the entry for Sheyh Gâlib below).

At the end, however, Nef'î's magnificent poems of praise did not avail against the consequences of his habit of writing scathing and obscene satires about the very greats of the day whom he often praised. As the historian Nâ'imâ tells it:

> *But the aforementioned [Nef'î] was exceedingly evil-tongued in the manner of writing satire; he dared to annoy the greats of his age with criticism, to malign the honor of intellectual leaders and noble viziers, and to satirize the famed notables of the time. Because his lordship Sultan Murâd, in his private gatherings, was inclined to jests as a way of setting aside his cares, he now and then would send for Nef'î and listen to some of his satires. However, one day in the year 1039 [1630 CE], while the ruler was in the Villa of Sultan Ahmed in Beshiktash reading a copy of Nef'î's collection of satires called Sihâm-i Kazâ* [The Shafts of Doom]*, the weather turned to thunder and lightning. When a thunderbolt struck near the royal throne, the Sultan tore the book to pieces and vowed never again to look at such trash. To discipline him, he dismissed Nef'î from his job and forced him to repent of doing satires.*

Neither the Sultan's disfavor nor the poet's repentance lasted very long. Nef'î was returned to a responsible position and again had access to the ruler's private entertainments. However, basking in his pride at having achieved such royal attention, he turned again to satire and produced a piece that greatly annoyed one Bayrâm Pasha, who complained to the Sultan. As a result, or so it is told, the Sultan (or Bayram Pasha with the Sultan's permission) had Nef'î imprisoned in the palace woodshed, where he was then strangled and his body thrown into the sea. This event occurred on 27 February 1635.

Sheyhülislâm Bahâyî

Bahâyî was born in 1601 into a family with a long history in the intellectual/religious establishment. His paternal grandfather was the famous Hoja Sa'deddîn Efendi, author of the *Crown of Histories* (*Tâj'üt-Tevârîh*) and his mother was a descendent of Ebusu'ûd Efendi, the great jurist of the age of Süleymân. It was only natural that young Mehmed would follow in the family tradition.

Bahâyî went through the traditional theological school education and studied for a time with his uncle. After returning from the pilgrimage to Mecca in 1617, he began a career which led from the usual professorships to the judgeships first of Salonika and then of Aleppo in 1633. During his tenure in Aleppo he quarreled with Ahmed Pasha, the Ottoman governor of the city. At the same time Sultan Murâd IV was engaged in several reform projects, among them an attempt to curtail the use of narcotics—including tobacco—in the Empire. Bahâyî, it seems, was a confirmed smoker, and the governor reported this to the palace, which resulted in Bahâyî's dismissal and exile to the island of Cyprus.

By 1636 he had been pardoned and returned to his career in Islamic Law. He served in several important judgeships, including the positions of Chief Military Magistrate of the European and Anatolian provinces. Finally, in 1649 he was appointed as Sheyhülislâm for the first time. His rivals were said to have claimed that he was favored by the powers in the Harem, led by the Sultan-Mother and the Grand Vizier because he was thought to be so befuddled by drugs that he would be easy to manipulate. In fact, Bahâyî proved to be quite strong in his position, resisting political pressures from palace factions and standing up to the opposition of a religious orthodoxy which objected to his support for dervish practices of music and dancing and his legalizing of coffee and tobacco. He is reported to have been a tolerant jurist who believed that the essence of Islamic Law was wherever possible to make licit that which the people customarily did.

In 1651 Bahâyî intervened in a jurisdictional dispute between the British Ambassador and the Chief Judge of Izmir, which culminated in his placing the Ambassador under house arrest. This breach of diplomatic etiquette displeased the Palace, and Bahâyî was dismissed and ostensibly exiled to the island of Midilli. He actually remained in Gallipoli from which he returned in 1653. He was subsequently reappointed to his position where he remained until his death, possibly from a throat cancer, in 1654.

Bahâyî was a brilliant scholar and a very talented poet whose production of poems was rather small and limited, for the most part, to secular lyrics.

Nâbî

Yûsuf, who was to become famous by the pen name Nâbî (the High or Pure) was born sometime in 1642 or 1643. His birthplace was the town of Urfa (also known as Ruhâ and Edessa) in the Euphrates basin in southeastern Anatolia. Although he moved to Istanbul in his early twenties, he seems to have retained an affection for his hometown, which he mentions in several poems.

Little is known of Nâbî's life in Urfa except that he came from a distinguished family—by most accounts descendants of the Prophet and sufi elders—that he had three brothers, and received an excellent education. One of the stories about him says that in his youth he attached himself to an adept of the Kâdirî dervish order named Ya'kûb Hâlife. As part of his training, Nâbî's master (*sheyh*) gave him the job of tending a lamb . The brilliant and ambitious young man in time grew tired of being a shepherd and began to complain about his *sheyh*, who, through his spiritual insight, soon became aware of this dissatisfaction. The master summoned the disciple into his presence. Their conversation wrought a change in Nâbî's attitude, and the *sheyh* suggested that he take himself to Istanbul, the center of the Ottoman universe, to finish his training.

Whatever the impetus, Nâbî did go to Istanbul, most likely at the age of twenty-three. Apparently he was greatly disappointed during his early days in the capital, but later made the acquaintance of an important figure, Mustafâ Pasha, Second Vizier, son-in-law of the Sultan, and a member of the ruler's intimate conversational circle. The acquaintance soon grew into the kind of patronage attachment that the Ottomans called "*intisâb*" and Nâbî was appointed as the Pasha's Council (Dîvân) Secretary. In Mustafâ Pasha's wake, Nâbî made the acquaintance of the Sultan—Mehmed IV, known as Mehmed the Hunter in honor of his favorite amusement. He subsequently joined the Sultan on hunting parties and accompanied him on the campaign to Poland.

This was also a period in which Nâbî completed his education in the cultural arts and began to achieve a reputation as a poet. Soon he made the acquaintance of the noted poets of the day including the old master, Nâ'ilî, who regarded him highly. And it was, in part, his masterful lyrics filled with popular sayings and critiques of the age and verses commemorating innumerable important occasions that won him the support of the Pasha and the Sultan.

In 1678-1679 he made the pilgrimage to Mecca in the company of a youthful protégé, Mehmed Râmî. This trip became the subject of one of his several prose works, a travel-book called *A Present on the Two Sanctuaries* (*Tuhfet'ul-Haremeyn*). Upon his return, Mustafâ Pasha promoted him to the position of steward. Although his subsequent career had its ups and downs, he remained faithful to his patron until the latter's death in 1686.

Following the death of his patron, Nâbî seems to have grown weary of life in Istanbul. He soon moved to Aleppo, the major center nearest to his hometown of Urfa. There he was to remain for nearly a quarter century, there he would enjoy the patronage of the local governor, and there his two sons would be born and grow into young manhood. For one of them, Ebulhayr Mehmed, he wrote his famous *Hayriyye*, a verse book of advice for young men. The reigns of two sultans passed without recognition by the great poet, but as some of his old friends, among them his former protégé Mehmed Râmî (now a pasha and vizier), rose to high office, he again began sending poems of praise to the capital. In 1710 with his patron, Baltajı Mehmed Pasha, he returned to Istanbul, where he enjoyed both lucrative positions and the respect of a poet community that included such brilliant figures as the young Nedîm.

Only two years following his return to Istanbul, the great Nâbî, now recognized as the Sultan of Poets in the Ottoman Empire, died shortly after writing a chronogram (a couplet, hemistich, or phrase in which the numerical values of the letters add up to a specific date) to commemorate his own demise. The year was 1712 and the poet was seventy years old.

Nâ'ilî

Nâ'ilî, whose common name was Mustafâ and who is often referred to as Nâ'ilî the Older to distinguish him from a nineteenth century poet who took the same pen name, is one of the two or three finest poets of the seventeenth century and perhaps the most exciting lyricist of them all. Nonetheless, we know little of his life, because he never attained high office or the patronage of a significant power-holder and so was not of much interest to the recorders of history. He was born in Istanbul sometime around 1608–1611. His father, Pîrî Hâlife, was a secretary in the Department of Mines, the bureaucratic office in which Nâ'ilî himself would work for most of his life.

From indications in his poetry it appears that his parents died when he was still rather young and that he lost a beloved brother sometime later. He seems to have had a good education but did not finish the usual full course of study. It also seems that he was an adherent of the Halvetî order of dervishes, although nothing is specifically said of this in the sources.

We do know that his poetry is unusual and striking and that it seems to have done him little material good. He submitted sheaves of wonderful poems to all manner of officials, but even the rare support he received soon passed without real consequence. His most recent modern biographer reached the conclusion that he was a nervous, unsympathetic, and somewhat paranoid person who complained constantly of plots against him—which may have really existed in the highly competitive atmosphere of Istanbul art-politics. In any case, some such plot or Nâ'ilî's own complaining caused the powerful Grand Vizier Köprülüzâde Fâzıl Ahmed Pasha to send him from his lifetime home to exile in the European city of Edirne.

This exile was a great tragedy for the poor poet, and his occasional poetry of the time reflects his agony. Finally, as a result of a *kasîde* to Fâzıl Ahmed Pasha, he was pardoned and allowed to return to Istanbul. Nâ'ilî was overjoyed, and that joy also reflects in his poetry. However, in 1666, within a year of his return, the great poet, who had always been slight and sickly, died while still in his late fifties.

Neshâtî

Neshâtî was from Edirne. He must have been born sometime around the turn of the seventeenth century because in his collected poems we find a verse chronogram that celebrates the terrible winter of 1622 when the Bosphorus was covered with ice. We could assume that Ottoman poets usually begin writing decent poetry (the kind one would include in a *dîvân*) in their early twenties. His name was Ahmed, and it is said that he first took the pen name Semendî (Of the Roan Horse) and later, at the suggestion of the Chief Justice of the day or at the urging of his *sheyh*, changed it to Neshâtî (the Cheerful).

Details about Neshâtî's life and background are few. He was a dervish, one of the many famous Mevlevî poets. The *sheyh* to whom he was attached was Ağazâde Mehmed Dede, who served as master of the Mevlevî dervish lodges of Gallipoli and Beshiktash (in Istanbul). Neshâtî apparently began as a disciple in Gallipoli and followed his master to Istanbul. Following Ağazâde's death in 1652, Neshâtî made his way to Konya, the spiritual center of the Mevlevîs. Sometime later he returned to Istanbul and in 1670 was appointed *sheyh* of the Mevlevî lodge in Edirne.

Neshâtî was a Mevlevî poet whose poems creatively reflect the philosophy of Rûmî, but he was also a master poet of the Ottoman tradition. He knew Persian well and in many ways modeled himself on the Indian style (*sebk-i hindî*; see the explanation following poem no. 67) poet 'Urfî of Shiraz for whose work he wrote an exegesis. He also seems to have admired Nef'î and among his many *kasîdes* are several that contain clear echoes of this admiration.

Although Neshâtî never attained either the high-level patronage or the renown of several of his contemporaries, his poetry is strikingly beautiful and seems to have been recognized as such by the poets of his day. When he died an old man in Edirne, in 1674, a large number of famous poets, including Nâbî, honored him by writing chronograms on his death.

Nedîm

Ahmed Nedîm (*nedîm* means "party-companion") was an Istanbulite from an old and distinguished family of the intellectual elite. He was born sometime in the last ten or twelve years of the seventeenth century. Nedîm's father was judge in several Anatolian towns. His grandfather, Mustafâ Musliheddîn Efendi from Merzifon, was a famous but rather unpopular Chief Military Justice during the reign of Sultan İbrâhîm (1640-48). His paternal grandmother was the daughter of the Justice Cheshmî Mehmed Efendi, from whom Mustafâ Musliheddîn received his official permission to practice law. On his mother's side he was related to a family that had held important government positions back to the time of Mehmed the Conqueror (fifteenth century).

As the child of such a family, Nedîm partook of the best education, learning Arabic and Persian as well as the required religious/legal studies and the study of rhetoric. Upon graduation from theological school he was examined by the Chief Justice of the Empire and admitted to the highest rank of legal scholars.

This was a normal progression for a bright young man of the educated elite. However, neither Nedîm nor his times were entirely normal. The Empire for years had been reeling under weak rulers, economic troubles, and military losses culminating in the disastrous treaty with the Europeans signed at Karlowitz. The new Sultan, Ahmed III, was no power himself, inclined as he was to poetry, parties, and cultural pursuits. But a few military successes under strong viziers and the signing of a peace-at-any-cost treaty with Austria at Passarowitz set the stage for a period of exceptional cultural fluorescence.

Nedîm had achieved his first real poetic success with *kasîdes* to the Grand Vizier 'Alî Pasha, but his real blossoming came during the viziership of Dâmâd (Son-in-Law) İbrâhîm Pasha. The period of peace authored by İbrâhîm Pasha at Passarowitz in 1718 saw the Ottoman elites turn in great relief to a round of entertainments on the lawns or in the pavilions of pleasure parks and newly constructed gardens inspired by European formal gardens, discovered by Ottoman emissaries sent to seek out the secrets of European military superiority. Then there were the tulips ... The fad for buying, raising, and developing tulips reached such a frenzy that the period between 1718 and 1730 in Turkey is often referred to as the Age of Tulips. And Nedîm was the poet of his age. He wrote brilliant *kasîdes* praising the pleasure and poetry-loving Sultan, his powerful Grand Vizier, and other notables of the court. His poems commemorated parties, buildings, ceremonies, and holidays of every sort. But above all his poems expand the range of Ottoman poetry from the highly polished, multilingual gems of the high court tradition to simpler and joyful lyrics that draw on the vernacular songs of the common people. This was a stunning departure from the practice of centuries, a departure for which Nedîm would become the emblem even though it was also the product of a number of prior experiments.

Nedîm's close ties to İbrâhîm Pasha would clothe him in success and glory. He would hold prestigious professorships, receive rapid promotions, and enjoy innumerable gifts and favors, yet none of this would bring him as much future fame as his revolutionary relaxation of barriers that had grown up between the language of art and the language of the streets and countryside.

Under İbrâhîm Pasha many barriers had come down. The first printing press was established, new manufacturing enterprises were begun, a fire brigade was instituted, public works were increased. But this required vast expenditures from an already depleted treasury and with the expenditures came inflation and the need to raise taxes, both of which severely squeezed the lower classes. While the wealthy built pleasure gardens and villas where they indulged in ever more lavish amusements, life simply grew worse for the lower classes, including the Janissary troops, many of whom worked as artisans to supplement grossly inadequate salaries.

In the end, in an ever-spreading aura of discontent, a revolt broke out on 28 September 1730 against İbrâhîm Pasha's viziership, led by a small group of artisan-Janissaries in collusion with disgruntled members of the learned class. The uprising quickly gained momentum and the Sultan was forced to sacrifice his highest officials to the mob. The strangled bodies of İbrâhîm Pasha and two other notables were turned over to the revolutionaries, and the Sultan was finally forced to abdicate.

And somehow, in the midst of this turmoil, the poet Nedîm lost his life. There are several stories about this death: that he died of fright, that he died as a result of alcoholism, and—the most interesting, and perhaps most accurate, story—that he died during the height of the revolt, falling off the roof of one of the palace buildings while trying to make his escape from the rampaging mob.

At his death Nedîm left behind a daughter, three sisters, and an scintillating poetic legacy.

Koja Râgıb Pasha

Koja (the Great) Râgıb Pasha was born Mehmed to the family of Shevkî Mustafâ Efendi, a secretary in the Office of Registers, in 1699. Nothing is known of his education, which would seem to indicate that he was educated privately. He was apparently extremely intelligent and talented. His exceptional abilities soon launched him on a spectacular career that began as a secretary in his father's bureau. At the early age of twenty-five, he was appointed as secretary to the governor of Erivan, with the task of recording lands taken in the wars with Iran. From this position he moved on to successively higher secretarial postings, in each of which he seems to have favorably impressed the men he served. He also distinguished himself as a delegate to the peace talks with Austrian and Russian representatives in Nemirova. As a result, in 1741 he was promoted to Chief Secretary (of Foreign Affairs) and became a vizier in 1744. Subsequently he was governor of Egypt, Aleppo, and Damascus. Finally, in 1756, he was made Grand Vizier and served in this role under the sultans Osmân III and Mustafâ III. He later married a sister of Sultan Mustafâ.

When he died in 1763, Koja Râgıb Pasha was buried in the garden of the library he had built in the district of Lâleli. He is remembered, on the one hand, as an exceptional statesman who guided the Empire through some extremely difficult times. On the other hand, he is known as a vastly talented writer and poet, perhaps the greatest poet between Nedîm and Sheyh Gâlib. In addition to his poetry, which is often said to have been the culmination of the "wisdom or philosophical" style associated with Nâbî, he was a master of prose style and the author of a famous collection called the *Samples (münshe'ât)* containing examples of letters, memoranda, official documents, and the like.

Râsih Bey

Very little is known for sure about Râsih Bey except that he was from Balıkesir (Zâtî's hometown) and that his common name was Ahmed. It is said that he was a descendant of Zağanos Pasha, one of the notables of Mehmed the Conqueror's time (1451– 1481). His mother and father were from noble families, but it is unclear what—if anything—Râsih did for a living, and it is almost certain that he did not do anything or hold a position that would justify the title *bey* (lord). It is most likely that, as the biographer Sâlim indicates, he considered himself a "lord" of the domain of poetic talent and so lived his life as a *bey*.

Even the date of his death is obscured by the fact that several biographers have confused him with another poet with the pen name Râsih. The best guess is that he died in 1731 and was buried in Balıkesir.

Râsih Bey's fame rests mostly on the poem translated for this volume, which was paralleled and expanded upon by many poets of his age including Nedîm who embedded a parallel *gazel* in a *kasîde* to the Grand Vizier Shehîd 'Alî Pasha. It begins with Râsih's opening:

> Don't lower your languid eyes, don't aim your pointed lashes
> Don't fire black arrow after arrow into my wounded heart

And then it continues in Nedîm's own style. For example:

> Don't imagine disease has inflamed the white of a rosy narcissus-eye
> The tyrant glance has again made it bleed on top of blood

Fıtnat Hanım

Fıtnat (Natural Wit) Hanım was the daughter of one Ebuishakzâde Mehmed Es'ad Efendi who had been sheyhülislâm during the reign of Sultan Mahmûd I (1730-1754). Her everyday name was Zübeyde.

Fıtnat's family were not only highly placed members of the intellectual elites but had a distinctly artistic and perhaps even unconventional bent. Her grandfather, an uncle, and her brother were also well-known poets, and her father was said to be an accomplished musician, an unusual pursuit for an upper-class intellectual as the performance of music was more commonly identified with the lower classes and minorities. Very little is known about Fıtnat's life except the obvious surmise that she was permitted and even encouraged by her family to become educated and to indulge her remarkable talent for poetry to a degree far beyond what was customary for women of her class. She has a complete collection of poems of all the usual varieties, including some famous verse riddles. Most recent commentators point out that her poetry is is difficult to distinguish from the poetry of her male counterparts and they express a disappointment that it is not in some undefined way more "womanly." However, we must remember that to our eyes and ears the poetry of the sultans doesn't seem very "monarchical"; nor does the poetry of many theologians seem very "religious." The problem certainly stems in part from our understandable inability to appreciate how a poem by a woman or a sultan might have been received by its audiences.

There is a rather rich tradition of often obscene anecdotes about Fıtnat, who is portrayed as sharp-witted and inclined to engage in risqué exchanges with her male acquaintances. The wide circulation and popularity of such tales would seem to indicate that, despite the fact that most Ottoman women did not lead public lives, they were recognized as potentially powerful, capable, and independent persons. Contemporary reports of Fıtnat's unfortunate marriage to a dull and unimaginative member of the religious establishment are clearly tinged by a sincere regret that such a clever and lively woman should be yoked to an unworthy companion. Nonetheless, however unhappy the marriage may have been, it does not seem to have prevented Fıtnat from continuing a very successful career as a poet that ended only with her death in 1780.

Esrâr Dede

The Mevlevî poet and biographer of Mevlevî poets Esrâr Dede was born in the Sütlüce quarter of Istanbul in 1748. Because his father, Ahmed (known as Bîzebân, "the Tongueless, Mute") was himself a Mevlevî dervish, he was raised in a mystical climate and at an early age entered the Mevlevî House at Galata. There he studied a number of subjects, including Arabic, Persian, Latin, and Italian. Later in life he would publish a Turkish-Italian dictionary.

Because the greater part of his life was spent pursuing the stages of spiritual enlightenment in the seclusion of a dervish retreat, we have little knowledge of Esrâr Dede's doings during his many years of service to his order. We do know that in 1790 the great poet Sheyh Gâlib came to be master of the Galata House. In him Esrâr Dede found both a fellow poet and a dear friend. At Gâlib's urging he wrote the collection of biographies of Mevlevî poets for which he is justly famed.

During this time Esrâr was advanced to the post of Master of the Cauldron (Kazancı Dede). In this position he was responsible for guiding those who wished to go beyond being lay adherents of a Master and occasional participants in the rituals to become fully committed dervishes themselves. His was the highly respected role of helping such initiates pass though the 1,001 day period of retreat, prayer, and fasting (*chîle*) that confirmed their abandonment of the concerns of the material world. They would begin by affirming "I will divest myself [of this-worldly things]"; and the Master of the Cauldron would address them saying, "Being a dervish is difficult and breaking your retreat is not a good thing. Being a dervish is a shirt of fire, a pea of iron. One must go hungry, be beaten, be reviled without reason. Being a dervish means dying [to this world] before death. If you can endure all this, then enter." Those who were so willing would then begin the rituals of their long retreat.

When Esrâr Dede died in 1796-1797 at the relatively early age of forty-nine his younger friend and spiritual master Gâlib was devastated and memorialized his grief in a touching elegy that begins:

Let it weep blood, weep, this my pearl scattering eye
Let it recall my dear, faithful friend and weep

Let my eye, my mouth, my face, my cheek weep
Let this eye all clad in black deeds weep

Let my rival weep for me and the one I love weep too
Let them all weep who hear the tale of my Esrâr

I have lost the rarest of pearls, alas and woe is me
I have buried him in the earth and come back, alas and woe is me

Among the works the self-effacing dervish left behind him was a lovely collection of inspired lyrics, which include some beautiful quatrains.

Sheyh Gâlib

Sheyh Gâlib was born Mehmed Es'ad in Istanbul in 1757. His family had long been associated with the Mevlevî dervishes, the order that traces its ancestry to the great master Mevlânâ Jelâleddîn Rûmî (see the article on Rûmî's Mirror following poem no. 50). He was the descendant of intellectual, scholarly, and sufi elites including his father, Mustafâ Reshîd, who was a poet, bureaucrat, and second-level adept of the dervish house (*tekke, hânkâh*) at Yenikapı.

Gâlib did not go through the theological school (*medrese*) education usual for Ottoman elites but was educated at home by his father and tutors from various Mevlevî houses. He was clearly a talented student and became an exceptional poet, who in his justly famed verse romance

Beauty and Love (*Hüsn ü 'Ashk*) has nothing good to say of the elite bureaucratic scribes with their formal educations.

And then there are the would-be-poet scribes
Most the bosses and elites of scribes

Each a mohair cloak all bloat with pride
Each a ripple on the sea of jargon

The most stupendous wish of any one
To memorize the *Samples* of Râgıb*

Then add to this a few attractive boys
A lute, a glass of wine, some books of poems

If one became fed-up with doing one's work
With these one's powers could surely be restored

Is this not what "pederast" should mean?
Is not such poetry deprived of taste?

Gâlib was certainly precocious. He assembled a *dîvân* (collection of poems) at the age of twenty-four and was only a year older when he composed his *Beauty and Love*, which has been so highly praised that his magnificent lyrics are often overlooked. The poet Nesh'et gave him the pen name Es'ad (Most Happy/Fortunate), which he later changed to Gâlib (the Victorious).

Although he grew up among the dervishes and dervish houses of Istanbul, Gâlib did not immediately follow the mystic's path. He seems to have worked in various bureaucratic positions while he studied the works of Rûmî. Suddenly, in 1783, he decided to join the Mevlevî order. Instead of applying to his father's and grandfather's *tekke*, he left home and presented himself to the master (*sheyh*, *dede*) of the Tomb of Rûmî in Konya, the spiritual and administrative center of the Mevlevîs. There, over his father's objections, he began the required 1,001 days of seclusion, which he completed at the Mevlevî dervish house of Yenikapı in Istanbul. After a brief period of seclusion at his home in Sütlüce, he accepted an assignment to become *sheyh* (master) of the famed Mevlevî House of Kulekapı in Galata (1791 C.E.).

In this position Gâlib prospered. He became an intimate of Sultan Selîm III, who was himself a poet, musician, and Mevlevî. He was an avid supporter with his poetry of the controversial reforms of the young Sultan.

* The *Samples* are a collection of exemplary writings (*münshe'ât*) by Koja Râgıb Pasha (see the above article).

The Sultan in turn aided the equally young *sheyh* in the development of his *tekke*, which became a center of intellectual activity. Although his position allowed Gâlib to avoid reliance on royal patronage, his social intimacy with the palace went beyond the Sultan and extended to the Sultan's sister, Princess Beyhân, a cultured woman who became a great supporter of the poet-*sheyh*. Among his other close friends was the poet Esrâr Dede, who was to write an important biography of Mevlevî poets.

Sadly, Gâlib contracted tuberculosis while still at the height of his powers and died in 1799 at the age of forty-two. His friend, the reformist Sultan Selîm, would be assassinated by reactionary elements only eight years later.

Sünbülzâde Vehbî

Vehbî (the Naturally Talented/Gifted) was born Mehmed in the town of Marash in the province of Aleppo sometime late in the first half of the eighteenth century. He is usually referred to by both his pen name and his family name, Sünbülzâde (Hyacinth-son), to distinguish him from another famous poet. The story is that Vehbî's father, Râshid Efendi, had been a judicial assistant to the distinguished poet Seyyid Vehbî while the latter was serving as magistrate in Marash. When Râshid's son Mehmed was born, Seyyid Vehbî, who had lost his own son, bestowed his pen name on the infant. In any case, Vehbî grew up as the son of a scholar and poet in surroundings where poetry was highly valued.

Vehbî was educated in Marash but soon departed for Istanbul, where the opportunities for a bright young man were far more numerous. Once in the capital he employed his poetic talents to attract the attention and support of powerful patrons. With their help he successfully passed the examinations for the judiciary and served as a magistrate in several cities in the European provinces. Upon returning to Istanbul, his reputation as a poet helped him shift his career and become one of the higher echelon of royal secretaries. As a result of his work in the bureau that handled foreign affairs and his excellent knowledge of Persian, he was sent on an embassy to Iran in 1775 with the job of reporting on a dispute between 'Ömer Pasha, the Ottoman Governor of Baghdad, and Zand Kerîm Khan, the ruler of Iran.

For an Ottoman poet, a trip to Iran meant returning to the sentimental source of poetic art. Vehbî was thrilled by the opportunity. He apparently enjoyed himself immensely, engaged in friendly poetic contests with the Persian masters of the day, and entered whole-heartedly into their entertainments. Subsequently his poetry would be full of references to this experience.

However, on his way home 'Ömer Pasha learned that Vehbî's report indicated that the trouble had been caused by the Pasha's mismanagement. The Pasha was incensed and secretly reported to the Sultan that Vehbî had formed an improper friendship with Kerîm Khan and acted in a biased manner unbecoming an ambassador and contrary to the interests of the Ottomans. As a result, an order was issued for Vehbî's execution, but the poet was warned by friends and returned secretly to Istanbul, where he hid himself until the Sultan's anger cooled and the Pasha's misdeeds came to light. Then, with the submission of a *kasîde* begging forgiveness and fancifully describing his Iranian trip, Vehbî was restored to favor. He immediately resigned his position and again took up the career of a magistrate. After serving all over the Empire for many years, the aging poet finally retired to Istanbul.

With the succession of Selîm III, a great friend of poets, in celebration of whose birth he had written a *kasîde* many years earlier, Vehbî achieved a position of great respect and spent his waning years living the comfortable life of a poet and libertine. His longtime friend and judicial assistant was the famous poet and chronogram writer Surûrî. From the time when the two were thrown into a provincial jail as a result of Vehbî's scandalous behavior, they carried on an amusing exchange of obscene lampoons.

When Vehbî was more than eighty years old, ill and growing senile, he gathered his friends and said farewell to them. Shortly thereafter, in 1809, he died and his friend Surûrî created three lovely and famed chronograms on the date of his death.

Enderunlu Vâsıf

Vâsıf Osmân was born sometime in the latter half of the eighteenth century to a niece of the famous Gardener-Corps Captain Halîl Pasha the Albanian who became Grand Vizier of Ahmed III. The *enderûn* is the inner circle of the palace, where the most elite of the Janissary guard were educated and served. Through the intercession of Halîl Pasha, Vâsıf was brought up during his childhood years in this inner service and later returned to it for much of his adult career. His path, however, was not easy. After finishing the Galatasaray school he was, for some reason, not admitted into the palace service as one would have expected. This failure cast Vâsıf into hard times from which he was rescued by Süleymân Pasha, who took him on as his personal Keeper of the Robes. Near the end of the reign of 'Abdülhamîd I (1774–1789), he entered the corps of the Royal Larder, where he served throughout the reign of Selîm III.

The several poems he wrote to the Sultan indicate that he must have been a part of the circle of poets and scholars that attended upon Selîm, a group that included the master poet Sheyh Gâlib. Upon the enthronement of Mustafâ IV (1807), Vâsıf was promoted to the service of the Royal Chamber, which was the highest level of the interior staff because it directly served the Sultan. He would later hold several other important positions, finally being invested in the presence of the Sultan himself with the ceremonial robes of Master of the Larder. In 1818, after serving for thirty years during the reigns of four sultans, he retired from the palace and lived the rest of his life at his home in Istanbul, where he died at a great old age in 1824.

Vâsıf seems to have been an amusing, fun-loving, and active person fond of food and drink. His poems are full of references to the favorite Janissary sports: riding, archery, and *jirit* (a game in which riders try to hit each other with blunted javelins). Both Vâsıf and his close friend 'İzzet Mollâ (see below) were large men, as is attested by a poem the two wrote together humorously begging the Sultan for favors:

> Oh Solomon of the age, we are two great masters of poetry
> Our bodies the size of elephants our luck the size of an ant
>
> With all this corpulence of ours, please do us justice
> We have no home in this world even the size of a beehive

Vâsıf left a large collection of poems, many of them light pieces in a rather colloquial Turkish and a style reminiscent of Nedîm where it is not overtly modeled on him. With its elegant traditional lyrics and rather more vulgar and popular verses, which were often set to music, his work seems to evidence the transitional character of his period. Although his poetry has been severely treated by some later scholars for its technical failings, others have treasured its original themes and glimpses of life in Istanbul and the Sultans' palaces. His friend 'İzzet, in a poem carved on Vâsıf's gravestone, mourned the loss of "two jewels in a single day," the first being "the anthology of his [Vâsıf's] life" the other "his verses."

Kechejizâde 'İzzet Mollâ

'İzzet Mollâ was born in Istanbul in 1786 to a family of the learned classes with ties to the Mevlevî dervishes, which traced its roots to the city of Konya. The family name, Kechejizâde went back to an ancestor who was a felt-maker (*kecheji*).

'İzzet's father and grandfather were Islamic jurists. In the troubled times of the late eighteenth and early nineteenth centuries, high position, even a judgeship, was fraught with dramatic reversals and 'İzzet's father led a tumultuous life of alternating favor and exile that ended with his early death when his son was only thirteen. Although two of his uncles took over his education and prepared him for a career in canon law, he was more attracted to the wilder life of the poet-uncle, Es'ad. He seems to have become addicted to alcohol and squandered a meager inheritance on riotous living. As a result, his law career was terminated and he was left with the problems of supporting both a family and an addiction. In the end the distraught young man decided to commit suicide. As the story goes, 'İzzet arose early one morning intending to take his own life. He boarded a rowboat near his home for a trip up the Bosphorus to the park at Göksu on the Anatolian shore. With him he took a huge bottle of *rakı* (a strong anise-flavored liquor like the Greek ouzo), apparently with the idea of drinking himself to death in the park. As he passed the houses along the shore, in one of them the famous lexicographer Hancherli Bey happened to have run into a difficult passage in a collection of poems he was reading. Seeing what was by his dress an educated man passing by in a boat, the *bey* called out to 'İzzet and asked him for help. The suicidal young man managed a clever answer, and the duly impressed older man engaged him in a pleasant conversation, at the end of which 'İzzet gave up on accomplishing his own death and the two became fast friends.

Concerning the success that 'İzzet enjoyed next there are several stories. In one of them, Hancherli Bey pays off a debt to the immensely powerful Hâlet Efendi by introducing 'İzzet to him as an extravagant gift. The Efendi, at first reluctant to accept as a protégé someone who had been dropped from theological school, soon was won over and started 'İzzet on a successful government career. Hâlet was also an adherent of the Mevlevî dervishes and it is probably through him that 'İzzet began the attachment to the Mevlevîs and Rûmî that figures so prominently in his poetry. One of his most highly regarded works is a narrative poem entitled *The Rosebower of Love* (*Gülshen-i 'Ashk*) that deals with Mevlevî theology much in the manner of Sheyh Gâlib's famous *Beauty and Love*.

In another story, sometime after Hâlet Efendi's demise, the young poet had a dream that he met Sultan Mahmud II in a mosque; the Sultan said to him that although they had not yet met in person, he felt that he knew 'İzzet from his poetry. Sometime later, while visiting a mosque with a friend, 'İzzet did indeed meet the Sultan and events transpired more or less as he had dreamt them. This convinced the poet of the Sultan's miraculous powers and he conveyed this in a few lines of verse. The Sultan was impressed and took 'İzzet under his wing.

However it may have happened, 'İzzet transcended his previous problems and served in a number of important positions including the chief judgeship of Galata. He married a woman from one of the noble families and had at least four children. He survived the downfall and execution of his one-time patron Hâlet Efendi but could not refrain from satirizing his patron's ill-wishers with a risqué couplet.

The Sultan could not tolerate such an assault on his Grand Vizier, so 'İzzet was exiled to the province of Keshan, a stay which he memorialized in a narrative poem entitled *The Sufferers* (*Mihnet-keshân*) or, as the pun in Persian goes, *Suffering in Keshan* (*Mihnet-i Keshân*). After almost a year, 'İzzet (now 'İzzet Mollâ, with the addition of a title proper to high judges) presented a *kasîde* to the Sultan and eventually was pardoned and returned to the good graces of the ruler. He subsequently held several high positions in the government. However, in 1828 he strongly opposed a declaration of war against the Russians who had invaded Ottoman territories. When the decision went against him, he wrote a letter of objection spelling out his position. When this was circulated and his arguments found to be without merit, the Mollâ was sentenced to death, a sentence later commuted to exile in the eastern Anatolian city of Sivas.

When the war turned out to be the mistake 'İzzet said it would be, a royal command was sent to Sivas pardoning him. But two hours before it arrived, the unfortunate Mollâ died under mysterious circumstances. The year was 1829 and the poet was forty three years old. He was buried with the royal pardon pinned to his chest.

Yenishehirli 'Avnî

Hüseyin, the son of Sıdkî Ebubekir Pasha, who would be known by the name 'Avnî (the Divinely Aided) was born in the town of Yenishehir, now the Greek town of Larissa. He was educated in the household of 'Abdürrahmân Sâmî Pasha, for whom his father was head steward. He is said to have read Rûmî's *Mesnevî* under the Pasha's tutelage. Eventually, Hüseyin too joined the entourage of Sâmî Pasha, serving as the Pasha's secretary during his tenure as Governor of Vidin. Sometime after 1854 he came to Istanbul where he became involved with the Mevlevî dervishes and married the daughter of the master of the Mevlevî lodge in Beshiktash. In 1859/60 he worked as secretary to the Governor of Baghdad.

After returning to Istanbul he held mostly insignificant jobs. He is said to have had two children, a son and a daughter, but both his son and his wife died tragically one after the other. 'Avnî apparently suffered from alcoholism and upon the deaths of his wife and child seems to have given in entirely to his addiction. He is said to have been of a naturally otherworldly and retiring temperament and under the influence of alcohol he appears to have become incapable of holding to any project or rising above a life of genteel poverty.

Although he was afflicted by stuttering, 'Avnî became a respected member of the Society of Poets, which included some of the most famous names of the day. He was fluent in Greek and Arabic, knew a little French, and was noted as an expert in Persian literature.

'Avnî's life also coincided with the first great revolution in Turkish culture known as the period of Tanzîmât (Reforms). He was one of the last skilled poets of the Ottoman tradition in a cultural, political, and intellectual age increasingly dominated by the nationalizing and Westernizing ideologies that would, in the next century, give birth to the Turkish Republic. The tide of poetry had shifted dramatically, and 'Avnî—a vastly talented poet, escaped into mysticism, alcoholism, and personal misery, unable to complete his most ambitious works—seems like a sadly appropriate emblem of the impending close of a long and productive literary era.

A NOTE ON SOURCES

Most of the material for the preceding short biographies was drawn from a range of sources, including standard reference works such as *The Encyclopaedia of Islam (New Edition; Leiden: Brill)* and its Turkish version, the *İslâm Ansiklopedisi* (Istanbul: Milli Eğitim Basımevi), which are not cited in the bibliography. The listing of sources below does not represent all or even a large fraction of the sources actually used, but rather identifies the location of material translated directly from Ottoman sources or referred to specifically.

Sheyhî:	'Âşık: 253b–254b; Kınalızâde Hasan Çelebî: 533–536
Ahmed Pasha:	Latîfî: 76–79; 'Âşık: 35b–37a
Nejâtî:	Kınalızâde Hasan Çelebî: 969–982; 'Âşık: 130a–132a
Mihrî:	Latîfî: 319–322; Tarlan, *Necâtî Beg Dîvânı*: 123-124; Erünsal
Zeyneb:	Latîfî: 178–179; 'Âşık: 83b
Revânî:	Kınalızâde Hasan Çelebî: 419–423; Latîfî: 169–172; 'Âşık: 240a–241b; 'Âlî (İsen): *Selîm I*, 176–177
Lâmi'î:	Burmaoğlu: 2; 'Âşık: 108b–111a
Zâtî:	'Âşık: 277a–284a; 'Âlî (İsen): *Süleymân*, 215–218; Kınalızâde Hasan Çelebî: 382–393
Hayretî:	'Âşık: 90b–91b; 'Alî (İsen): *Süleymân*, 208–209
Figânî:	Latîfî: 204–205
Fevrî:	'Âşık: 203a–212a
Hayâlî:	'Âşık: 271a–277a; 'Âlî (İsen): *Süleymân* (Kandî), 212–215
Fuzûlî:	*Dîvân-i Fârsî*: 10–12
Nisâyî:	Çavuşoğlu (1978): 405–416
Bâkî:	Kınalızâde Hasan Çelebî: 199–209
Yahyâ:	'Âşık: 95b–97a; Kınalızâde Hasan Çelebî: 1077–1083

Rûhî:	Gölpınarlı (1953)
Sheyhülislâm Yahyâ:	Bayraktutan
Nef'î:	Karahan (1972): 2–3; Nâ'imâ III: 234–236
Râsih Bey:	Sâlim: 273–274; Nedîm, *Dîvân*: 10–12
Esrâr Dede:	Pakalin II: 228; Şeyh Gâlib, *Dîvân*: 432
Sheyh Gâlib:	Gölpınarlı, *Hüsn ü 'Işk*: 91 (756)
Vâsıf:	İpekten (1989): 3
'İzzet:	Bülbül: 182

Ottoman Turkish Texts

Nesîmî

1. *Oh my idol*

Senden ırağ ey ṣanem şâm u seḥer yanaram
Vaṣlını ârzûlaram daḫi beter yanaram

'Aşḳ ile şevḳın odu cânuma kâr eyledi
Gör nice tâbende uşşems ü ḳamer yanaram

Senden ırağ olduğum bağrumı ḳan eyledi
Oldı gözümden revân ḫûn-ı ciger yanaram

Şems-i ruḫuñ ṣûreti ḳarşuma gelmiş durur
Şa'şa'asından baña şu'le düşer yanaram

Ṣabr ile ârâm-ı dil ḳapdı elümden ġamuñ
Bâd-ı hevâdan degül ġamdan eger yanaram

Çıḳdı içümden tütün çarḫı boyadı bütün
Gör ki ne âteşdeyem gör ne ḳadar yanaram

Yanduğumı yâr içün gizlü degül ben daḫi
Her ne ḳadar kim anuñ göñlü diler yanaram

Müdde'î yanar dimiş ġamda Nesîmî belî
Ġamda yanan yârı yâr çünki sever yanaram

Aḥmed-i Dâ'î

2. *The torture of the beloved*

Ma'şûḳanuñ cefâsı egerçi cefâ degül
Şükr iderem ki bâri özüñ bî-vefâ degül

Çoḳ servi boylu câdu gözi fitne ḳaşlu var
Maḥbûb olursa sencileyin müntehâ degül

La'l-i lebüñ şarâbına her kim ki ṣuṣadı
Biñ cân virürse cür'asına çoḳ bahâ degül

Senden egerçi ṣûret ile ben cüdâ olam
Bir laḥẓa cân içinde ḫayâlüñ cüdâ degül

Cânâ revâ mı vaṣlı dırıġ idesin bize
İtme bu cevri ben ḳuluña kim revâ degül

Luṭf eyle 'âşıḳa vü göñüller ele getür
Ḫulḳ u vefâ gerek çü güzellik baḳâ degül

Cândan 'azîzrek severem ben seni inan
Dâ'ı sözinde Tañrı ṭanuḳ kim ḫaṭâ degül

Şeyḫî

3. *Your sun face*

Ṣanemâ gün yüzüñ âyîne-i cândur bilürem
Dü cihân naḳşı ḳamu anda 'ayândur bilürem

Ḳangı naḳḳâş kim ol dâyire-i ḥüsnüñden
Noḳṭa taṣvîr ide üstâd-ı cihândur bilürem

Ġamzeñ eydür ki göñül şehrini vîrân iderem
Şehriyâruñ eline ḥükmi revândur bilürem

Gözüñüñ ḳaşuñuñ añlayımazam ḥîlelerin
İlle bu fitne vü ol âfet-i cândur bilürem

Ni'met-i ḳahr ile kim ḳullaruñı añar idüñ
Bizi yâd eylemedüñ ḫayli zamândur bilürem

Ey riyâlı 'ameli aṣṣilu bilen ṣûfî
Gider ol fikr ki îmâna ziyândur bilürem

Çemen ü yâr u mey ü sâz gerek Şeyḫîye bes
Ḳalanı ġuṣṣa vu ġam 'ayş-ı hemândur bilürem

4. *It's the season of spring*

Bahâr mevsimidür hem-dem-i ṣabâ olalum
Gül ile dôst ḳoḫusına âşinâ olalum

Çü devr-i lâledür iḫlâṣ ile ḳadeḥ dutalum
Nite ki nergis olur mest-i bî-riyâ olalum

Zamâne sırrını ḳo ġonca bigi ser-beste
Çemen ṣafâsını gül bigi dil-güşâ olalum

Cihân fütûḥına Cem câmdur dimiş miftâḥ
Gelüñ mülâzım-ı câm-ı cihân-nümâ olalum

'Amelden ücret umınca ġurûr-ı tâ'at ile
Günehde muntaẓır-ı raḥmet-i Ḫudâ olalum

Bahâr-ı tevbeye Şeyḫî cünûn dimiş 'âḳil
Bugün muvâfaḳat it irte pârsâ olalum

Aḥmed Paşa

5. *Ask about my wailing*

Nâlemi zemzeme-i murġ-ı seḥerden ṣorasın
Derd-mend olduġumı ḫasta cigerden ṣorasın

Ġuṣṣamuñ ḳıṣṣaların yazar iken âhumdan
Ḫâmeler yanduġını nâme-i terden ṣorasın

Şevḳını ruḫlarınuñ şem'-i ḳamerden bilüben
Ẕevḳını leblerinüñ şehd ü şekerden ṣorasın

Kîse-i 'ömri tehî itdügümi yoluñda
Olıcaḳ ḫâk beden kâse-i serden ṣorasın

Ḫâk olduġuma inanmaz iseñ bâd-ı ṣabâ
Ayaġı tozı ile geldi seferden ṣorasın

Gözlerüm yaşı gibi dilbere ey peyk-i nesîm
Ne içün ṣaldı beni 'ayn-ı naẓardan ṣorasın

Vâdî-i hecrde Aḥmed ḳuluñ üftâde ġarîb
Cevrler çekdügini devr-i ḳamerden ṣorasın

6. *Is there any heart*

Bir dil mi ḳalmışdur bu tîr-i ġamzeden ḳan olmamış
Bir cân mı vardur ol kemân-ebrûya ḳurbân olmamış

Şol 'ömr kim sensüz geçer ol 'ömr żâyi' 'ömr imiş
Bir cân k'anuñ cânânı yoḳ ol cân daḫi cân olmamış

Ne fitnedür yâ Rab bu kim bir dilberüñ her ġamzesi
Bir demde biñ cân almasa dirler bu fettân olmamış

Zülfin gidermiş ol ṣanem kâfirligin ḳomaz henûz
Zünnârını kesmiş velî daḫi müselmân olmamış

Şehrüñde la'lüñ şevḳine şol deñlü ḳan aġlamışam
Kim bir der ü dîvâr yoḳ yâḳût u mercân olmamış

Añup çerâġ-ı ḥüsnüñi pervâne göñlüm şem'-vâr
Meclis mi var kim germ olup sûzân u giryân olmamış

Mecmû'-ı diller mecma'ı zülfüñdür anı çözse bâd
Cem'iyyet-i ḫâṭır m'olur andan perîşân olmamış

Gülden ḳoḫuñ alup seḥer âh itse Aḥmed derd ile
Bülbül bulınmaz bâġda kim baġrı biryân olmamış

Necâtî

7. *Those glances rain down arrows*

Ġamzeler kim cân iline tîr-i müjgân yaġdurur
Beñzer ol tâtâra kim siḥr ile bârân yaġdurur

Fürḳatüñden gözlerüm geh yaş aḳıdur gâh ḳan
Yoluña îs̱âr içün dürr ile mercân yaġdurur

Dûd-ı âhumdan duyar aġladuġum ḫalḳ-ı cihân
Ḳara yil esdükce bilürler ki ṭûfân yaġdurur

Ol ḳadar aḳdı gözümüñ yaşları kim geldi ḳan
Şimdiden gerü aḳan seyl-âbı ḳandan yaġdurur

Leblerinüñ sâġarından sâḳî-i 'Îsî-nefes
Cür'a diyü ehl-i meclis üstine cân yaġdurur

İşigüñde âhum işiden döker göz yaşların
Nitekim ḳıble yili esse firâvân yaġdurur

Ṣan yaġar bârân-ı ḫışm ile tekerk-i pür-belâ
Ol kemân-ebrû ḳaçan tîr ile peykân yaġdurur

Zülfüñ ucından göñüller düşdügin gören ṣanur
Ejdehâdur kim aġızdan nâr-ı sûzân yaġdurur

Ey Necâtî kilk-i gevher-bâruña ḳıymet mi var
Dürr olur her ḳaṭre kim ol ebr-i nîsân yaġdurur

8. *The heart is pleased*

Dil sevinür yañaġuñda ḫaṭ-ı ḫôş-bû olıcaḳ
Uġrınuñ güni doġar ay ḳarañu olıcaḳ

Dôstum böyle yabanlar mı gözetmek yaraşur
Ġamze-i mest ḥarâmî gözüñ âhû olıcaḳ

Ḫâk-i kûyuñ var iken cennet añılmaḳ ṣanemâ
Şuña beñzer ki teyemmüm ideler ṣu olıcaḳ

'Âşıḳ olalı ġam u ġuṣṣa durur hep yidügüm
Ki muḫâlif yimek ister kişi ṣayru olıcaḳ

Umaruz kim baḳa bizden yaña ol rûḥ-ı revân
'Aḳabınca işümüz na'ra-i yâ-hû olıcaḳ

Bûy-i zülfüñi ṣabâdan işidüp nâfe-i Çîn
Didi ben Rûma varup neyleyeyüm bû olıcaḳ

Söze uymaz diyü siz baña delü dimeñ kim
İşini ġayra inanmaz kişi uṣlu olıcaḳ

Ey göñül ben 'acebâ nice gelem kendüme kim
Göricek bî-ḫôd olup ölürin ayru olıcaḳ

Kim ḳabûl ide Necâtî seni kim dôst dimiş
Varmazam ṣoḥbete şimden gerü ben o olıcaḳ

9. *Those tulip-cheeked ones*

Lâle-ḫadler yine gülşende neler itmediler
Servi yürütmediler ġoncayı söyletmediler

Ṭaşradan geldi çemen mülkine bîgâne diyü
Devr-i gül ṣoḥbetine lâleyi iletmediler

'Âdeti ḫûblaruñ cevr ü cefâdur ammâ
Baña itdüklerini kimselere itmediler

Hele ol ḳaşları ya oḳları peykânlarını
Sîneden çekmediler yüregi oynatmadılar

Biñ güzeller bulınur Yûsufa mânend ammâ
Bu ḳadar var ki bular kendülerin ṣatmadılar

Ḥamdü li'llâh mey-i cân-baḫş ile sâḳîlerümüz
Âb-ı Ḥayvân ile Kevs̱er ṣuyın istetmediler

Ey Necâtî yüri ṣabr eyle elüñden ne gelür
Ḫûblar cevr ü cefâyı kime ögretmediler

10. *Spiraling, the sparks*

Çıḳalı göklere âhum şereri döne döne
Yandı ḳandîl-i sipihrüñ cigeri döne döne

Ayaġı yer mi baṣar zülfüñe ber-dâr olanuñ
Ẕevḳ u şevḳ ile virür cân u seri döne döne

Şâm-ı zülfüñle göñül Mıṣrı ḫarâb oldı diyü
Saña iletdi kebûter ḫaberi döne döne

Ka'be olmasa ḳapuñ ay ile gün leyl ü nehâr
Eylemezlerdi ṭavâf ol güẕeri döne döne

Sen olasın diyü yer yer aṣılup âyîneler
Gelene gidene eyler naẓarı döne döne

Sen ṭurup raḳs idesin ḳarşıña ben boynum egem
İne zülfüñ ḳoça sen sîm-beri döne döne

Ey Necâtî yaraşur muṭribi şeh meclisinüñ
Raḳs urup oḳıya bu şi'r-i teri döne döne

Mihrî Ḫ̱âṭûn

11. *I opened my eyes from sleep*

Ḫ̱âbdan açdum gözüm nâgehân ḳaldurdum seri
Ḳarşuma gördüm ṭurur bir mâh-çehre dilberi

Ṭâli'üm sa'd oldı yâḫ̱ud ḳadre irdüm ġâlibâ
Kim maḥallem içre gördüm gice doġmış Müşterî

Nûr aḳar gördüm cemâlinden egerçi ẓâhirâ
Kendüsi beñzer müselmâna libâsı kâferî

Gözümi açup yumınca oldı çeşmümden nihân
Şöyle teşḫ̱îṣ iderem kim ya melekdür ya perî

İrdi çün Âb-ı Ḥayâta Mihri ölmez ḥaşra dek
Gördi çün şeb ẓulmetinde ol 'ayân İskenderi

12. *At times, my longing*

Geh hecr-i yâr u gâh beni ġamlar öldürür
Geh vaṣl-ı dilber ile geçen demler öldürür

Düşmen güler bu ḥâlüme ben aġlaram müdâm
Hey buña cân mı ḳatlanur âdemler öldürür

Ḫ̱aste dile ḫ̱ayâliyle ey emsem eyleyen
Müşkil budur ki şimdi beni emler öldürür

Aġlañ gelüñ ki bir gün eyâ dôstlar raḳîb
Ecel irişmeden beni derhemler öldürür

Ḫ̱âr-ı cefâda Mihrî ölürse ne ġam raḳîb
İt ḳabırcı seni anı gül-femler öldürür

13. *My heart burns*

Âteş-i ġamda kebâb oldı ciger döne döne
Göklere çıḳdı duḫ̱ânumla şerer döne döne

Dil derûnumda ṭuṭuşdi yine bir şem' gibi
Ten ḫ̱ayâlüñle fener oldu yanar döne döne

Cân cânbâzını gör la'lüñle irişmek içün
Rîsmân-ı ser-i zülfüñden iner döne döne

Ḫâk-i pâyuña yüzin sürmek içün şems ü ḳamer
Ser-i kûyuña gelir şâm u seḥer döne döne

Ḳaşuña beñzemek içün senüñ ey zühre-cebîn
Kendüzin ṭutdı hilâl itdi ḳamer döne döne

Düşeli şevḳ-i ḫayâl-i lebüñ Mihrî dile
Âteş-i ġamda kebâb oldu ciger döne döne

Zeynep Ḫâṭûn

14. *Remove your veil*

Keşf it niḳâbuñı yeri gögi münevver it
Bu 'âlem-i 'anâṣırı firdevs-i enver it

Depret lebüñi cûşâ getir ḥavż-ı Kevs̱eri
'Anber ṣaçıñı çöz bu cihânı mu'aṭṭar it

Ḫaṭṭuñ berât yazdı ṣabâya didi ki tîz
Var milket-i Ḫıtây ile Çîni musaḫḫar it

Âb-ı Ḥayât olmayıcaḳ ḳısmet ey göñül
Biñ yıl gerekse Ḫıżr ile seyr-i Sikender it

Zeyneb ḳo meyli ziynet-i dünyâya zen gibi
Merdâne-vâr sâde-dil ol terk-i zîver it

Revânî

15. *What do you say*

Şol serv gibi ḳâmet-i dil-cûya ne dirsin
Şol güller ile sünbül-i ḫôş-bûya ne dirsin

Hîç añmayalum ḫâl ü ḫaṭ u zülfini nâṣıḥ
Şol şîve ile ḥâlet-i ebrûya ne dirsin

Bir ḫûyuñ ile ṣûfî cihâna ṣıġamazsın
Üftâdelerüñ itdügi yâ-hûya ne dirsin

Cânânelerüñ va'desi çoḳ 'âşıḳa cânâ
Ġayrıyı ḳoyalum hele pehlûya ne dirsin

Zâhid dir imiş tevbelüyem câm-ı şarâba
Bi'llâhi Revânî ya şu bed-ḫûya ne dirsin

Lâmi'î

16. *Yesterday I saw*

Âsumânî ṭon geyer dün gördüm ol gün yüzli yâr
Sâye-veş pâyine düşmek istedüm itdi firâr

Şâm idi beñzer anuñçün tîz ṭolandı ol güneş
Berḳ iki yâ ṣıçradı olup bulutdan âşikâr

Yâ raḳîb-i kelb vehminden yatağın özledi
Ḳurd ṣandı 'âşıḳın yâ ol geyik gözli nigâr

Gözlerüm ardınca ḳaldı irmedi gerdine vehm
Ṣan perî idi görindi yâ ḫayâl idi o yâr

Ṭâli'-i ferḫunde idi gösterüp yüz oldı ġayb
Ya hümâ-yı devlet idi geldi geçdi sâye-vâr

Göz ḳarardup ol tezerv ardınca ṣaldum bilmedüm
Çıḳdı dil şâhbâzı destümden ne ol var ne bu var

Ol perînüñ şîvesinden Lâmi'î bildüm yaḳîn
Kim ḫayâl-i ḫâb imiş dünyâ-yı dûn bî-i'tibâr

Ẕâtî

17. *Oh heavens why do you cry*

N'olduñ iñlersin felek her-câyî cânânuñ mı var
Seyr ider her menzili bir mâh-ı tâbânuñ mı var

Beñzüñi ey bûstân faṣl-ı ḫazân mı itdi zerd
Yoḫsa başı ṭaşra bir serv-i ḫırâmânuñ mı var

Aġlayup feryâd idersin her nefes ey 'andelîb
Ḫâr ile hem-sâye olmış verd-i ḫandânuñ mı var

Yoluña cânum revân itsem gerek cânâ didüm
Yüzüme biñ ḫışm ile baḳdı didi cânuñ mı var

Zülf-i dilber gibi ey Ẕâtî perîşânsın yine
Cevri bî-ḥad yoḫsa bir yâr-i perîşânuñ mı var

Ḥayretî

18. *We are not slaves*

Ne Süleymâna esîrüz ne Selîmüñ ḳulıyuz
Kimse bilmez bizi bir şâh-ı Kerîmüñ ḳulıyuz

Ḳul olan ʿaşḳa cihân beglerine egmedi baş
Başḳa sulṭân-ı cihânuz gör e kimüñ ḳulıyuz

Ġam yirüz ḳan yudaruz gûşe-i miḥnetde müdâm
Ṣanma biz Kevs̱er-i cennât-ı naʿîmüñ ḳulıyuz

Ḥüsn-i ḥâdis̱ ḳulıyuz ṣanma bizi sulṭânum
Vech-i pâküñde olan ân-ı ḳadîmüñ ḳulıyuz

Terk idüp Ḥayretiyâ tâc u ḳabâdan geçdük
Anca bu dünyede bir köhne kilîmüñ ḳulıyuz

Fiġânî

19. *My sad heart is burnt*

Tennûr-i sînem içre bağrum kebâba beñzer
ʿAks-i lebüñle yaşum ḳanlu şarâba beñzer

Seyl-i revân-i eşküm üstinde çarḫ-ı gerdân
Ṣu üzredür binâsı bir âsiyâba beñzer

Göñlüm vilâyetini ol seng-dil yıḳaldan
Ṭaş üzre ṭaşı yoḳdur şehr-i ḫarâba beñzer

Bu nüh revâḳ-ı gerdûn ʿArş-ı ʿAẓîmi ile
ʿUmmân-ı eşküm üzre bir ḳaç ḥabâba beñzer

Bu âh-i serd içinde ḫâk-i tenüñ Fiġânî
Ṣarṣar yili ṣavurmış bir kef türâba beñzer

20. *Your kiss does not satisfy*

Bûseñe dil ḳâniʿ olmaz vaṣluñuñ şeydâsıdur
Dôstum maʿẕûr ṭut dünyâ ṭamaʿ dünyâsıdur

Âh kim ölmezden öñ bir gün beni ḫâk eyleyen
Ol ḳıyâmet ḳâmetüñ bu vaʿde-i ferdâsıdur

Dimek olmaz adını bir mâh sevdüm tâzece
Edrine şehrinüñ ol ġâyetde müstes̱nâsıdur

Ḳıpḳızıl dîvâne idüp ḳara çullar geydüren
Baña ol ḳaşı ḳaranuñ gözleri alasıdur

Bilmek isterseñ Fiġânî kim durur ol ġonca-leb
Gülsitân-ı ḥüsninüñ bir bülbül-i gûyâsıdur

Fevrî

21. *The arrow of your glance*

Geh ḫayâl-i tîr-i ġamzeñ sîne-çâk eyler beni
Geh firâḳ-ı la'l-i nâbuñ derd-nâk eyler beni
Geh ġubâr-ı ḫaṭṭ-ı sebzüñ fikri ḫâk eyler beni
Gel gel ey cân yoḫsa hicrânuñ helâk eyler beni

Dûr idelden âl ile devrân beni sen mâhdan
Yidi ḳat gökler göge boyandı dûd-ı âhdan
İki 'âlemde murâduñ var ise Allâhdan
Gel gel ey cân yoḫsa hicrânuñ helâk eyler beni

Sen gidelden derd ile şol deñlü bîmâr oldı dil
Kim dil aġız virmeyüp dünyâyı bilmez şöyle bil
Bir daḫi görsün seni luṭf it ḳadem-rencîde ḳıl
Gel gel ey cân yoḫsa hicrânuñ helâk eyler beni

Derd ü ġam ben ḫastayı şol deñlü itdi nâtüvân
Kim vedâ' itmek hevâsı üzredür cism ile cân
Tende sensüz bir nefes ḳaldı ḥayâtumdan hemân
Gel gel ey cân yoḫsa hicrânuñ helâk eyler beni

Tîġ-i ḥasret çâk çâk itdi dil-i ṣad-pâreyi
Ḫançer-i hecr urdı her bir pâreye biñ yâreyi
Vaḳtidür vaṣluñla eyle çâre-i bî-çâreyi
Gel gel ey cân yoḫsa hicrânuñ helâk eyler beni

Görmeyelden sen güneş yüzlü ḳamer ruḫsârını
Ḫasta göñlüm göklere irgürdi âh u zârını
Ḥażret-i Ḥaḳḳuñ görem dirseñ eger dîdârını
Gel gel ey cân yoḫsa hicrânuñ helâk eyler beni

Fevri senden olalı ey ruḫları cennet cüdâ
Oldı cânı dûzaḫ-ı derd ü firâḳa mübtelâ
Ben günehkâra şefâ'at ḳıl bi-ḥaḳḳ-ı Muṣṭafâ
Gel gel ey cân yoḫsa hicrânuñ helâk eyler beni

Ḫayâlî

22. *They do not know how to search*

Cihân-ârâ cihân içindedür arayı bilmezler
O mâhîler ki deryâ içredür deryâyı bilmezler

Ḫarâbât ehline dûzaḫ ‘aẕâbın añma ey zâhid
Ki bunlar ibn-i vaḳt oldu ġam-ı ferdâyı bilmezler

Şafaḳ-gûn ḳan içinde dâġını seyr etse ‘âşıḳlar
Güneşde ẕerre görmezler felekde ayı bilmezler

Ḫamîde ḳadlerine rişte-i eşki ṭaḳup bunlar
Atarlar tîr-i maḳṣûdu nedendür yayı bilmezler

Ḫayâlî faḳr şâlına çekenler cism-i ‘uryânı
Anuñla faḫr iderler aṭlas u dîbâyı bilmezler

23. *We are among those*

Bu cemâlüñ şem‘ine pervâne gelmişlerdenüz
Yanalum ey şem‘-i rûşen yana gelmişlerdenüz

Cerr idüp eytâm-ı eşküm kûyuñu devrân eder
Merḥamet ḳıl dôstum iḥsâna gelmişlerdenüz

İtlerüñle âşinâ olmaġ içün ey nâzenîn
Nâzükâne kûyuñu seyrâna gelmişlerdenüz

Zâhidâ maḥbûb u meyden gel bizi men‘ eyleme
Biz ezelden bu yola rindâne gelmişlerdenüz

Vaṣf-ı ḫaddüñle Ḫayâlî tâze dîvân baġladı
Pâdişâhum ṣunmaġa dîvâna gelmişlerdenüz

24. *When dawn hennas her hands*

Ṣubḥ-dem kim yaḳınup ḫûn-ı şafaḳdan ḥınnâ
Nev-‘arûs-ı tutuḳ-ı çârüm ola çihre-güşâ

Felegi reşk-i ṭarab-ḫâne-i Cemşîd edüp
Vire eknâfa ‘iẕârı leme‘âtiyle żıyâ

Sâzına şa‘şa‘ayı târ edüb Zühre-i çarḫ
Naġme-i sünbüleden eyleye âheng-i nevâ

Cür‘a-i feyż döke arża inâ’-i ḫôrşîd
Cümle ẕerrât girüp raḳṣa ola mest-i liḳâ

Ben hem ol âyîne-i câmı alam destüme kim
Naẓar etdükce olur çihre-i maḳṣûd-nümâ

Nice göz dikmeyeyin bâdeye mânend-i ḥabâb
Görünür iki cihân anda *ke-naḳşün fi'l-mâ'*

Sâġar u bâdeye derlerse Ḫayâlî yeridür
Âb-ı rûy-ı ḥükemâ çeşm-i çerâġ-ı şu'arâ

Fużûlî

25. *Oh God, don't let anyone*

Menüm tek hîç kim zâr ü perîşân olmasun yâ Rab
Esîr-i derd-i 'aşḳ u dâġ-ı hicrân olmasun yâ Rab

Demâdem cevrlerdür çekdügüm bî-raḥm bütlerden
Bu kâfirler esîri bir müselmân olmasun yâ Rab

Görüp endîşe-i ḳatlümde ol mâhı budur derdüm
Ki bu endîşeden ol meh peşîmân olmasun yâ Rab

Çıḳarmaḳ etseler tenden çeküp peykânın ol servüñ
Çıḳan olsun dil-i mecrûḥ peykân olmasun yâ Rab

Demen kim 'adli yoḫ yâ ẓulmü çoḫ her ḥal ile olsa
Göñül taḫtına andan özge sulṭân olmasun yâ Rab

Cefâ vü cevr ile mu'tâdem añlarsuz n'olur ḥâlüm
Cefâsına ḥad ü cevrine pâyân olmasun yâ Rab

Fużûlî buldı genc-i 'âfiyet meyḫâne küncinde
Mübârek mülkdür ol mülk vîrân olmasun yâ Rab

26. *If my heart were a wild bird*

Âşiyân-ı murġ-i dil zülf-i perîşânuñdadur
Ḳanda olsam ey perî göñlüm senüñ yanuñdadur

'Aşḳ derdiyle ḫoşem el çek 'ilâcumdan ṭabîb
Ḳılma dermân kim helâküm zehri dermânuñdadur

Çekme dâmen nâz idüp üftâdelerden vehm ḳıl
Göklere açılmasun eller ki dâmânuñdadur

Mest-i ḫâb-ı nâz ol cem' it dil-i ṣad-pâremi
Kim anuñ her pâresi bir nevk-i müjgânuñdadur

Bes ki hicrânuñdadur ḫâṣiyyet-i ḳaṭ'-i ḥayât
Ol ḥayât ehline ḥayrânem ki hicrânuñdadur

Ey Fużûlî şem'-veş mutlaḳ açılmaz yanmadın
Tâblar kim sünbülinden rişte-i cânuñdadur

27. *For long years*

Nice yıllardur ser-i kûy-i melâmet beklerüz
Leşker-i sulṭân-ı 'irfânuz velâyet beklerüz

Sâkin-i ḫâk-i der-i meyḫâneyüz şâm ü seḥer
İrtifâ'-i ḳadr içün bâb-ı sa'âdet beklerüz

Cîfe-i dünya degül kerkes kimi maṭlûbumuz
Bir bölük 'Anḳâlaruz Ḳâf-i ḳanâ'at beklerüz

Ḫâb görmez çeşmümüz endîşe-i aġyârdan
Pâs-bânuz genc-i esrâr-ı maḥabbet beklerüz

Ṣûret-i dîvâr idüpdür ḥayret-i 'aşḳuñ bizi
Ġayr seyr-i bâġ ider biz künc-i miḥnet beklerüz

Kârbân-ı râh-ı tecrîdüz ḫaṭar ḫavfın çeküp
Gâh Mecnûn gâh men devr ile nevbet beklerüz

Ṣanmañuz kim giceler bî-hûdedür efġânumuz
Mülk-i 'aşḳ içre ḥiṣâr-ı istiḳâmet beklerüz

Yatdılar Ferhâd u Mecnûn mest-i câm-ı 'aşḳ olup
Ey Fużûlî biz olar yatduḳça ṣoḥbet beklerüz

28. *The pointed reproach of the enemy*

Kâr-ger düşmez ḫadeng-i ṭa'ne-i düşmen maña
Keṡret-i peykânüñ itmişdür demürden ten maña

Îmenem seng-i melâmetden kim alup çevremi
Oldı zencîr-i cünûn bir ḳal'a-i âhen maña

Andanam rüsvâ ki seylâb-ı sirişküm çâk eder
Zaḫm-ı tîġuñ ḳanı geydürdükçe pîrâhen maña

Dem-be-dem şem'-i cemâlüñden münevver olmasa
Ey gözüm nûrı gerekmez dîde-i rûşen maña

Hîç meskende ḳarârum yoḳdurur ol źevḳden
Kim ḳaçan ḫâk-i ser-i kûyuñ ola mesken maña

Başda bir serv-i semen-ber vaṣlınuñ sevdâsı var
Sûd ḳılmaz bâġ-bân neźźâre-i gülşen maña

Ey Fużûlî odlara yansun bisâṭ-ı salṭanat
Yegdür andan Ḥaḳ bilür bir gûşe-i külḫan maña

Nisâ'î

29. *We are the Mejnûn*

Biz de Mecnûn-ı zamânuz deşt-i ʻuzlet beklerüz
Kes̱reti vaḥdetle terk itdük ḥalvet beklerüz
Bezm-i ġamda hem-demüz nây ile ṣoḥbet beklerüz
Ṣanma ey zâhid bizi râh-ı selâmet beklerüz
Bir belâ-keş ʻâşıḳuz kûy-ı melâmet beklerüz

Ṭutmışuz Mecnûn gibi deşt-i ferâġatde mekân
Yapmışuz ʻAnḳâ gibi Ḳâf-ı ʻademde âşiyân
Gizli gencüz itmezüz râz-ı dili ḫalḳa ʻayân
Bulmışuz künc-i ferâġatde niçe genc-i nihân
Tâc u taḫtı terk idüp kûy-ı ferâġat beklerüz

Cân u dil mest ü melâmet bir iki sersemlerüz
Bezm-i ġamda Vâmıḳ u Ferhâd ile hem-demlerüz
ʻAşḳ câmın nûş idüp her ḥâl ile ḫurremlerüz
Bende-i pîr-i muġân olduḳda niçe demlerüz
ʻÂlemüñ sulṭânıyuz bâb-ı saʻâdet beklerüz

Ḫânumânı terk idüp ḳodum yoluñda baş u cân
Eşk-i çeşmüm gibi nem var ise ḳıldum der-miyân
Dönmezin bir yaña olursa eger ḫalḳ-ı cihân
Almaġa vaṣluñ metâʻını virüp rûḥ-ı revân
Naḳd-i ʻömri ṣarf idüp hey ḫâce nevbet beklerüz

Ḫusrev-i dehrüz bu eşk-i çeşm-i pür-ḫûnîn ile
Bîsütûnı seyle virdük dîde-i nemgîn ile
Kûhken ṣanur görenler bu dil-i sengîn ile
Biz belâ Ferhâdıyuz yâd-ı leb-i Şîrîn ile
Niçe demdür ey Nisâ derbend-i miḥnet beklerüz

Nevʻî

30. *We don't need the cup of pleasure*

Câm-ı ṣafâ gerekmez dünyâ-yı dûn elinden
Merdâneler şikârı almaz zebûn elinden

Ġam çekme câm-ı mergi yeksân ṣunar zamâne
Ol zehri Cem de çekmiş gerdûn-ı dûn elinden

Dil ṣafḥasına baḳdum eṭrâfı cümle meşrûḥ
Bildim bu nüsḫa çıḳmış bir ẕû-fünûn elinden

Kef kef geçer deñizler 'aşḳ ile mużṭarib-ḥâl
Dağlar şikâyet eyler ṣabr ü sükûn elinden

Ferhâda öz vücûdı ṭağlarca ḥâ'il idi
Yoḫsa degüldi 'âciz ol Bîsütûn elinden

Ḫâlî degül göñülden hergiz o zülf ü şâne
Kârum ḳatı müşevveş ḥâl-i derûn elinden

Ehl-i ṣafâ dilinden bir şi'r dedi Nev'î
Geh şükr ü geh şikâyet 'aşḳ-ı cünûn elinden

31. *Help me, oh sapling*

Meded ey gülşen-i nâzuñ nihâl-i lâle-ruḫsârı
Leṭâfet sebze-zârınuñ tezerv-i kebk-reftârı
Vefâsuz dil-rübâlar 'askerinüñ şâh-ı serdârı
Ağardı giryeden luṭf it esirge çeşm-i ḫûn-bârı
Gözümüñ nûrı göñlümüñ sürûrı 'ömrümüñ varı
Bizümle dôst olmazsañ 'adâvet eyleme bârî

Revâ mıdur bu ey şâh-ı serîr-i milk-i istiğnâ
Raḳîb-i rû-siyeh sâyeñ gibi saña ola hem-tâ
Yaşum gibi ayaḳlarda ḳalam ben 'âşıḳ-ı şeydâ
Ġam-ı zülfüñle oldum ağlamaḳdan şimdi nâ-bînâ
Gözümüñ nûrı gönlümüñ sürûrı 'ömrümüñ varı
Bizümle dôst olmazsañ 'adâvet eyleme bârî

Ser-i kûyuñdan özge Ka'be-i maḳṣûda râhum yoḳ
Ḳapuñdan ġayrı bu deyr-i fenâda secdegâhum yoḳ
Kime yalvarayın ben senden artuḳ dâd-ḫâhum yoḳ
Beni öldürdi ġam ey cevri çoḳ cürmüm günâhum yoḳ
Gözümüñ nûrı gönlümüñ sürûrı 'ömrümüñ varı
Bizümle dôst olmazsañ 'adâvet eyleme bârî

Naṣîb olmazsa vuṣlat ey sipihr-i 'izzetüñ mâhı
Iraḳdan merḥabâñ ile ḳanâ'at eylerüz gâhî
Esirge alma âhumla yaşum isterseñ Allah'ı
Unutma ẓulmet-i şâm-ı ġamuñda cân-ı güm-râhı
Gözümüñ nûrı gönlümüñ sürûrı 'ömrümüñ varı
Bizümle dôst olmazsañ 'adâvet eyleme bârî

Saña ġamz itse Nev'î bî-günâhı dôstum düşmen
Ümîd itmezdüm anı gül gibi gûş eylemek senden
Ne bâ'iṡ oldı bilmem yüz çevirdüñ bülbülüñden sen
Ne çâre fürḳatüñ yazu imiş başumda evvelden
Gözümüñ nûrı göñlümüñ sürûrı 'ömrümüñ varı
Bizümle dôst olmazsañ 'adâvet eyleme bârî

Bâḳî (Mânî)

32. *That tyrant*

'Aceb ol şâh-ı ẓâlim 'âşıḳuñ ḫûnına ḳanmaz mı
Bu deñlü nâle bir gün aña te'ṡîr ide ṣanmaz mı
Ḳıyâmet yoḳ mıdur ṣanur yâḫôd ḥaşre inanmaz mı
Beni cândan uṣandurdı cefâdan yâr uṣanmaz mı
Felekler yandı âhumdan murâdum şem'i yanmaz mı

Dem-â-dem ol gül-i ḫandân ider cân bülbülin seyrân
Naṣîbi illerüñ iḥsân benüm endûh-i bî-pâyân
İder ġayrıları ḫandân beni biñ derd ile giryân
Ḳamu bîmârına cânân devâ-yı derd ider iḥsân
Niçün ḳılmaz baña dermân beni bîmârı ṣanmaz mı

Duyuldu râz-ı pinhânum dükenmez âh ü efġânum
Yıḳıldı ḳalb-i vîrânum ferâġat üzredür cânum
Aḳar eşk-i firâvânum çıḳar eflâke nâlânum
Şeb-i firḳat yanar cânum döker ḳan çeşm-i giryânum
Uyarur ḫalḳı efġânum ḳara baḫtum uyanmaz mı

Olaldan dilde ġam mesken ḥużûrum gitdi 'âlemden
Görinür çeşmüme gülşen belâ-yı 'aşḳ ile külḫan
Nice demler o sîmîn-ten ḫaber almadı dâmîden
Ġamum pinhân ṭutardum ben didiler yâre ḳıl rûşen
Disem ol bî-vefâ bilmem inanur mı inanmaz mı

Firâḳ-ı 'âriż-ı gül-bû ider cân bülbülin ṣayru
Gözümden devr derer incû figânumdan cihân memlû
Ruḫuñ gördükde ey meh-rû sirişküm ṣaçılur her sû
Gül-i ruḫsâruña ḳarşu gözümden ḳanlu aḳar ṣu
Ḥabîbüm faṣl-ı güldür bu aḳan ṣular bulanmaz mı

Ruḫuñ seyr eyleyen ġâfil olursa mest-i *lâ-ya'ḳil*
Degildir sevmemek ḳâbil maḥabbet itmemek müşkil
Ne deñlü olsa sengîn dil ṣaraḳdı meyl ider ḥâṣıl

Degüldüm ben saña mâ'il sen itdün 'aḳlumı zâ'il
Baña ṭa'n eyleyen ġâfil seni görgeç untanmaz mı

Ḳuluñ Bâḳî (Mânî) şeker-ḫâdur lebüñ vaṣfında gûyâdur
İşi seyr ü temâşâdur ser-i kûyüñda ġavġâdur
Gedâ-yı bî-ser ü pâdur ġarîb-i deşt-i bîmâdur
Fużûlî rind-i şeydâdur hemîşe ḫalḳa rüsvâdur
Ṣoruñ kim bu ne sevdâdur o sevdâdan uṣanmaz mı

🎴 Bâḳî

33. *Oh beloved, since the origin*

Ezelden şâh-ı 'aşḳıñ bende-i fermânıyuz cânâ
Maḥabbet mülkinüñ sulṭân-ı 'âlî-şânıyuz cânâ

Seḥâb-ı luṭfuñ âbın teşne-dillerden dirîġ itme
Bu deştüñ baġrı yanmış lâle-i nu'mânıyuz cânâ

Zamâne bizde gevher sezdigiçün dil-ḫırâş eyler
Anuñçün baġrımuz ḫûndur ma'ârif kânıyuz cânâ

Mükedder ḳılmasun gerd-i küdûret çeşme-i cânı
Bilürsün âb-ı rûy-ı milket-i 'Oṣmânıyuz cânâ

Cihânı câm-ı naẓmum şi'r-i Bâḳî gibi devr eyler
Bu bezmüñ şimdi biz de câmî-i devrânıyuz cânâ

34. *The fountain of my spirit*

Âb-ı Ḥayât-ı la'lüñe ser-çeşme-i cân teşnedür
Ṣun cür'a-i câm-ı lebüñ kim Âb-ı Ḥayvân teşnedür

Cân la'lin eyler ârzû yâr içmek ister ḳanumı
Yâ Rab ne vâdîdür bu kim cân teşne cânân teşnedür

Âb-ı zülâl-ı vaṣluña muḥtâc tenhâ dil degil
Ḥâk üzre ḳalmış ḫuşk-leb deryâ-yı 'ummân teşnedür

Bezm-i ġamuñda cân u dil yandı yaḳıldı sâḳiyâ
Depret elüñ sür ayaġın meclisde yârân teşnedür

Cânâ zülâl-i vaṣluñı aġyâr umar 'uşşâḳ umar
Âb-ı zülâl-i raḥmete kâfir müselmân teşnedür

Giryân ol Leylî-veş n'ola ṣaḥrâya ṣalsa Bâḳî'yi
Mecnûn'uñ âb-ı çeşmine ḫâk-i beyâbân teşnedür

35. *If only the bud would open*

Açılsa ġonca mânend-i leb-i la'l-i nigâr olsa
Şaçılsa ḫurde-i pîrûze ṣaḥrâ sebze-zâr olsa

Getürsem pendini bir bir yerine vâ'iẓ-i şehrüñ
Bahâr olsa nigâr olsa şarâb-ı ḫôş-güvâr olsa

Elinden sâḳî-yi dehrüñ ne ḳanlar yuṭduġum her dem
Açılsa lâle-veş dâġ-ı derûnum âşikâr olsa

N'olur bî-raḥm sengîn-dil cefâ-ḫû tond serkeşden
Göñüller iñlese şûḫ olsa dilber şîvekâr olsa

Piyâle dönse ey Bâḳî yine gül devrini görsek
Kenâr-ı cûda 'ayş itdükçe dilber der-kenâr olsa

36. *Sparks from my heart*

Çıḳar eflâke derûnum şereri döne döne
Dökülür ḫâke yaşum ḳaṭreleri döne döne

'Âşıḳ-ı ḫaste-dilüñ niteki fânûs-ı ḫayâl
Nâr-ı 'aşḳuñla yanupdur cigeri döne döne

Bister-i ġamda gözüm giceler uyḫu görmez
İderin ṣubḥa degin nâleleri döne döne

Zevraḳ-âsâ ġam-ı 'aşḳuñla yaşum girdâbı
Ġarḳ idüpdür ṣanemâ çeşm-i teri döne döne

'Îd-gâhuñ göreyin iñlesün ol dôlâbı
K'ile seyr itdürür ol sîmberi döne döne

Dîde-i encüme küḥl olmaġıçün eflâke
Gird-bâd ile çıḳar ḫâk-i deri döne döne

Ṭolaşaldan ruḫı şem'ine dil-i ser-geşte
Yaḳdı pervâne-ṣıfat bâl ü peri döne döne

Ḳaṭre-i eşkine öykündi diyü Bâḳî'nüñ
Çarḫ ḥakkâki yonupdür güheri döne döne

37. *Your rebellious glance*

Müje ḫaylin dizer ol ġamze-i fettân ṣaf ṣaf
Gûyiyâ cenge ṭurur nîze-güẕârân ṣaf ṣaf

Seni seyr itmegiçün reh-güẕer-i gülşende
İki cânibde ṭurur serv-i ḫırâmân ṣaf ṣaf

Leşger-i eşk-i firâvân ile ceng itmegiçün
Gönderür mevclerin lücce-i 'ummân ṣaf ṣaf

Gökde efġân iderek ṣanma geçer ḫayl-i küleng
Çekilür kûyuña murġân-ı dil ü cân ṣaf ṣaf

Câmi' içre göre tâ kimlere hem-zânûsın
Şekl-i saḳḳâda gezer dîde-i giryân ṣaf ṣaf

Ehl-i dil derd ü ġamuñ ni'metine müstaġraḳ
Dizilürler keremüñ ḫânına mihmân ṣaf ṣaf

Vaṣf-ı ḳaddüñle ḫırâm itse 'alem gibi ḳalem
Leşger-i saṭrı çeker defter ü dîvân ṣaf ṣaf

Kûyuñ eṭrafına 'uşşâḳ dizilmiş gûyâ
Ḥarem-i Ka'bede her cânibe erkân ṣaf ṣaf

Ḳadrüñi seng-i muṣallâda bilüp ey Bâḳî
Ṭurup el baġlayalar ḳarşuña yârân ṣaf ṣaf

Yaḥyâ

38. *Come wander through the city*

Gel ayaḳ seyrini ḳıl nûş it meyi peymâneden
'Âḳil olanlar ḳaçar mı zâhidâ meyḫâneden

Bezme ebr-i âhum eşkümden ṭolular yaġdurur
Aġlayup âh eylesem ol gözleri mestâneden

Göñlümüzden ṭoġmadı bir gice ol bedr-i tamâm
Ben ḳara günlü n'olaydı ṭoġmayaydum anadan

Bir yalıñ yüzlü göricek cân atar pür-şevḳ olup
Yanmaġı pervâneden ögren göñül pervâneden

İntiẓâr ile hemân ey ḫaste-dil cânum çıḳa
Şîve vü nâz ile ol âfet çıḳınca ḫâneden

Ḳanı ol dem bir sehî-ḳâmetle hem-pehlû olup
Sînemi ḳılsam ṣadef ol gevher-i yekdâneden

Yârdan bir bûse cerr eyler didi Yaḥyâ göñül
Bilmiş ol uṣlu ḫaberdür bu dil-i dîvâneden

39. *Poetry holds the written veil*

Yüzine ṭutmuş niḳâb-ı ḫaṭṭı Yûsuf-vâr şi'r
Şîvesindendür ḥicâb ile ider güftâr şi'r

Çekdügüm derdi bilürdi nâlemi gûş eylese
Ḥâlüme vâkıf olurdı oḳusa dildâr şi'r

Yâruñ ebrûsı gibi baḥr-i melâḥat mevcidür
Yaraşur olursa manẓûr-ı ülü'l-ebṣâr şi'r

Pâre pâre itdi endâmın yaḳasın çâk idüp
Ṭûr-ı Mûsâ gibi görmişdür meger dîdâr şi'r

'Âşıḳ-ı dîvâneye dîvanum oldı ḥasb-i ḥâl
Ehl-i derdüñ derdini eyler müdâm iş'âr şi'r

Bir lisân-ı ġaybdur gûyâ anuñ her mıṣra'ı
'Âlem-i ma'nâdan eyler kendüyi iẓhâr şi'r

Şevḳ ile Yaḥyâ gibi güller yaḳasın çâk ider
Söylesem ol ḳâmeti mevzûn içün her bâr şi'r

Rûḥî

40. *Curse the thorns of fate*

Yûf ḫârına dehrüñ gül ü gül-zârına hem yûf
Aġyârına yûf yâr-ı cefâ-kârına hem yûf

Bir 'ayş ki mevḳûf ola keyfiyyet-i ḫamre
'Ayyâşına yûf ḫamrına ḫammârına hem yûf

Çün ehl-i vücûduñ yeri ṣaḥrâ-yı 'ademdür
Yûf ḳâfile vü ḳâfile-sâlârına hem yûf

Ẕî-ḳıymet olunca nidelim câh ü celâli
Yûf anı ṣatan dûna ḫarîdârına hem yûf

'Âlemde ki bengîler ola vâḳıf-ı esrâr
Ḥayrânına yûf anlaruñ esrârına hem yûf

'Ârif kim ola müdbir ü nâdân ola muḳbil
İḳbâline yûf 'âlemiñ idbârına hem yûf

Çarḫ-ı felegüñ sa'dine vü naḥsine la'net
Kevkeblerinüñ s̱âbit ü seyyârına hem yûf

Çün oldu ḥarâm ehl-i Ḥaḳ'a dünye vü 'uḳbâ
Cehd eyle ne 'uḳbâ ola ḫâṭırda ne dünyâ

Şeyḫülislâm Yaḥyâ

41. *Saki, offer the cup*

Ṣun sâġarı sâḳî baña mestâne disünler
Uṣlanmadı gitdi gör o dîvâne disünler

Peymânesini her kişi doldurmada bunda
Şimden gerü bu meclise meyḫâne disünler

Dil ḫânesini yıḳ ḳoma ṭaş üstüne bir ṭaş
Sen yap anı iller aña vîrâne disünler

Göñlüñde senüñ ġayr ü sivâ ṣûreti neyler
Lâyıḳ mı bu kim Ka'be'ye büthâne disünler

Yaḥyâ'nuñ olup sözleri hep sırr-ı maḥabbet
Yârân işidüp söyleme yabane disünler

42. *Let the hypocrites*

Mescidde riyâ-pîşeler itsün ḳo riyâyı
Meyḫâneye gel kim ne riyâ var ne mürâyî

Ey câm-ı ṣafâ ṭâlibi bî-hûde özenme
Cem'le bile defn eylediler câm-ı ṣafâyı

Redd itmiş idi yâr raḳîbi işiginden
Gelmiş o siyeh-rû yine gördüñ mü belâyı

Def' idemedik ceyş-i ġamı sa'y idegördük
Tedbîr ne mümkin boza taḳdîr-i Ḫudâ'yı

Yaḥyâ nice âvâre-i 'aşḳ olmayayın ben
Dilberse güzel dilse nihâyetde havâyî

43. *Is there no heart*

'Aşḳa ḳâbil dil mi yoḳ şehr içre yâ dilber mi yoḳ
Mest yoḳ meclisde bilmem mey mi yoḳ sâġar mı yoḳ

Ġonca-i dil açılup ḫâṭır nice şâd olmaya
Bâġda güller mi yoḳ gülşende bülbüller mi yoḳ

Görmezüz bir dil ki ṭûṭî gibi güftâr eyleye
Söyledür mi yoḳ cihânda bilmezin söyler mi yoḳ

Sengden dil kem mi yâ seng-i siyâhı la'l ider
Âfitâb-ı feyż-baḫşâ-yı bülend-aḫter mi yoḳ

Niçün ebkâr-ı ma'ânî beslemez erbâb-ı naẓm
Yoḫsa Yaḥyâ gibi üstâd-ı süḫan-perver mi yoḳ

Nef'î

44. *That black drunken eye*

Meyḫâne-i nâz olmış o çeşm-i siyeh-mest
Her gûşe-i pür-fitnesi bir ḫâb-geh-i mest

Ḫışm ile çeker ġamzesi peymâne-i nâzı
Âşûb-ı cihân olsa n'ola her nigeh-i mest

Bezm-i Cem'e revnaḳ viremez olmayıcaḳ tâ
Cârûb-ı der-i meykede perr-i külâh-i mest

Mestâne-i niyâz eylese Nef'î n'ola yâra
Ma'żûr-ı kirâm-ı 'uḳalâdur güneh-i mest

Almış ele Rüstem gibi şemşîrini ġamze
Olmış saña müjgânları ṣaf ṣaf sipeh-i mest

45. *Those who painted my portrait*

Yazanlar peykerim destimde bir peymâne yazmışlar
Görüp mest-i mey-i 'aşḳ olduġum mestâne yazmışlar

Baña teklîf-i zühd etmezdi idrâk olsa zâhidde
Yazıḳlar kim anı 'âḳil beni dîvâne yazmışlar

Degildir gözlerinde sâye-i müjgânı 'uşşâḳıñ
Ḫaṭıñ resmin beyâżı dîde-i giryâna yazmışlar

Benim 'âşıḳ ki rüsvâlıḳla ṭutdu şöhretim şehri
Yazanlar ḳıṣṣa-i Mecnûnu hep yabana yazmışlar

Nice ẓâhirdir ey Nef'î sözüñden dildeki sûzuñ
Yazınca nüsḫa-i şi'riñ ḳalemler yana yazmışlar

46. *The heart is both the cup and the wine*

Hem ḳadeh hem bâde hem bir şûḫ sâḳîdir göñül
Ehl-i 'aşḳıñ ḥâṣılı ṣâḥib-meẕâḳıdır göñül

Bir nefes dîdâr içün biñ cân fedâ etsem n'ola
Nice demlerdir esîr-i iştiyâḳıdır göñül

Dildedir mihriñ ḳo ḫâk olsun yoluñda cân ü ten
Ben ölürsem 'âlem-i ma'nîde bâḳîdir göñül

Ẕerredir ammâ ki tâb-ı âfitâb-ı 'aşḳ ile
Rûzigârıñ şemse-i tâḳ u revâḳıdır göñül

Etse Nef'î n'ola ger göñliyle dâ'im bezm-i ḫâṣ
Hem ḳadeh hem bâde hem bir şûḫ sâḳîdir göñül

Şeyḫülislâm Bahâyî

47. *Oh cry, what are you doing*

Dağıttın ḫâb-ı nâz-ı yârı ey feryâd neylersin
İdip fitneyle dünyâyı ḫarâb-âbâd neylersin

Dil-i mecrûḥuma raḥm eyle ḳalsın dâm-ı zülfiñde
Şikeste-bâl olan murġu idüp âzâd neylersin

İdersin gerçi her derde ṭabîbim devâ ammâ
Cünûn-ı ehl-i 'aşḳ olınca mâder-zâd neylersin

Varup gîsû vü zülf-i yârı biri birine ḳattıñ
Yine bir fitne taḥrîḳ eylediñ ey bâd neylersin

Şehîd-i tîġ-i 'aşḳ-ı yârdır ser-cümle-i 'âlem
Urup şemşîre dest ey ġamze-i cellâd neylersin

Güzel taṣvîr idersin ḥâl ü ḫaṭṭ-ı dilberi ammâ
Füṣûn u fitneye geldükde ey Behzâd neylersin

Bahâyî-veş degilsin kâbil-i feyż ü ṣafâ sen de
Tekellüf ber-ṭaraf ey ḫâṭır-ı nâ-şâd neylersin

Nâbî

48. *When we watch the spinning of the sky*

Sipihriñ gerdişin yâd eyleyip aḫterden el çekdik
Yemiñ çîn-i cebînin seyr idip gevherden el çekdik

Bu bezmiñ ṭâlib olduḳ biz daḫi ṣahbâsına ammâ
Görüp sâḳîde rûy-i imtinân sâġardan el çekdik

Ṭuyup meylin ḫazâna şâhid-i gülzârı terk itdik
Görüp destâr-ı aġyâr üzre verd-i terden el çekdik

Olup dil bûte gibi tâb-ı hicrân ile germ-ülfet
Temennâ-yı viṣâl-i yâr-ı sîmîn-berden el çekdik

Ṣafâ-yı ḫâṭır üzre olmayan iḥsânı neylerler
Görüp sûz-ı derûnın micmerüñ 'anberden el çekdik

Virip ser-rişte-i ġavġâya fayṣal baḫt u ṭâli'le
Ferâġat eyledik şemşîrden ḫançerden el çekdik

Gelû-yı şîşe ile pây-ı ḫumla eglenip Nâbî
Girîbân-ı hevesden dâmen-i dilberden el çekdik

49. *In the garden of time and destiny*

Bâġ-ı dehriñ hem ḫazânın hem bahârın görmüşüz
Biz neşâṭıñ da ġamıñ da rûzgârın görmüşüz

Çoḳ da maġrûr olma kim meyḫâne-i iḳbâlde
Biz hezârân mest-i maġrûruñ ḫumârın görmüşüz

Ṭop-ı âh-ı inkisâra pây-dâr olmaz yine
Kişver-i câhıñ nice sengîn ḥiṣârın görmüşüz

Bir ḫurûşiyle eder biñ ḫâne-i iḳbâli pest
Ehl-i derdiñ seyl-i eşk-i inkisârın görmüşüz

Bir ḫadeng-i cân-güdâz-ı âhdır sermâyesi
Biz bu meydânıñ nice çâbük-süvârın görmüşüz

Bir gün eyler dest-beste pây-gâhı cây-gâh
Bî-'aded maġrûr-ı ṣadr-ı i'tibârın görmüşüz

Kâse-i deryûzeye tebdîl olur câm-ı murâd
Biz bu bezmiñ Nâbiyâ çoḳ bâde-ḫârın görmüşüz

50. *At the gathering of joy*

Bezm-i ṣafâya sâġar-ı ṣaḥbâ gelir gider
Gûyâ ki cezr ü medd ile deryâ gelir gider

Açıldıġuñ ḫaber virür aġyâra gül gibi
Her dem bize nesîm-i sebük-pâ gelir gider

Olmaz yine marîż-i maḫabbet şifâ-pezîr
Rûy-ı zemîne bir daḫi Îsâ gelir gider

Sulṭân-ı ġam neşîmen idelden derûnumu
Ṣaḥrâ-yı ḳalbe leşker-i sevdâ gelir gider

Bir gün dimez o şûḫ ki âyâ murâdı ne
Çoḳdan bu kûya Nâbi-i şeydâ gelir gider

Nâ’ilî

51. *We are the snake*

Mârız ki ‘aṣâ-yı kef-i Mûsâda nihânız
Mâr añlama mûruz ki kef-i pâda nihânız

Görmez bizi âyînede ger ‘aks-dih olsaḳ
Pîş-i naẓar-ı ‘aḳl-ı ḫôd-ârâda nihânız

Güncâyişimiz dîde-i Mecnûnadır ancaḳ
Nîreng-i cemâliz ruḫ-ı Leylâda nihânız

Elmâs ise de kârger olmaz bize merhem
Ol dâġ-ı cünûnuz ki süveydâda nihânız

Mûsâ göremez Ṭûr u şecerde bizi bi’llâh
Biz şu‘le-i sîmâ-yı tecellâda nihânız

Derdiz ki devâ şîfte-i ṣıḥḥatimizdir
‘Aşḳız ki nihân-ḫâne-i sevdâda nihânız

Destiñde daġal mühreyiz ey çarḫ-ı müşa‘biẕ
Her laḥẓada biñ çeşm-i temâşâda nihânız

Biz Nâ’iliyâ sözde füsûn-kâr-ı ḫayâliz
Elfâẓda peydâ dil-i ma‘nâda nihânız

52. *My tears became desire*

Oldu eşkim gülşen-ârâ-yı heves cûlar gibi
Aḳdı göñlüm bir nihâl-i ‘işveye ṣular gibi

Ṭurfa Mecnûnam ki pey-der-pey ḫayâl-i çeşm-i yâr
Devr eder eṭrâfımı ser-geşte âhûlar gibi

Hep siyeh-pûş oldular ḳaṣd-ı şebîḫûn-ı dile
Girdiler müjgânlarıñ bir renge câdûlar gibi

Bir nihâl-i âhdur ḳaddiñ hevâsıyla göñül
Ṣaḥn-ı gülşende ḫırâmân serv-i dil-cûlar gibi

Âb ü tâb-ı ṭal‘at-ı ebkâr-ı naẓmıñ Nâ’ilî
Ṭa‘n eder âyine-i ḫurşîde meh-rûlar gibi

53. *Since the thunderbolt of disaster*

Tâ cilve-geh-i berk-i belâ ḫarmenimizdir
Ḫâkister-i dûzaḫ çemen-i gülşenimizdir

Vâ sûḫtegân-ı ḥarem-i Ka'be-i 'aşḳız
Peyġûle-i ġam-ḫâne-yi dil meskenimizdir

Ol 'âşıḳ-ı pâkız ki serâ-perde-i 'iṣmet
Âlûde-i ḫûn-ı dil olan dâmenimizdir

Biz sâḳî-i ḫûn-ı cigeriz ġamze-yi dilber
Peymâne be-kef serḫôş-ı derd-efgenimizdir

Sûr-efgen olan Nâ'iliyâ kişver-i nażma
Ḥükm-i raḳam-ı ḫâme-i câdû-fenimizdir

54. *What witch are you*

Baġlanur zülfüñe diller nice câdûsun sen
Ḥarem-i Ka'beyi dâm eyleyen âhûsun sen

Döndi Baġdâd-ı dile kişver-i cân 'ahdiñde
Müjeler leşker-i Tâtâr u Ḫulâgûsun sen

Cân virür Âb-ı Ḥayât-ı lebine Ḫıżr u Mesîḥ
Teşnesi rûḥ-ı Sikender bir içim ṣusun sen

Zîb-i nüh-ravża-i eflâksin ey mihr ammâ
Beñzemezsin ruḫ-ı yâra gül-i ḫod-rûsun sen

Olur ebrûları pür-çîn-i ġażab Nâ'iliyâ
Dehen-i yâra diñildükçe ser-i mûsun sen

Neşâṭî

55. *We are desire*

Şevḳız ki dem-i bülbül-i şeydâda nihânız
Ḫûnuz ki dil-i ġonca-i ḥamrâda nihânız

Biz cism-i niẕâr üzre döküp dâne-i eşki
Çün rişte-i cân gevher-i ma'nâda nihânız

Olsaḳ n'ola bî-nâm u nişân şöhre-i 'âlem
Biz dil gibi bir ṭurfa mu'ammâda nihânız

Maḥrem yine her ḥâlimize bâd-ı ṣabâdır
Dâ'im şiken-i zülf-i dil-ârâda nihânız

Hem gül gibi rengînî-i ma'nâ ile ẓâhir
Hem neş'e gibi ḥâlet-i ṣahbâda nihânız

Geh ḫâme gibi şekve-ṭırâz-ı ġam-ı 'aşḳız
Geh nâle gibi ḫâme-i şekvâda nihânız

Etdik o ḳadar ref'-i ta'ayyün ki Neşâṭî
Âyine-i pür-tâb-ı mücellâda nihânız

56. *You're gone—I'm alone*

Gitdiñ ammâ ki ḳoduñ ḥasret ile cânı bile
İstemem sensiz olan ṣoḥbet-i yârânı bile

Bâġa sensiz varamam çeşmime âteş görünür
Gül-i ḫandânı degil serv-i ḫırâmânı bile

Sîneden derd ile bir âh edeyim kim dönsün
'Aksine çarḫ-ı felek mihr-i dıraḫşânı bile

Devr-i meclis baña girdâb-ı belâdır sensiz
Mey-i raḫşânı degil sâġar-ı gerdânı bile

Ḫâr-i firḳatle Neşâṭî-i ḥazînin vâ ḥayf
Dâmen-i ülfeti çâḳ oldu girîbânı bile

57. *The sky's face has turned dark*

Gögerdi rûy-ı hevâ ẓâhir oldu ṣanma seḥâb
Çemende berf ile bâz-ı sefîde döndü ġurâb

Ne naḳş göstere âyâ müşa'biẕ-i sermâ
Ki hemçü âyîne yaḫ-beste oldu safḥa-i âb

Cihân ki yek-sere yaḫ-bestedür n'ola şimdi
Olursa bezmde yaḫ-pûş âteşîn mey-i nâb

Nedir bu şiddet-i sermâ ki ṣanma ḫâkister
Giyirdi aḫker-i sûzâna ḫavfden sincâb

Gezend-i bâd-ı şitâdan Neşâṭiyâ şimdi
Seḥâbı perde ṭutar şem'-i mihr-i 'âlem-tâb

Nedîm

58. *At the gathering of desire*

Bir şeker-ḫand ile bezm-i şevḳa câm ettiñ beni
Nîm ṣun peymâneyi sâḳî tamâm ettiñ beni

Şu'le-i serv çıḳar ḫâkimden ol yerlerde kim
Pây-mâl-i tevsen-i âteş-ḫırâm ettiñ beni

Nükhet-i gîysû ile geldiñ bize âh ey nesîm
Ṭurra-i sünbül-ṣıfat âşüfte-kâm ettiñ beni

Cilve-i ḥüsnüñle her mûyum perî-ḫîz olmada
'Aşḳ ile ser-tâ-ḳadem âyîne-fâm ettiñ beni

Böyle ser-mest ü ḫarâb etme Nedîm-i zârıñı
Nîm ṣun peymâneyi sâḳî tamâm ettiñ beni

59. *When the east wind*

Ṣabâ ki dest ura ol zülfe müşk-i nâb ḳoḳar
Açarsa 'uḳde-i pîrâhenin gül-âb ḳoḳar

Ne berg-i güldür o leb çignesem şeker ṣanırım
Ne ġoncadir o dehen ḳoḳlasam şarâb ḳoḳar

'Aceb ne bezmde şeb-zinde-dâr-ı ṣoḥbet idiñ
Henûz nergis-i mestinde bûy-ı ḫâb ḳoḳar

Nikâb ile göremezken biz anı vâ ḥayfâ
Raḳîb o gerden-i sîmîni bî-nikâb ḳoḳar

Seni meger ki gül-efsûn-ı nâz terletmiş
Ki sîb-i ġabġabıñ ey ġonca-leb gül-âb ḳoḳar

Nedîm sen yine ma'nî-şikâflıḳta mısın
Ki nevk-i ṭîğ-ı ḳalem ḫûn-ı intiḫâb ḳoḳar

60. *As the morning wind blows*

Esdikçe bâd-ı ṣubḥ perîşânsın ey göñül
Beñzer esîr-i ṭurra-ı cânânsın ey göñül

Gül mevsiminde tevbe-i meyden benim gibi
Ẓannım budur ki sen de peşîmânsın ey göñül

Eşkimde böyle şu'le nedendir meger ki sen
Çün sûz u tâb giryede pinhânsın ey göñül

Ben saña bâde içme güzel sevme mi dedim
Benden niçin bu gûne girîzânsın ey göñül

Bîgânedir mu'âmeleñiz 'aḳl ü hûş ile
Gûyâ derûn-ı sînede mihmânsın ey göñül

Âyîne oldu bir nigeh-i ḥayretiñle âb
Billâh ne saḫt âteş-i sûzânsın ey göñül

Ḥac yollarında meş'ale-i kârbân gibi
Erbâb-ı 'aşḳ içinde nümâyânsın ey göñül

Feyż-âşiyânı mihr-i hüner cilvegâhsın
Ṣubḥ-ı bahâr-ı şevḳe girîbânsın ey göñül

Peymâne-i maḥabbet ṣundum Nedîme çün
Luṭf eyle alma câmı biraz ḳansın ey göñül

61. *Take yourself to the rose-garden*

Gülzâra ṣalın mevsimidir geşt ü güẕârıñ
Ver ḥükmünü ey serv-i revân köhne bahârıñ
Dök zülfüñü semmûr giyinsin ḳo 'iẕârıñ
Ver ḥükmünü ey serv-i revân köhne bahârıñ

Bülbülleriñ ister seni ey ġonca-dehen gel
Gül gitdigini añmayalum gülşene sen gel
Pâmâl-i şitâ olmadan iḳlîm-i çemen gel
Ver ḥükmünü ey serv-i revân köhne bahârıñ

Ṣal ḫaṭṭ-ı siyeh-kârıñ o ruḫsâre-i âle
Semmûruñu ḳaplat bu sene ḳırmızı şâle
Al deste eger lâle bulunmazsa piyâle
Ver ḥükmünü ey serv-i revân köhne bahârıñ

Cennet gibi 'âlem yine her meyve firâvân
Sen meyve-i vaṣlın daḫi itmez misin erzân
'Uşşâḳa birer bûse idüp gizlice iḥsân
Ver ḥükmünü ey serv-i revân köhne bahârıñ

Bir mıṣrâ' işitdim yine ey şûḫ-ı dilârâ
Bir ḫôşça da bilmem ne dimek istedi ammâ
Ma'ḳûl didi ẓann iderem anı Nedîmâ
Ver ḥükmünü ey serv-i revân köhne bahârıñ

62. *Delicacy was drawn out*

Ḥaddeden geçmiş nezâket yâl ü bâl olmuş saña
Mey süzülmüş şîşeden ruḫsâr-ı âl olmuş saña

Bûy-ı gül taḳṭîr olınmış nâzın işlenmiş ucu
Biri olmuş ḫoy birisi dest-mâl olmuş saña

Siḥr ü efsûn ile dolmuştur derûnuñ ey ḳalem
Zülfü Ḥârûtuñ dimek mümkin ki nâl olmuş saña

Şöyle gerd olmuş Firengistân birikmiş bir yere
Ṣoñra gelmiş gûşe-i ebrûda ḫâl olmuş saña

Ol büt-i tersâ saña mey nûş ider misin dimiş
El-amân ey dil ne müşkil-ter su'âl olmuş saña

Sen ne câmın mestisin âyâ kimin ḫayrânısın
Kendiñ aldırdıñ göñül n'olduñ ne ḥâl olmuş saña

Lebleriñ mecrûḥ olur dendân-ı sîn-i bûseden
La'liñ öptürmek bu ḥâletle muḥâl olmuş saña

Yoḳ bu şehr içre senüñ vaṣf itdigiñ dilber Nedîm
Bir perî-ṣûret görünmüş bir ḫayâl olmuş saña

Koca Râğıb Paşa

63. *Dark thought is revealed*

Pîç u tâb-ı sîneden efkâr kendin gösterir
Cevher-i âyîneden jengâr kendin gösterir

Iżṭırâb-ı nâ-be-hengâm istemez taḥṣîl-i kâm
Mevḳi'inde bî-tekellüf kâr kendin gösterir

Ḫûb u zişt âsârıdır âyîne-i kirdâr-ı ḫalḳ
Her ne ṣûret çarḫ eder seḥḥâr kendin gösterir

Perde-i nâmûs ṣığmaz berk-i 'âlem-sûz-ı 'aşḳ
Bî-muḥâbâ teşne-i serşâr kendin gösterir

Kimseyi maḥrûm-ı feyż etmez tecellî-zâr-ı ḥüsn
Cünbiş-i kûhsârdan dîdâr kendin gösterir

Cilve-i ḥüsne mezâyâ-yı meẓâhirdür nüfûs
Her kime etse işâret yâr kendin gösterir

Böyledir Râğıb mükâfât-ı 'amel kim fi'l-meṯel
Ṣorsalar mağdûrunu ġaddâr kendin gösterir

Râsiḫ

64. *Don't lower your languid eyes*

Süzme çeşmiñ gelmesin müjgân müjgân üstüne
Urma zaḫm-ı sîneme peykân peykân üstüne

Dilde ġam var şimdilik luṭf eyle gelme ey sürûr
Olamaz bir ḫânede mihmân mihmân üstünde

Rîze-i elmâs eker her açtıġı zaḫma o şûḫ
Luṭfu var olsun eder iḥsân iḥsân üstüne

Yârdan mehcûr iken düştük diyâr-ı ġurbete
Dehr gösterdi bize hicrân hicrân üstüne

Hem mey içmez hem güzel sevmez demişler ḥaḳḳına
Eylemişler Râsiḫe bühtân bühtân üstüne

Fıṭnat

65. *In a heart*

Bir dilde kim ḫayâl-i leb-i cân-fežâsı var
Ma'nî-i rûḥ-perver-i rengîn-edâsı var

Etmez nigâh o şûḫ ḫarîdâr-ı vuṣlata
Kûyunda cân-be-kef nice biñ mübtelâsı var

Efzûni-i ḫıredle Felâṭûn-ı ḫum-nişîn
Deşt-i cünûnu geşt ile Ḳays'ın ṣafâsı var

Cevr ü cefâ mihr ü vefâ firḳate viṣâl
Her derdiñ ey göñül bu cihânda devâsı var

Elbette bir mu'âmelesi vardır 'âşıḳa
Yârıñ vefâsı yoġısa Fıṭnat cefâsı var

Esrâr Dede

66. *In the ruins*

Yapmaḳ da yapılmaḳ da meyḫânede ḳalmışdır
Âs̱âr-ı 'imâret hep vîrânede ḳalmışdır

Girdâb-ı şu'ûr içre ser-geştedir 'âḳiller
Âzâdeligin ẕevḳi dîvânede ḳalmışdır

Ṣûfî arayıp gezme beyhûde mesâcidde
Feyżiñ es̱eri şimdi ḫum-ḫânede ḳalmışdır

Da'vâsını terk itsin bülbülde fedâ yoḳdur
Bir nüktecigi 'aşḳuñ pervânede ḳalmışdır

Derd-i dilim 'arż itdim güldü didi ol kâfir
N'olmış yine Esrâra efsânede ḳalmışdır

67. *You left, but don't forget*

'Azm-i sefer etdiñ dil-i nâçârı unutma
Gittiñ güzel ammâ bu dil-efgârı unutma

Gâhîce uyandıḳça şebistân-i ṣafâda
Şol gice olan ṣoḥbet-i hemvârı unutma

Vardıḳça şeker-ḫâba girip bister-i nâza
Ne zehr içer dîde-i bîdârı unutma

Ben ṣabr edeyim derd ü ġam-ı hecriñe ammâ
Sen de güzelim etdigiñ iḳrârı unutma

Aġlatmıyacaḳdıñ yola baḳtırmıyacaḳdıñ
Ol va'de-i tekrâr-be-tekrârı unutma

Yoḳ ṭâḳatı hicrânıña luṭf eyle efendim
Dil-ḫaste-i 'aşḳıñ olan Esrâr'ı unutma

Şeyḫ Ġâlib

68. *You are my effendi*

Efendimsin cihânda i'tibârım varsa sendendir
Miyân-ı 'âşıḳânda iştihârım varsa sendendir

Benim feyż-i ḥayâtım ḥâṣılı rûḥ-ı revânımsın
Eger ser-mâye-i 'ömrümde kârım varsa sendendir

Viren bu ṣûret-i mevhûma revnaḳ reng-i ḥüsnüñdür
Gülistân-ı ḫayâlim nev-bahârım varsa sendendir

Felekden ẕerre miḳdâr olmadım devrüñde rencîde
Ger ey mihr-i münevver âh u zârım varsa sendendir

Senüñ pervâne-i hicrânuñam sen şem'-i vuṣlatsın
Be-her şeb ḫâhiş-i bûs u kinârım varsa sendendir

Şehîd-i 'aşḳuñ oldum lâle-zâr-ı dâġdur sînem
Çerâġ-ı türbetim şem'-i mezârım varsa sendendir

Gören ser-geştelikde gird-bâd-ı deşt ẓann eyler
Fenâ-ender-fenâyım her ne varım varsa sendendir

Niçün âvâre ḳılduñ gevher-i ġalṭânuñ olmışken
Göñül âyînesinde bir ġubârım varsa sendendir

Şafaḳ-tâb eylediñ peymânemi ḫûn-âb ile sâḳî
Ṣabâḥ-ı ṣoḥbet-i meyde ḫumârım varsa sendendir

Sañadur ilticâsı Ġâlib'iñ yâ ḥażret-i Monlâ
Başımda bir külâh-ı iftiḫârım varsa sendendir

69. *I won't abandon you*

Fâriġ olmam eylesen yüz biñ cefâ sevdim seni
Böyle yazmış alnıma kilk-i ḳażâ sevdim seni
Ben bu sözden dönmezem devr eyledikçe nüh felek
Şâhid olsun 'aşḳıma 'arż u semâ sevdim seni

Bend-i peyvend-i dilim ebrû-yı ġaddârıñdadır
Rişte-i cem'iyyetim zülf-i siyeh-kârıñdadır
Ḫastayım ümmîd-i ṣıḥḥat çeşm-i bîmârıñdadır
Bir devâsız derde oldum mübtelâ sevdim seni

Ey hilâl-ebrû diliñ meyli sañadır doġrusu
Sû-yı miḥrâba nigâhım kec-edâdır doġrusu
Râ ḳaşıñdan inḥirâf etsem riyâdır doġrusu
Yâ sevâb olmuş veya olmuş ḫaṭâ sevdim seni

Bî-ġubârım ḥasret-i ḫaṭṭıñla ḫâk olsam yine
Ṣoḥbetiñ ruḫ ü lebiñdedir helâk olsam yine
Tîġ-i ġamzeñden kesilmem çâk çâk olsam yine
Ḥâṣılı bî-hûde cevr itme baña sevdim seni

Ġâlib-i dîvâneyim Ferhâd ü Mecnûn'a ṣalâ
Yüz çevirmem olsa dünyâ bir yaña ben bir yaña
Şem'iñe pervâneyem pervâ ne lâzımdır baña
Añlasın bîgâne bilsin âşinâ sevdim seni

70. *To me love is the flame*

'Aşḳ âteş-i tecellî-i Manṣûr'dur baña
Her çûb-ı dâr bir şecer-i Ṭûr'dur baña

Ol serv-i gül-fürûş-ı tecellî-i cilveden
Her naḫl-i âh bir şecer-i nûrdur baña

Semt-i belâda bellemişim dâr-ı vaḥdeti
Seng-i nişân minâre-i Manṣûr'dur baña

Teb-lerze-zâd gevher-i ġalṭân-ı ġurbetem
Mihr-i ṣadef ṣabâḥ-ı Nişâbûr'dur baña

Reh-dân-ı ġaybam öyle ki 'Anḳâ-yı vaḥşetiñ
'Arż-ı refâḳat ettigi meşhûrdur baña

Gûyâ ḫayâl-i ḫaṭṭ-ı lebiñle müjemde ḫûn
Bâġ-ı vefâda tûṭî-i zenbûrdur baña

Çekmem ḫumâr-ı çîn-i cebîn sergüzeşt-i Cem
Naḳş-ı gül-i piyâle-i faġfûrdur baña

Baḳmaz ṣafâ-yı sâġar-ı zerrîne mest-i 'aşḳ
Kîmyâ-yı 'ayn o nergis-i maḫmûrdur baña

Ṣad mîḫ-i tîr-i hecr ile bu sîne-i ḫarâb
Meşk-i fiġâna taḫta-i ṣanṭûrdur baña

Mânend-i jâle sâlik-i meczûb-ı 'aşḳıyam
Ġâlib demem ki şems-i Ḫudâ dûrdur baña

Sünbülzâde Vehbî

71. *Oh east wind, come*

Gel ey ṣabâ yine ol gül-'iẕârdan ne ḫaber
Ḫazân-dîde hezâr-ı bahârdan ne ḫaber

Gör ey sirişk-i revân kimlerin kinârında
O serv-i tâze-res-i 'işve-kârdan ne ḫaber

Nesîm geldi ayaġı tozuyla ey dîde
'Aceb ġubâr-ı ser-i râh-ı yârdan ne ḫaber

Diyâr-ı ḥüsnüñe gitmiş ḫayâl câsûsu
Yine o ḫusrev-i mülk-i vekârdan ne ḫaber

Berîd-i âh gidip gelmek üzre ey Vehbî
Peyâm-ı vuṣlata dâ'ir nigârdan ne ḫaber

Enderûnlu Vâṣıf

72. *The gazelles have bound their hearts*

O ḳudretten mükeḥḥal çeşmiñe dil-beste âhûlar
Nigâhıñdan oḳurlar nüsḫa-i efsûnu câdûlar

Gece sermest iken gülşende almış nükhet-i zülfüñ
Meşâm-ı ehl-i 'aşḳı eyliyor ta'ṭîr şebbûlar

Naṣîb-i aġniyâdır iḫtiyâc erbâbını naḳdi
Olur deryâya cârî ol sebepten sû-be-sû ṣular

Ḥaḳîḳatte mecâzı etme isti'mâl her yerde
Ruḫuñ ister mi ġâze hîç diler mi vesme ebrûlar

Muṣanna' bir ġazeldir Es'adı tanẓîrdir Vâṣıf
Sezâdır etseler taḥsîn bu naẓma hem suḫen-gûlar

'İzzet Mollâ

73. *Everyone knows*

Meşhûrdur ki fısḳ ile olmaz cihân ḫarâb
Eyler anı müdâhane-i 'âlimân ḫarâb

Bilmez ki iki ḳat yıḳılur kendi ḫalḳdan
İster cihân yıḳıldıġını ḫânümân-ḫarâb

A'mâl-i ḥayr süllemidir ḳaṣr-ı Cennetiñ
Mümkin mi çıḳma olsa eger nerdübân ḫarâb

Bir mevsim-i bahârına geldik ki 'âlemiñ
Bülbül ḫamûş ḥavż tehî gül-sitân ḫarâb

Çıḳmaz bahâra degmede bî-çâre 'andelîb
Pejmürde-bâl vaḳt şitâ âşiyân ḫarâb

Elbet de bir sütûnu olurdu bu ḳubbeniñ
'İzzet nihâyet olmasa kevn ü mekân ḫarâb

Teslîm olursa Pîre medeng-i irâdesi
Olmaz diyâr-ı Rûm'da bir ḫanedân ḫarâb

74. *I am a nightingale*

Hezâr-ı bâġ-ı ġamam âşiyân gözümde degil
Degil bu köhne ḳafes gülsitân gözümde degil

Perî-veşim saña maḫṣûṣ şîşe-i çeşmim
Ḫayâle gelse de ḥûr-ı cinân gözümde degil

Sevâd-ı dîde reh-i intiẓâra oldı ġubâr
O nûr çeşmi görürsem cihân gözümde degil

Ġaraż o gül-ruḫûnu yoḫsa feyż-i sirişk
Müjemde ġonca bitürse inan gözümde degil

Bu feyżi dûzaḫ-ı âh ile buldı bâġ-ı derûn
Sirişkim olsa da nehr-i cinân gözümde degil

Ḫayâlini daḫi dilden çıḳardı bâġ-ı derûn
Yer etse şimdi o serv-i revân gözümde degil

O rütbe dûd-ı firâḳ aldı dîdemi 'İzzet
Degil o çeşm-i kebûd âsumân gözümde degil

Ḳapanmasın da baña bâb-ı luṭf-ı Mevlânâ
Ḫudâ bilir bunu bir âsitân gözümde degil

Yeñişehirli 'Avnî

75. *Don't think we came to ask*

Ṣanmañ ṭaleb-i devlet ü câh itmege geldik
Biz 'âleme bir yâr içün âh itmege geldik

Ṣad ḳâfile şekvâ ile âẕâr-ı felekden
Ḫâk-i der-i cânâna penâh itmege geldik

Ser-tâ-be-ḳadem dîde olup dâġ-ı hevesden
Âyîne-i dîdâra nigâh itmege geldik

Ey ḫâce günâh ise naẓar rûy-ı bütâna
Biz 'âlem-i 'îcâda günâh itmege geldik

Ḫâr olmasın a'dâ ki bu gülzâr-ı fenâya
Bir gül ḳoparup zîb-i külâh itmege geldik

Bu meykede-i miḥnete 'Avnî gibi biz de
Ḥâl-i dil-i şeydâya tebâh itmege geldik

Ottoman Script Texts

This new edition of *Ottoman Lyric Poetry* has been expanded by the addition of some examples of our translated texts as they appear in the Ottoman version of the Arabic script. Our primary purpose in including the texts is to give students, scholars, and other interested readers some idea of the variety of sources encountered by those who work with the large corpus of Ottoman-era texts. Our examples include typeset texts, lithographs, and handwritten manuscripts. They are presented in raw form with all the printing defects, writing idiosyncrasies, and variant versions that scholars struggle with in their efforts to create accurate texts, which translators and literature scholars can use in their work. Because our samples are black and white images, we have, in a few cases, digitally reduced the darkening effects of severely yellowed paper, but otherwise we have not corrected or enhanced the samples in any way. While these examples are not intended to constitute a mini-course in Ottoman paleography, we hope that they will be of value to students of Ottoman literature and introduce them to the joys of puzzling out readings of original Arabic script texts.

Poem 1, p. 27, by Nesîmî
From the *Dîvân-ı Nesîmî*. İstanbul, 1298, p. 113. Printed.

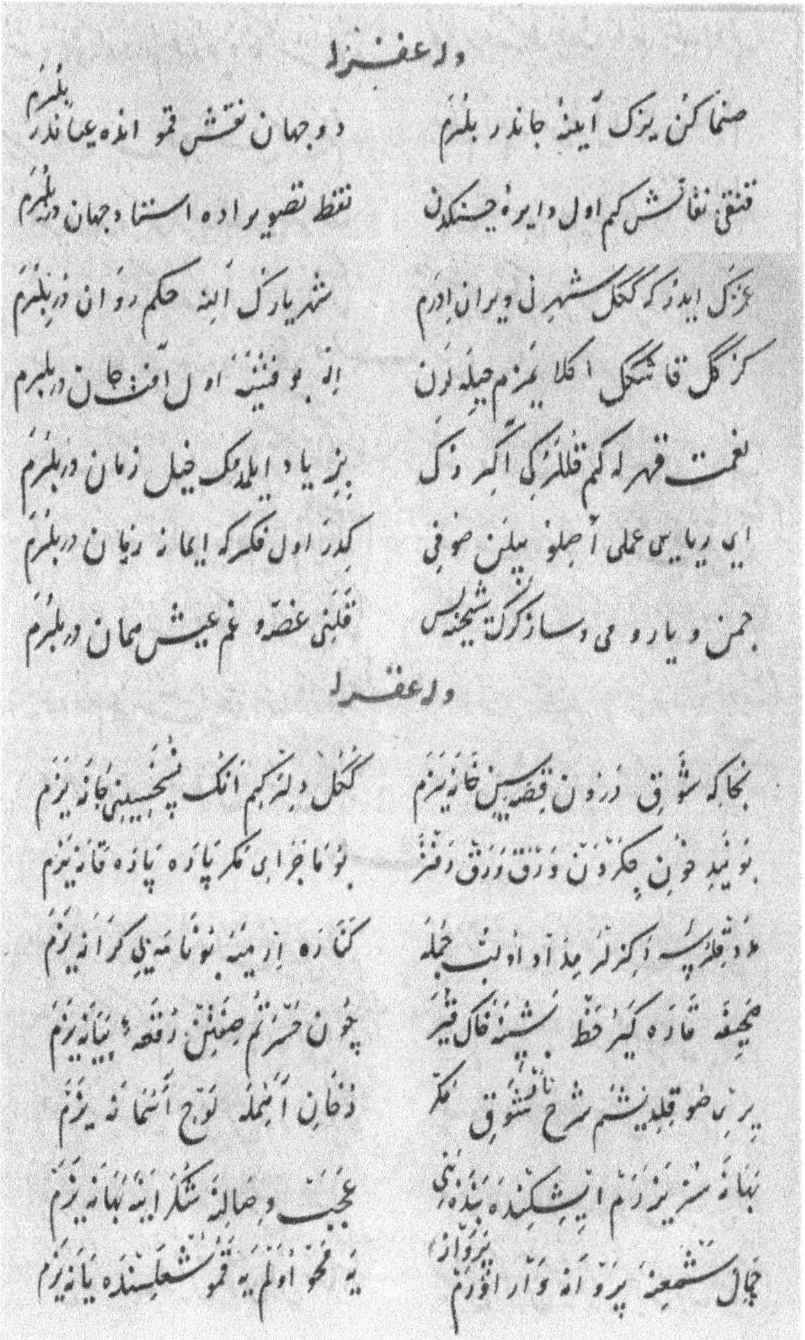

Poem 3, p. 29, by Şeyhî
From the *Şeyhi Divanı* edited by Ali Nihad Tarlan.
İstanbul: Maarif Matbaası, 1942, pp. 131–32. Facsimile.

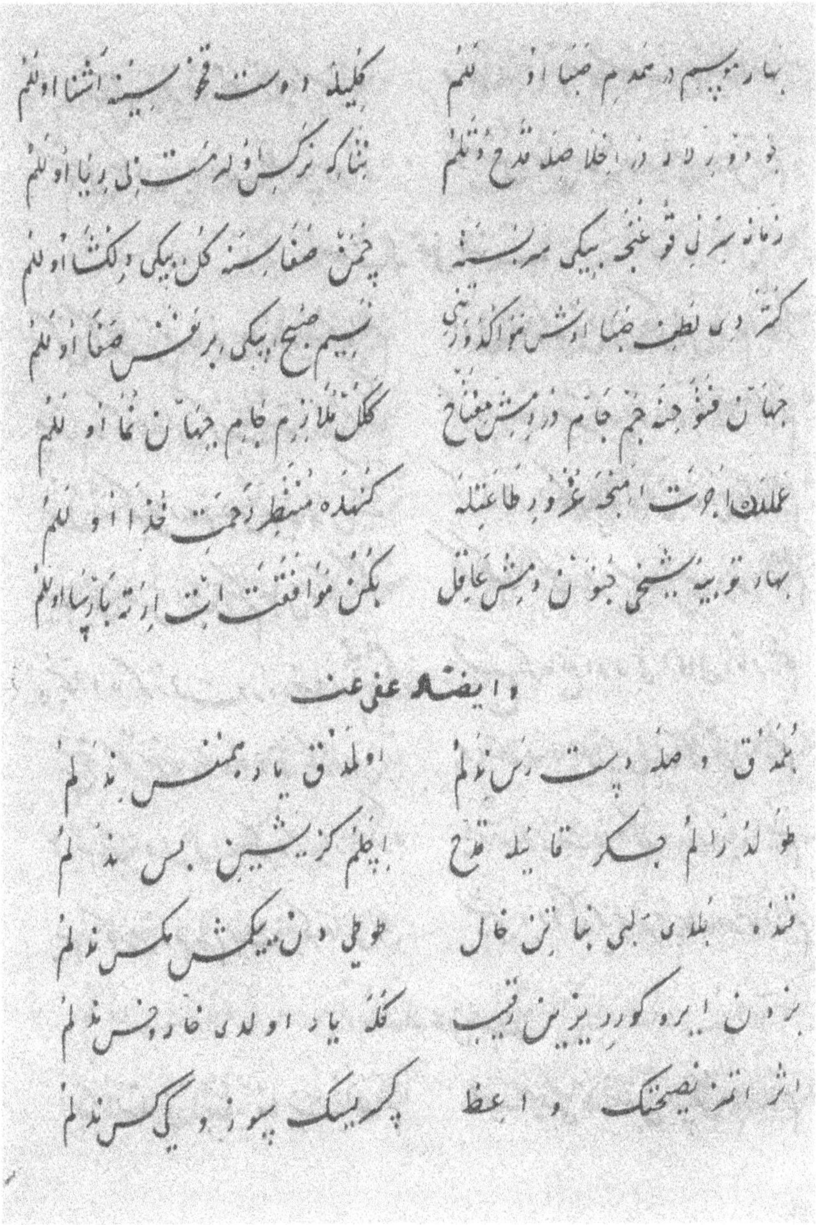

Poem 4, p. 31, by Şeyhî
From the *Şeyhi Divanı* edited by Ali Nihad Tarlan.
İstanbul: Maarif Matbaası, 1942, p. 128. Facsimile.

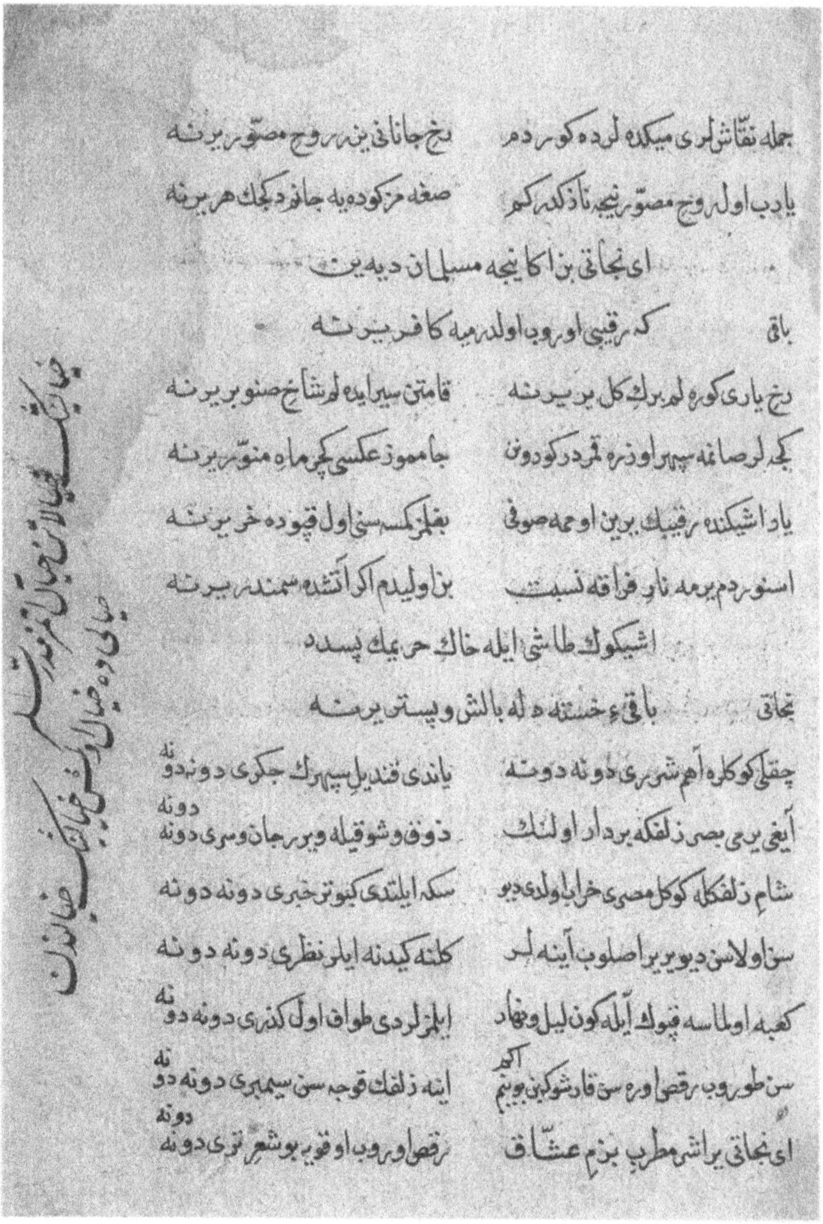

Poem 10, p. 43, by Necâtî
From the *Nazîre Mecmuası*. Private collection of Mehmet Kalpaklı.
Manuscript from the sixteenth-seventeenth century.

Poem 17, p. 56, by Zâtî
From the *Mecmuatü'n-Nezâ'ir*. Millet Library, Ali Emiri 673 (fol. 49a).
Manuscript.

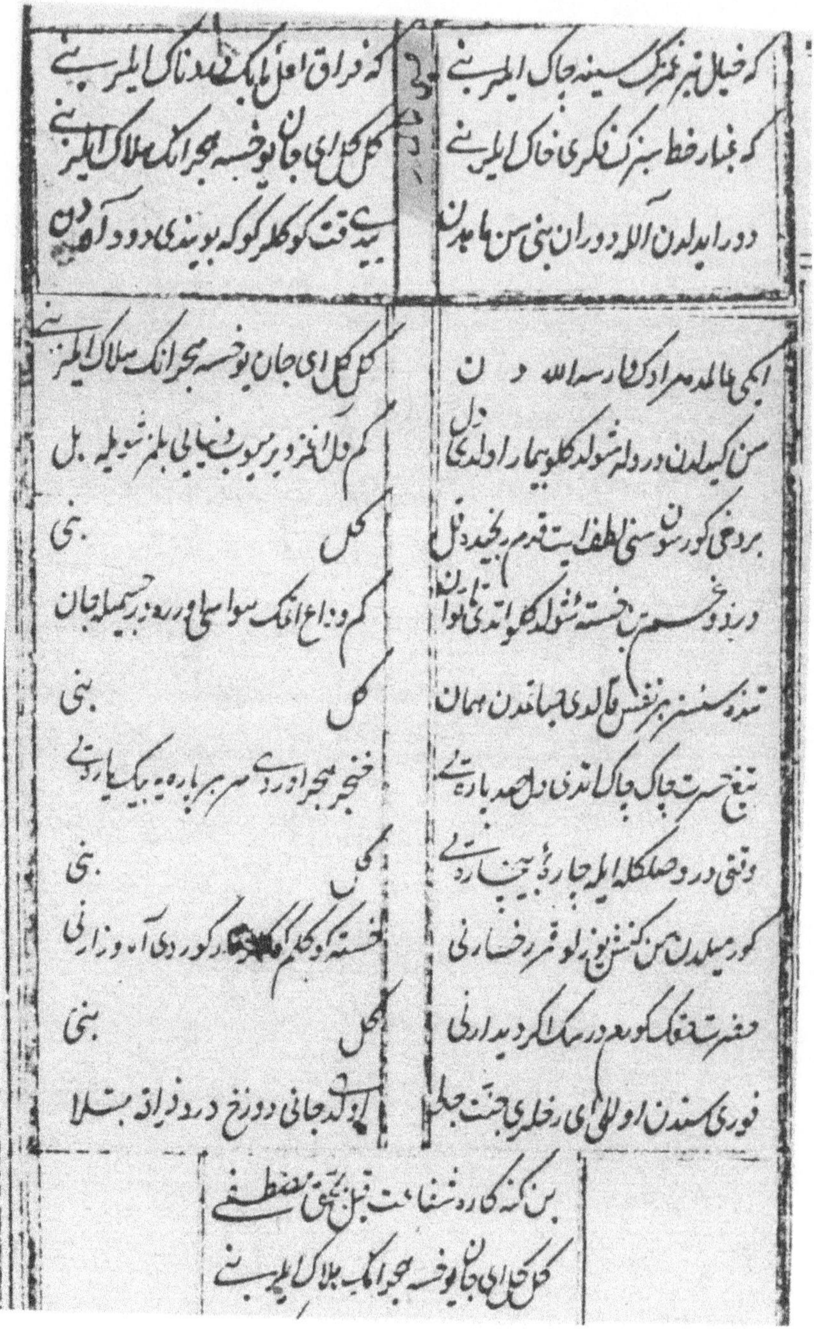

Poem 21, p. 64, by Fevrî
From the *Dîvân*. Topkapı Palace Museum Library, Revan 763 (fol. 90a-b).
Manuscript.

Poem 22, p. 66, by Hayâlî
From the *Mecmuatü'n-Nezâ'ir*. Millet Library, Ali Emiri 673 (fol. 56a).
Manuscript.

اهل تمکینم بنی بکرتمه ای گل بلبله ⁕ درده یوق صبری آنک هر لحظه بیک فریادی وار
اویله بدحالم که احوالم کورنده شاد اولور ⁕ هر کیمک کیم دور جورندن دل ناشادی وار
کزمه ای کوکلم قوشی غافل فضای عشقده ⁕ کیم بو صحرانک کذرکاهنده چوق صیادی وار

ای فضولی عشق منعن قیلمه ناصحدن قبول
عقل تدبیریدر اول صانمه که بر بنیادی وار

مقوس قاشلرک کیم وسمه ایله رنک دوتمشلر ⁕ قلیجلردر که قانلر دوکمک ایله ژنک دوتمشلر
قیلوب تغییر صورت وسمه‌دن یغما قیلورلر دل ⁕ حرامی قاشلرک رسم وره نیرنک دوتمشلر
کوکل مرآتنی ایلرمکدر عقل تکلیفی ⁕ خوش اول بی باکلر کیم ترک نام و ننک دوتمشلر
فضای عمردن کویا دکللر غنچه تک واقف ⁕ اولر کیم اوزلرین دنیا ایچون دلتنک دوتمشلر
بنم کیم سنکسار محنتم بازار عشق ایچره ⁕ بلا داغن چکن فرهاد ایله همسنک دوتمشلر
لبک دورنده زاهدلر طوتوب میخانه‌لر کنجن ⁕ قیلوب تسبیح ترکین تار زلف چنک دوتمشلر

سحر بلبللر افغانی دکل بیهوده کلشنده
فضولی ناله‌ء دلسوزینه آهنک دوتمشلر

آشیان مرغ دل زلف پریشانکده‌در ⁕ قنده اولسم ای پری کوکلم سنک یانکده‌در
عشق دردیله خوشم ال چک علاجمدن طبیب ⁕ قیلمه درمان کیم هلاکم زهری درمانکده‌در
چکمه دامن ناز ایدوب افتاده‌لردن وهم قیل ⁕ کوکلره آچلمسون اللر که دامانکده‌در
کوزلرم یاشن کوروب شور ایتمه نفرت کیم بو هم ⁕ اول نمکدندر که لعل شکرافشانکده‌در
مست خواب ناز اولوب جمع ایت دل صدپاره‌می ⁕ کیم انک هر پاره‌سی بر نوک مژکانکده‌در
بسکه هجرانکده‌در خاصیت قطع حیات ⁕ اول حیات اهلینه حیرانم که هجرانکده‌در

ای فضولی شمع تک مطلق آچلمز باشمدن
تابلر کیم سنبلندن رشته‌ء جانکده‌در

ساقیا اول عشقه طوت جام کیم قیغولودر ⁕ قیغو چکمک نه ایچون جام ایله عالم طولودر
تلخ کفتار سن اولمز لب یار ای عاشق ⁕ چوق هوس ایله اول شربته کیم آغولودر
قویه‌لم باشی خم باده ایاغینه کلک ⁕ طوتمامق اولمز انک حرمتنی بر اولودر
بو نجه کیم کوه صفت باشمه طاشلر اوریلور ⁕ دیده‌ء بختم اویانمز نه عجب اویقولودر

Poem 26, p. 75, by Fuzûlî
From the *Külliyât-ı Dîvân-ı Fuzûlî*. İstanbul, 1296, p. 109. Printed.

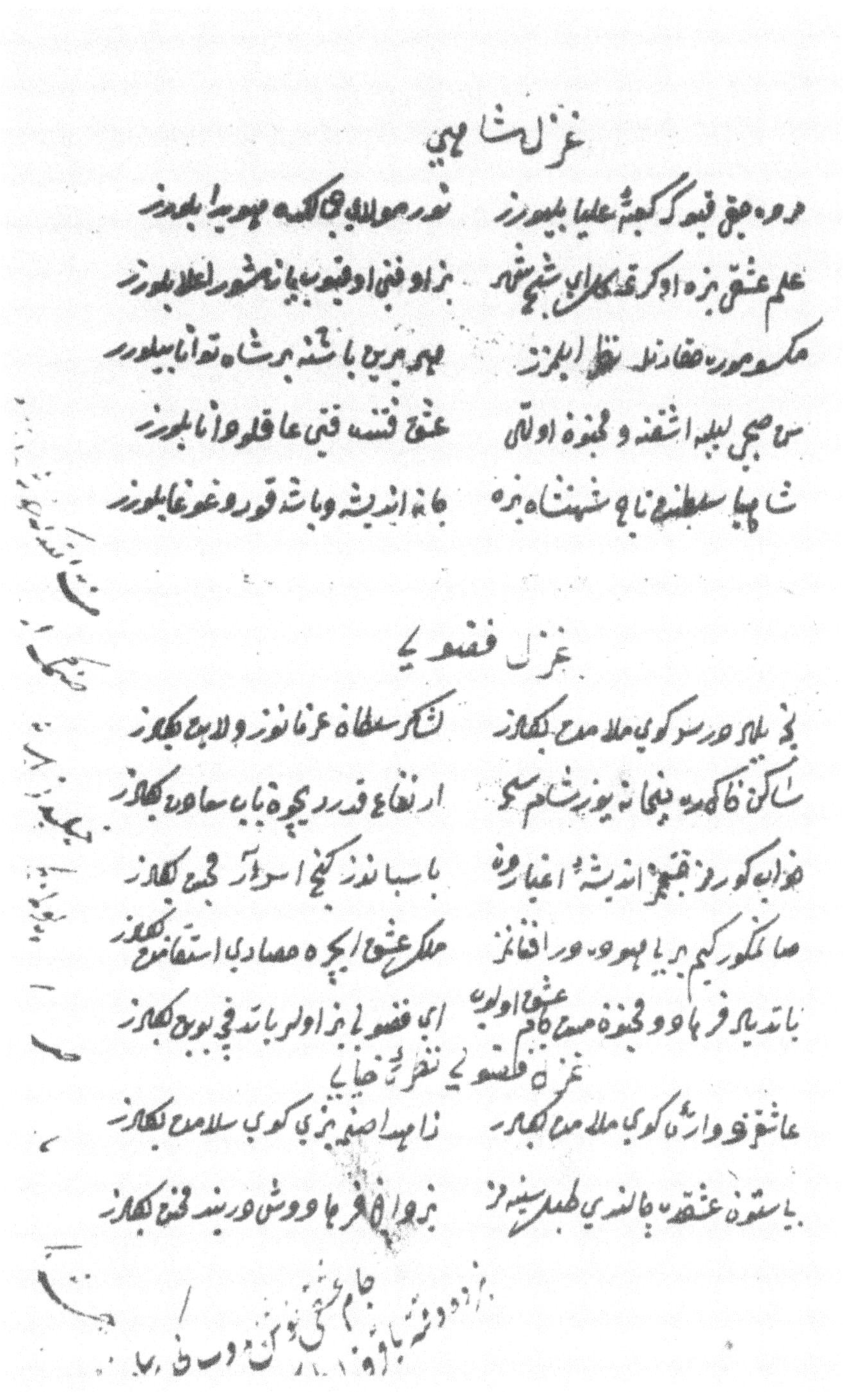

Poem 27, p. 76, by Fuzûlî
From the *Mecmuatü'n-Nezâ'ir*, Millet Library, Ali Emiri 673 (fol. 84a).
Manuscript.

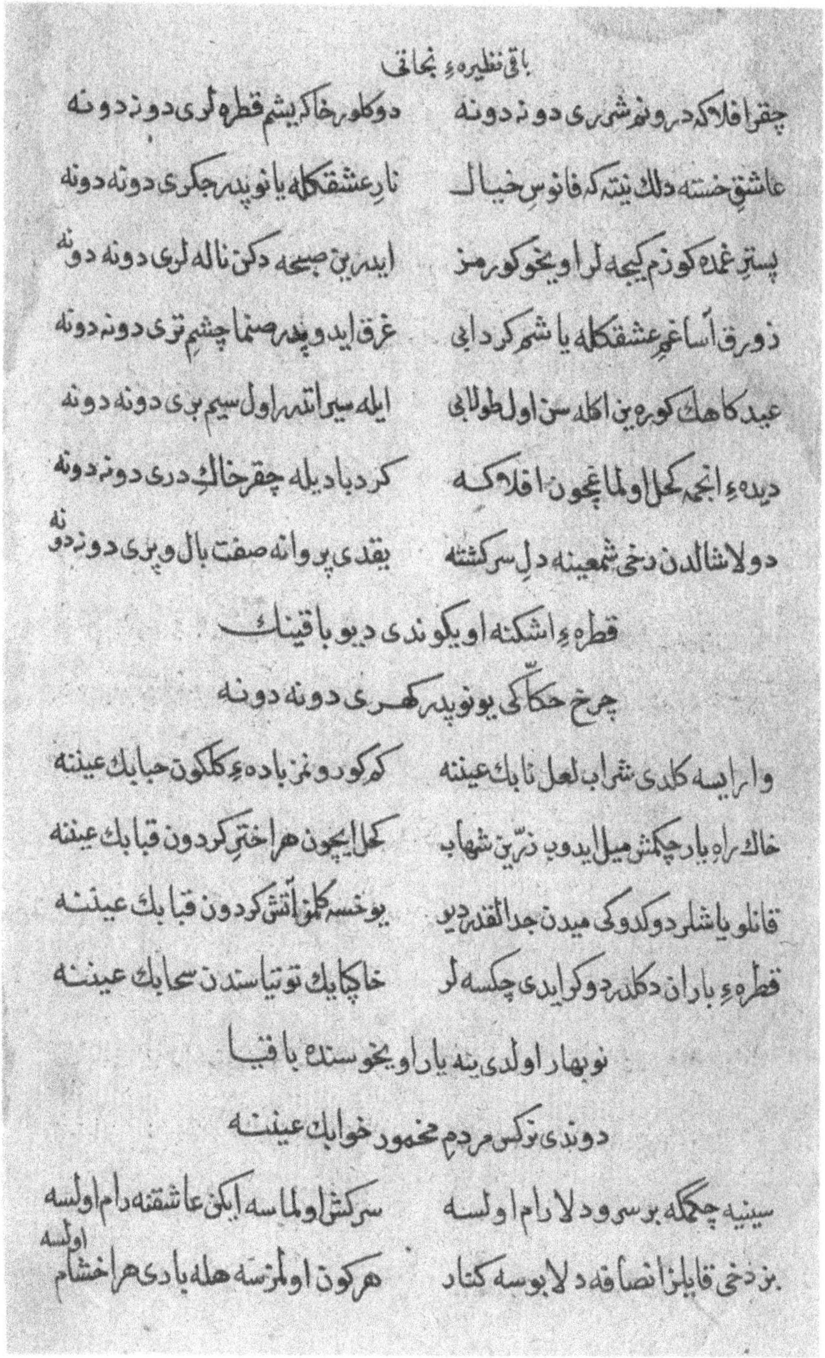

باقی نظیرهٔ نجاتی

چقر افلاکه درونم شرری دونه دونه دوکلور خاکه یشم قطره لری دونه دونه

عاشق خسته دلك بیته که فانوس خیال نار عشقکله یانوبدر جکری دونه دونه

پستی غمزه کوزم کیجه لر اویخو کورمز ایدر بن صبحه دکن ناله لری دونه دونه

ذورق آسا غم عشقکله یاشم کردابی غرق ایدوبدر صنما چشم تری دونه دونه

عید کاهك کوره بن اکلدسن اول طولابی ایله سیر اتدر اول سیم بری دونه دونه

دیدهٔ انجم کحل اولمغچون افلاککه کرد بادیله چقر خاك دری دونه دونه

دولاشالدن دخی شمعینه دل سرکشته یقدی پروانه صفت بال و پری دونه دونه

قطرهٔ اشکنه اویکوندی دیو باقینك

چرخ حکاکی یونوبدر کهری دونه دونه

وار ایسه کلدی شراب لعل نابك عیننه کم کوردونمز بادهٔ کلکون حبابك عیننه

خاك راه یار چکمش میل ایدوب نرکس شهاب کحل ایچون هر اختر کردون قبابك عیننه

قانلو یاشلر دوکدوکی میدن جدا القدر دیو یوخسه کلمز آتش کردون قبابك عیننه

قطرهٔ باران دکلدر دوکایدی چکسه لر خاکپایك توتیاسندن سحابك عیننه

نوبهار اولدی ینه یار اویخوسندن باقیا

دوندی نرکس مردم مخمور خوابك عیننه

سینیه چکمکه بوسی و دلارام اولسه سرکش اولماسه ایکن عاشقنه رام اولسه

بز دخی قایلز انصافه دلا بوسه کناد هر کون اولمزسه هله یادی هر اخشام اولسه

Poem 36, p. 97, by Bâkî
From the *Nazîre Mecmuası*. Private collection of Mehmet Kalpaklı.
Manuscript from the sixteenth-seventeenth century.

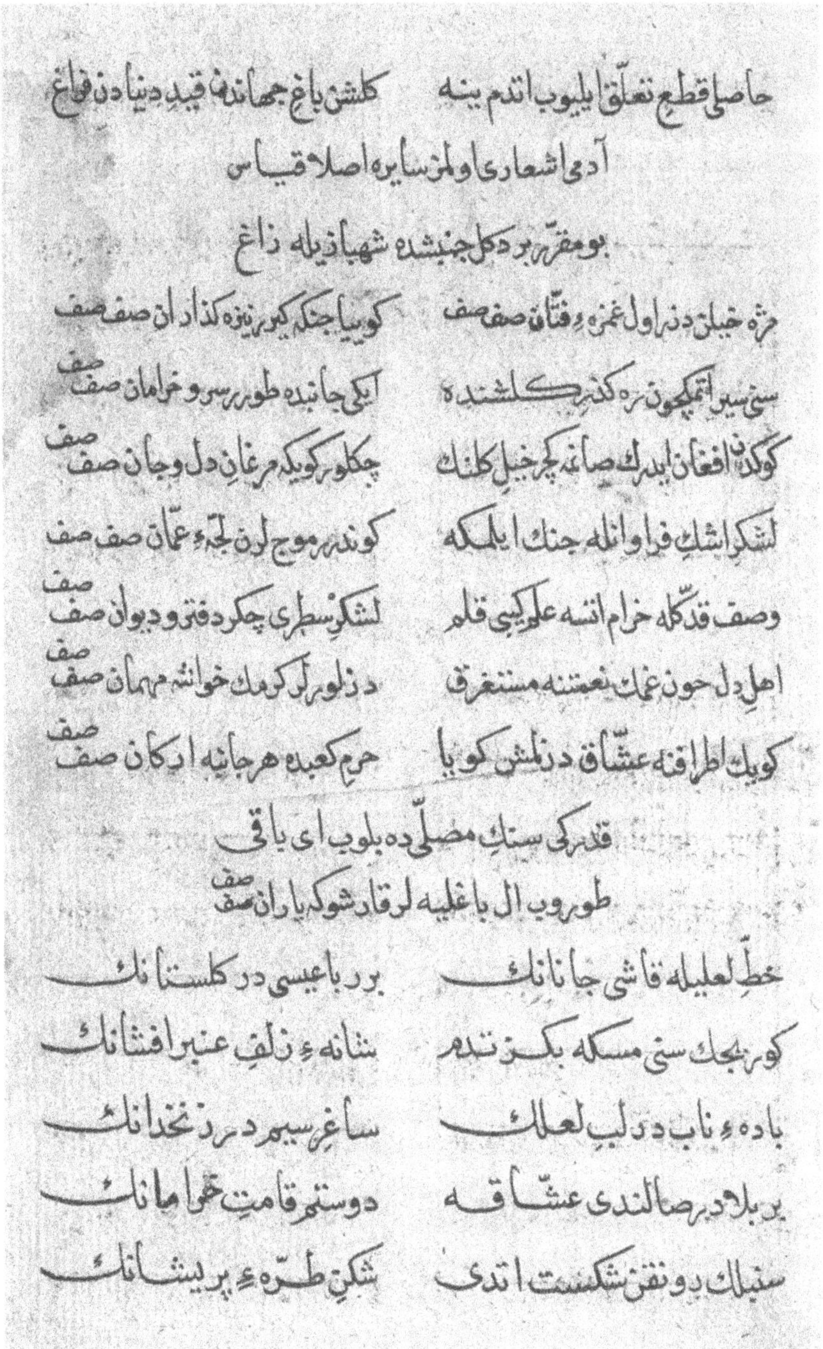
حاصلی قطع تعلق ایلیوب اتدم بینه　　کلشن باغ جهاندن قید دنیادن فراغ
آدمی اشعاری اولمز سایره اصلا قیاس
بو مقرر بر دکل جنبشده شهباز ایله زاغ

مژه خیلندن اول غمزهٔ فتانه صف صف　　کوییا جنکه کوره نیزه کذاران صف صف
سنی سیر اتمکیچون ره کذره کلشنده　　ایکی جانبده طورر سرو خرامان صف صف
کوکدن افغان ایدرک صانمه کچر خیل کلنک　　چکلور کویکم مرغان دل و جان صف صف
لشکر اشک فراوانله جنک ایلمکه　　کوندرر موج لرن لجهٔ عمان صف صف
وصف قدکله خرام اتسه علو کبی قلم　　لشکر سطری چکر دفتر و دیوان صف صف
اهل دل خون غمک نعمتنه مستغرق　　دزلورلر کرمک خواننه مهمان صف صف
کویک اطرافنه عشاق دزلمش کویا　　حرم کعبده هر جانبه ارکان صف صف
قدرکی سنک مصلیده بلوب ای باقی
طوروب ال باغلیه لر قارشوکه یاران صف صف

خط لعلیله قاشی جانانک　　بر رباعیسی در کلستانک
کوره جک سنی مسکه بکزتدم　　شانهٔ زلف عنبرافشانک
بادهٔ ناب در لب لعلک　　ساغر سیمدر زنخدانک
بر بلادر صالندی عشاقه　　دوستم قامت خرامانک
سنبلک دو نقش شکست اتدی　　شکن طرهٔ پریشانک

Poem 37, p. 98, by Bâkî
From the *Nazîre Mecmuası*. Private collection of Mehmet Kalpaklı.
Manuscript from the sixteenth-seventeenth century.

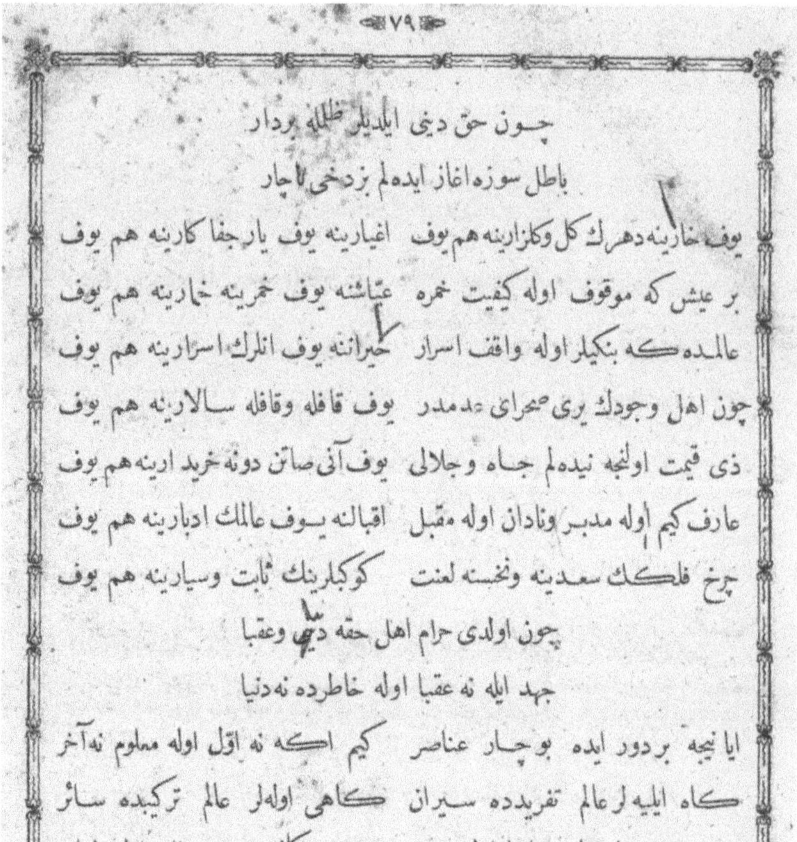

٧٩

چون حق دینی ایلدیلر ظلمله بردار

باطل سوزه اغاز ایدهلم بزدخی ناچار

یوف خارینه دهرك كل وكلزارینه هم یوف   اغیارینه یوف یارجفا كارینه هم یوف

بر عیش كه موقوف اوله كیفیت خمره   عیاشنه یوف خمرینه خمارینه هم یوف

عالمده كه بنكیلر اوله واقف اسرار   حیراننه یوف انلرك اسرارینه هم یوف

چون اهل وجودك یری صحرای عدمدر   یوف قافله وقافله سالارینه هم یوف

ذی قیمت اولنجه نیدهلم جاه وجلالی   یوف آنی صاتن دونه خریدارینه هم یوف

عارف كیم اوله مدبر ونادان اوله مقبل   اقبالنه یوف عالمك ادبارینه هم یوف

چرخ فلكك سعدینه ونحسنه لعنت   كوكبلرینك ثابت وسیارینه هم یوف

چون اولدی حرام اهل حقه دنیا وعقبا

جهد ایله نه عقبا اوله خاطرده نه دنیا

ایا نیجه بردور ایده بوچار عناصر   كیم اكه نه اول اوله معلوم نه آخر

كاه ایلیهلر عالم تفریدده سیران   كاهی اولهلر عالم تركیبده سائر

تفریدده چار اولهده ناچار اوله دوری   تركیبه كلنجه سه موالید اوله ظاهر

بو جمله مظاهردن اوله معتبر انسان   انسانك اوله جمله طفیلی بومظاهر

نفسنی بلنلر كوره خالقه ایمان   بلمزلره ایمان كورنلر دیه كافر

كافر كه یرین دوزخ ایدر جهلدن ایلر   چون جهل حقیقتده اوله كفر عجب سر

جاهللره دنیا ویره ال كامل اولنلر   آیقده قالوب اولمیهلر حبهیه قادر

چون جهلدهدر ذوق كمالی نیدهلم بز

مال اهلنه صفا ایلیه حالی نیدهلم بز

دنیا طلبیله كیمسی خلقك امكده   كیمی اوتوروب ذوقله دنیایی یمكده

Poem 40, p. 103, by Rûhî
From the *Dîvân-ı Rûhî*. İstanbul, 1287, p. 79. Printed.

مکر سوزدلمدن آگه یحیی بر شرر دوکدی [۱]
صباح اولنجه یاندی مجلسك شمع شبستانی

کوزم ایصردی کورنجه اولعل خندانی
نشانلادم لبنك یاره‌سیله جانانی
کیم اوله قارشو طوره خوبرولر ایچره آکا
مکرکه آیینه‌ده عکس روی رخشانی
تصور ایتمدیمی بی‌مثال تصویرك
نه صورتیله چیقردی که نقشنی مانی
جبینی چین ایله مسطرلی صفحه‌در یازمش
دبیر حسن آگه دیباجهٔ گلستانی
غزلده اول مهی یحیی لبیله وصف ایتسون
شکرله بسلسون اول طوطیٔ سخندانی

مسجدده ریا پیشه‌لر ایتسون قوء ریایی
میخانه‌یه کل کم نه ریا وار نه مرایی
ای جام صفا طالبی بیهوده اوزمه
جمله بیله دفن ایلدیلر جام صفایی
رد ایتمشدی یار رقیبی ایشیکندن
کلمش اوسیه‌رو ، ینه کوردکمی بلایی
دفع ایده‌مدك جیش غمی سعی ایده کوردك
تدبیر نه‌ممکن بوزه تقدیر خدایی
یحیی نیجه آوارهٔ عشق اولمیه‌یم بن
دلبرسه کوزل دلسه نهایتده هوایی

Poem 42, p. 105, by Şeyhülislâm Yahyâ
From the *Dîvân-ı Yahyâ*. İstanbul, 1334, pp. 310–11. Printed.

Poem 44, p. 109, by Nef'î
From the *Dîvân-ı Nef'î*. İstanbul, 1269, vol. 2, p. 8. Lithograph.

گوسترر دنیایی مرآت حبابنده تمام | کند و باشقه باشنه براوزکه عالمدر قدح

نوله برشوق ایتسه دنیایی دل نفعی کبی
روزکاره یادکار مجلس جمدر قدح

چکه مم درد فراقک مددای ماه مدد | کوردم بو بحلاین برغم جانکاه مدد
غزمک جان الیه غمزه که فرمان ایله | ایلسون تازیله برشیوهٔ دلخواه مدد
ضبط آه ایلمه دمد عاشقه اول چاره | بن الیه آه ایسز آرام ایده جم آه مدد
داغلر لاله کبی تازه لنور سیدی اکر | آتشی سینمه آه ایتمه مهرکاه مدد
چاین نه لفکده کرفتار قالوردی دل | ایرشوب بادصبا ایمسه ناکاه مدد
حال پک مشکل اکر ایتمز ایسه ای نفعی | همت آصف صاحب دل آکاه مدد
حافظ کنج کرم حضرت احمد پاشا | که ایدرا اهل رجایه که وبیکاه مدد
قالدم آیفده پریشان و مکدر احوال | دستکیر اول بکا ای آصف جمجاه مدد

بویله درمانده لرک دردینه درمان ایتکم
مهرایشکده پکاده ایلیه الله مدد

یازنلر پیکرم دستده بر پیمانه یازمشلر | کوروب مست می عشق اولدیغم مستانه یازمشلر
بکا تکلیف زهد ایتمزدی ادراک اولسنه هردم | یازقلر کیم آنی عاقل بنی دیوانه یازمشلر
دکلدر کوزلرنده پایهٔ مژکانی عشاقک | خطک رسمین بیاض دیدهٔ کریانه یازمشلر
بنم عاشق که رسوا القلبه طوتدی شهرتم شهری | یازنلر قصهٔ مجنونی صبیا بانه یازمشلر

بیچه ظاهردر ای نفعی سوزکدن دلده کی سوزک
یازیجه نسخهٔ شوقک قلملر یانه یازمشلر

اول ابرولرکه لوح جبههٔ جانانه یازمشلر | جمالی مطلعیدر کیم بسر دیوانه یازمشلر
دکل کرد لبنده خطی اول عیسی دمک کویا | دعای حضری برمر جاندن فنجانه یازمشلر
مصورلر یازه وب فرهادی کوه بیستون اوزره | دیروب دپسنیه تیشه خیلی استادانه یازمشلر
صانورلر حلقه حلقه دود آهمی اوج اعلاده | براثر در که سقف کنبد کردانه یازمشلر

بوطرز خاصه ای نفعی بنه صورت ویرن پنسناین
نظیره سویلینلر الکثر افسانه یازمشلر

Poem 45, p. 111, by Nef'î
From the *Dîvân-ı Nef'î*. İstanbul, 1269, vol. 2, p. 9. Lithograph.

﴿ ۱۳٤ ﴾

نقد امید ایله پردر جیب صبح ایدل همان — واتحواه آهك الدن قویمه‌سن دامانی
سیرایدوب اشك كلابی خنده‌ٔ كلغنچه‌ده — عاقبت بسین ایلینلر دیده‌ٔ عرفانی
روی تابانك سحر خواب ایچره بركز سیرایدن — پنجه‌ٔ خورشیددن كیرابولور مژكانی
سینه‌ده تنك اولمه ای دل كیم سنی دربند ایدن — مطلع كام ایلیندر یوسفك زندانی

نیلدك تشدك ندیما تیشه‌ٔ افكار ایله
بیستون فیض عشقك بولدك آخر كانی

برشكر خنده بله بزم شوقه جام ایتدك بنی — نیم صوون پیمانه‌یی ساقی تمام ایتدك بنی
شعله سروآساچیقر خاكدن اول یرلرده كیم — پایمال توسن آتشخرام ایتدك بنی
نكهت كیسو ایله كلدك بزه آه ای نسیم — طره‌ٔ سنبل صفت آشفته كام ایتدك بنی
جلوه‌ٔ حسنكله هرمویم پری خیز اولمده — عشقله سرتاقدم آیینه جام ایتدك بنی

بویله سرمست وخراب ایته ندیم زاربنی
نیم صوون پیمانه‌یی ساقی تمام ایتدك بنی

عیبدر كبری قالور دستكده یوزده قاره‌سی — درهم ودینار ایله آلدانمسه جانم باره‌سی
اویله بردر یتیم نازی ایلرپرورش — نوله اول طفلك صدفكاری ایسه كهواره‌سی
كردش ساغرقدر لذت وبردی عاشقه — طفل ایكن اول مست نازك نركس بیماره‌سی
ایتمسون بیهوده دللر مرهم لعلن هوس — خنجر مشكین ابرونك اوكلمز یاره‌سی
كوسترر آیینه‌ٔ زانوده بركرداب خون — حسرت آموزان عشقك كردش نظاره‌سی
نوله كتسه كندودن حیرتله جان ناصبور — یاسفر دریا تحمل چونكه عشقك چاره‌سی

دل نه سركشته درتیرهوایی وش ندیم
بركمان ابرونك اولمشدر مكر آواره‌سی

برنیم نشئه صای بوجهانك بهاربنی — برساغر كشیده‌یه طوت لاله زاربنی
دل كرد غمزه اولمه روامی كه كعبه‌نك — ای خواجه یلده برسپوررلر غباربنی
پیكان كبی لبكده كوتور آنی تیروش — عشقك جریده طی ایده كوررهكذاربنی
آهی یتشدی بلبل زارك كه باغبان — چوب دخان ایلدی كلك شاخساربنی
بر ذمی وار كه آه ایدرك آكیه كوكل — ای سرو قد سنكله كچن روزكاربنی
شوق تمام وعده‌ٔ فردایی دكله مز — رشك اكا كه جهانده بوكون بولدی یاربنی
ایران زمینه تحفه مز اولسون بونو غزل — ایركورسن اصفهانه ستانبول دیاربنی

(دشمن)

Poem 58, p. 134, by Nedîm
From the *Dîvân-ı Nedîm*. İstanbul, 1291, p. 134. Printed.

هر جلوه سی ساقینك بیك نكته بیان ایلر
قرآن مجیددن هر طوری بر آیتدر

بر نكته در عشق اما تكمیلی محال انجق
سر بند نهایاتی حیران بدایتدر

فقر عین غنا اولمش درد عین دوا اولمش
عارف ایكیسندنده مستغنئ الفتدر

میخانهٔ عشقنده رندان قدح نوشه
كستاخ روشلك هپ آیینهٔ طاعتدر

آثار تجلیده صورتده نمودارى
بى سایه‌لرك اسرار عصیانى اطاعتدر

یاعقده یامقده میخانه‌ده قالمشدر
آثار عمارت هپ ویرانه‌ده قالمشدر

كرداب شعور ایچره سركشته در عاقللر
آزاده لكن ذوقى دیوانه‌ده قالمشدر

صوفى اراپوب كزمه بیهوده مساجدده
فیضك اثرى شمدى خمخانه‌ده قالمشدر

اول چشم خموش اولمش همسایهٔ كفر زلف
عبسى بو كیجه كویا بتخانه‌ده قالمشدر

دعواسى ترك ایتسون بلبلده فدایوقدر
بر نكته جكى عشقك پروانه‌ده قالمشدر

درد دلم عرض ایتدم كولدى دیدى اول كافر
نوملش ینه اسراره افسانه‌ده قالمشدر

سیه پوشئ كلشن رنك سنبلدن عبارتدر
شب دیجور غم سوداى كاكلدن عبارتدر

هزارك ناله‌سى روى كلستانه ویر رخنده
نسیم نكهت كل آه بلبلدن عبارتدر

ایدوب بر جلوه ده افتاده صكره ایلر استغنا
المخارئ عاشق بر تغافلدن عبارتدر

نكات جامع حسنك كتاب خطن اخذ ایله
اوقیل وقالى زلفك هپ تسلسلدن عبارتدر

عبث در ره نورد عشقه فكر پیش و پس ایتمك
ره آزادكى ترك تأملدن عبارتدر

الاى كوچهٔ كردان تلون شرط درویشى
جفاى یاره اغیاره تحملدن عبارتدر

نه حاجت سوز سازه كرمئ مجلس ایچون اسرار
نواسى عشرتك فریاد قلقلدن عبارتدر

حسنك دقیقه سندن كوكل كرچه ساده در
دركاه دیر عشقه ولى سر نهاده در

جذب نكاه فیضنه اولسون مكر دوچار
دشت طلبده عاشق بیدل پیاده در

رندان الندن آل یورى جام محبتى
دل صنمه شمدى دل دینلن جام باده در

نفخ نفسیم بادهٔ جانبخشى بزده كور
عبسئ وحدتك سوزى توحید زاده در

اولمش فناى عشقله مست بى شعور
اسرار بى مدار بغایت فتاده در

هر كیمكه غم دلبر ایله زار دكلدر
لطف وكرم عشقه سزاوار دكلدر

عریان

Poem 66, p. 145, by Esrâr Dede
From the *Dîvân-ı Belâgat-unvân-ı Esrâr Dede Efendi*.
İstanbul, 1257, p. 58. Printed.

(٣٢)

بزمده اهل بصیرت سپاه افغانی | سواد شهر صفاهانه سورمه‌لی دیرلر
میان مویه یوقدن یلان شهادتیدوب | کروه اهل سخن اویله دربلی دیرلر

تحیفی نکته یه ای غالب ایله روحنی شاد
نظیره نکته بو در انجق محصلی دیرلر

ایتسم دیدم جمالنه ای پرجفا نظر | یار اجدی سینه سن دیدی عاشق صفا نظر
مانند برق تشنه کلوب کچدی بی خبر | بیکانه مشرب ایتمدی بر آشنا نظر
آخر دوشوب خسارته برکون بقا قاور | اهل فنایه هرکیم ایدرسه فنا نظر
کرداب فکره طالمه تهی سری وارانک | مرآت حسنه ایلمه حیرت نما نظر
ابروی ناز و غمزهٔ جاناندن اوسه ده | باللّه چکلمیور ایله هیچ کج ادا نظر
اغیاره قارشو کلدیکی خاطرنشانمیدر | سوزدکدی تیر غمزه که ای ماه یا نظر

غالب نحاس قلبی زر خالص ایتمده
اولمز جناب شمس کبی کیمیا نظر

افندمسین جهانده اعتبارم وارسه سندندر | میان عاشقانده اشتهارم وارسه سندندر
بنم فیض حیاتم حاصلی روح روانمسین | اکر سرمایهٔ عمرمده کارم وارسه سندندر
دیرن بوصورت موبهمه رونق رنک حسنکدر | کلستان خیالم نوبهارم وارسه سندندر
فلکدن ذره مقدار اولمدم دورکده رنجیده | کرای مهر منور آه و زارم وارسه سندندر
سنک پروانهٔ هجرانکم سن شمع وصلمسین | بهرشب خواهش بوس وکنارم وارسه سندندر
شهید عشقک اولدم لاله‌زار داغدر سینه‌م | چراغ تربتم شمع مزارم وارسه سندندر
کورن سرکشته لکده کردباد دشت ظن ایلر | فنا اندر فنایم هرنه وارم وارسه سندندر
نیچون آواره قیلدک که هر غلطانک اولمشکن | کوکل آیینه سنده بر غبارم وارسه سندندر
شفقتاب ایلدک پیمانهٔ می خونابله ساقی | صباح صحبت میده خمارم وارسه سندندر

سکادر التجاسی غالبک یا حضرت منلا
باشمده بر کلاه افتخارم وارسه سندندر

زاهدلرا و لعل لبی کیم نار کوریرلر | روشن نظران شعلهٔ دیدار کوریرلر
خوابیده نکهطرتیه بیلور جزیهٔ حسنی | اعمی کبی مرآته باقوب نار کوریرلر

خط

Poem 68, p. 149, by Şeyh Gâlib
From the *Dîvân-ı Şeyh Gâlib*. Bulak, 1252, vol. 2, p. 32. Lithograph.

ابتداء غزلیات
فی حرف الالف

عشق آتش تجلی منصور دربکا — هر چوب دار بر شجر طور دربکا
اول سرو گلفروش تجلی جلوه‌دن — هر نخل آه بر شجر طور دربکا
سمت بلاده بلبله شمع دار وحدتی — سنگ نشان مناره منصور دربکا
تبلرزه زاده گوهر غلطان غربتم — مهر صدف صباح نشابور دربکا
رهدان غبیم اوله که عنقای وحشتک — عرض رفاقت ایتدیکی مشهور دربکا
گویا خیال خط لبکله مژه مده خون — باغ وفاده طوطی زنبور دربکا
چکمم خمار چین جبین سرگذشت جم — نقش گل پیاله فغفور دربکا
باقر صفای ساغر زرینه مست عشق — کیمیای عین اونرگس مخمور دربکا
صد میخ تیر هجر له بوسینه خراب — مشق فغانه تخته سنطور دربکا
با قلندری تارکا کلنه نغمه جنون — زنجیرلر ترانه طنبور دربکا
قانلر اقر عجبکه بو چشم سفیددن — خونابه خیز اوچشمه کافور دربکا

ماننده ژاله سالک مجذوب عشقیم
غالب دیمکه شمس خداوند دربکا

بخش ایتدی خاکروبی اکسیر درگهن — اول حضرتک عنایتی موفور دربکا

(دیگر)

عشق و صحبت مطلع دیوان صحتدر بکا — مقطع نظم حیاتم قطع الفتدر بکا
ساغر گلگون شرار آه حسرتدر بکا — چشم پرخون غنچه گلزار وصلتدر بکا

ب

Poem 70, p. 153, by Şeyh Gâlib
From the *Dîvân-ı Şeyh Gâlib*. Bulak, 1252, vol. 2, p. 1. Lithograph.

(١٩)

حور جنان خیالی ایله آلمه ایکی زن — واعظ بیلور بسن زن دنیا دوزنلیدر

وهبی یاقشمش اول لب جانبخشه خط سبز
کویا کناری چشمهٔ خضرک چمنلیدر

سفر برده عشقک نیجه دیاره کیدر — کوزل آدک ایشیدوب تاکوز محصاره کیدر
غبار پایک ایچون اصفهانده در نظری — امید قند لبک ایله قندهاره کیدر
نیجه فتاده لی فتراک نازه بند ایتمش — نیچون او شاهسوار ارم بنه شکاره کیدر
جیغر سه حسرت ایله جانی عاشق زارک — حریم جنت ماوای کوی یاره کیدر
در جحیمی کشاد ایتدی غفله واعظ — بو آتشیله اوده قورقمکه ناره کیدر
مساعد اولسه ده کشتی بختکه ایام — بوروزکاری صاقین صانمه برقراره کیدر

منازل قمر یدی خانهٔ وهبی
کهی کاورسه ده طورمز او ماهپاره کیدر

نه تیر غمزه دن نه دیدهٔ جادولرندندر — بنم چکدکلرم آنجق کمان ابرولرندندر
صفاهانده کوروب برچار ابرولی خطن صوردم — دیدی بوچار باغک سنبل وشبو لرندندر
غم موی میانی نال ایدر امادل زاری — بورتبه پیچ وتابم حلقهٔ کیسولرندندر
کریزاندر غزال مشک وش وحشتله عاشقدن — خط آورلر که صحرای خطا آهولرندندر

قفس بند غم ایامدر حیرتله لال اولمش
بو باغک کرچه وهبی بلبل خوشکولرندندر

کل ای صبا نه اول کلعذاردن نه خبر — خزان دیده هزار بهاردن نه خبر
کورای سرشک روان کیملرک کنارنده — او سرو تازه رس عشوه کاردن نه خبر
نسیم کلدی ایاغی توزیله ای دیده — عجب غبار سر راه یاردن نه خبر
دیار حسننه کتمش خیال جاسوسی — ینه او خسرو ملک وقاردن نه خبر

بریدآه کیدوب کلمک اوزره ای وهبی
پیام وصلته دائر نکاردن نه خبر

٢٤٩

Poem 71, p. 155, by Sünbülzâde Vehbî
From the *Dîvân-ı Vehbî*. Bulak, 1253, p. 249. Lithograph.

(١٣٨)

صاره مم وصلتكي ايتمجك استمزاج
بكا اذن استمه اي شوخ نكار پاي دوشر

حسنكه مغرور اولوب ايتمه گدا كي تحقير
اعتبارندن اولور دمكه بكم پاي دوشر

خيري ترك ايله كه شرابتمه سن ديمك عبث
برخير اوله معادل دوشره جاي دوشر

واصف اول مرتبه زاربكه كف برزندن
دم اولور نالهٔ جانكاهم ايله ناي دوشر

اوقدرندن بكمل چشمكه دلبسته آهولر
نگاهكدن اوقورلر نسخهٔ افسوني جادولر

كيجه سرست ايكن كلشنده آلش نكهت زلفك
مشام اهل عشقي ايلبور تعطير شبولر

نصيب اغنيا دراحتياج اربابنك نقدي
اولور دريايه جاري اول سيبدن سوبسوجولر

حقيقتده مجازي ايتمه استعمال هرپرده
رخك استرمي غازه هيچ ديلرمي وسمه ابرولر

مصنع برغزلدر اسعدي تنظير در واصف
سزا دراتسه لر تحسين بونظمه سخنكولر

ديهمم سينهٔ براقي سمندن كيبدر
ياسمن بلكه او كلنخل سمنتن كيبدر

زلفي سنبل دهني غنچهٔ تر ساقي سمن
تپه‌دن طرنغه دك هرپري كلشن كيبدر

چشم وابرو ورخ ولعلنه سوزيوق اما
ابچلرنده ينه خال سيهي بن كيبدر

نعجب دوشمسه دلدارك الندن مرآت
حسننه سيل و محبنده او ده بن كيبدر

رنك وبوي كلي تعريفنه زحمت چكه يم
كل بنم بلديكم اي غنچه دهن سن كيبدر

يم دوكوب طوتمغه عشاقي نه حاجت اي شوخ
صيدمرغ دله خال رخك ارزن كيبدر

عاشق اسيرتنك اكر واصف زار ايله كورش
بنه اول سائره نسبت براز اهون كيبدر

اولسه غرق يم هجرانه ينه شن كيبدر
ظنم اغيار براز عقلنه بلكن كيبدر

الم ونشئه سي افتاده نك اولمز معلوم
عاشقك خنده سيه حالت شبون كيبدر

ايلسم نوله خدنك سخنندن فرياد
هرسوزك جانمه كار ايتمده دمرن كيبدر

برغم يا غمه درون دله ايتمز تأثير
جامهٔ عشق بنم كوكلمه جوشن كيبدر

Poem 72, p. 156, by Enderûnlu Vâsıf
From the *Dîvân-ı Gülşen-efkâr-ı Vâsıf-ı Enderûnî*. İstanbul, 1285, p. 138.
Lithograph.

BIBLIOGRAPHY

A NOTE ON BIBLIOGRAPHY

It was not within the scope of this book of translations and texts to compile a comprehensive bibliography on Ottoman literature or culture from the fourteenth to the twentieth centuries. We have, for the most part, listed the books that we used in some very specific way in producing this volume and want our readers to recognize that there are any number of valuable books that we did not use in this manner and, therefore, do not cite.

For those who want to know more about the Ottomans, their history, and their culture, this is a good time. Publication of exciting work on the Ottomans has burgeoned in recent years. The basic histories of the Ottoman state and the Turkish Republic in English—Stanford Shaw's 1976 history for example—have been supplemented and updated by a spate of innovative studies that provide fascinating and detailed glimpses into life and culture during Ottoman times. Among the exceptional books in English that do not appear in our bibliography, a few of our favorites and good starting points for those who want to know more are the following. The Ottoman palace, its public ceremonies, and its inner life are the topic of Gülru Necipoğlu's magnificent *Architecture, Ceremonial, and Power: The Topkapı Palace in the Fifteenth and Sixteenth Centuries* (Cambridge and London: MIT Press, 1991) and Leslie Peirce's immensely interesting *The Imperial Harem: Women and Sovereignty in the Ottoman Empire* (New York and Oxford: Oxford University Press, 1994). The outstanding biographical work on an Ottoman literary figure—the poet, intellectual, and historian Mustafa 'Âlî—is Cornell Fleischer's *Bureaucrat and Intellectual in the Ottoman Empire* (Princeton: Princeton University Press, 1986). Victoria Holbrook's brilliant study of Sheyh Gâlib's *Beauty and Heart* has already been mentioned in the introductory essay and appears in the bibliography. Among the newer historical writings that expand and modify the traditional story of the Ottomans are Rifa'at Abou-El-Haj's theoretical critique *Formation of the Modern State: the Ottoman Empire Sixteenth to Eighteenth Centuries* (Albany: SUNY Press, 1991), Palmira Brummett's insightful work on the Ottoman sea trade, *Ottoman Seapower and Levantine Diplomacy in the Age of Discovery* (Albany: SUNY Press, 1994), and Daniel Goffman's study *Izmir and the Levantine World, 1550–1650* (Seattle and London: University of Washington Press, 1990).

BIBLIOGRAPHY

Akkuş, Metin, ed. 1993. *Nef'î Dîvânı*. Ankara: Akçağ Yayınları.

'Âlî, Muṣṭafâ. 1994. *Künhü 'l-ahbâr'in tezkîre kısmı:* Ed. Mustafa İsen. Ankara: Atatürk Kültür Merkezi.

Alparslan, Ali. 1986. "Gazel Şerhi Örnekleri." *Türk Dili: Türk Şiiri Özel Sayısı II* 52 (415-416-417): 248–290.

———. 1987. *Ahmet Paşa*. Ankara: Kültür Bakanlığı.

Andrews, Walter G. 1976. *An Introduction to Ottoman Poetry*. Minneapolis and Chicago: Bibliotheca Islamica.

———. 1985. *Poetry's Voice, Society's Song*. Seattle and London: University of Washington Press.

———. 1989. "The Sexual Intertext of Ottoman Literature: The Story of Me'âlî, Magistrate of Mihalich." *Edebiyat*, n.s. 3(1): 31–56.

'Âşıḳ Çelebî. 1971. *Meşâ'ir üş-Şu'ârâ*. Ed. G. M. Meredith-Owens. London: Luzac.

Ayan, Hüseyin, ed. 1990. *Nesimî Divanı*. Ankara: Akçağ Yayınları.

Başlangıcından Günümüze Kadar Büyük Türk Klâsikleri: Tarih, Antoloji, Ansiklopedi 1985. 12 vols. Istanbul: Ötüken, Söğüt.

Bayraktutan, Lütfi. 1990. *Şeyhülislam Yahya Divanından Seçmeler*. Ankara: Kültür Bakanlığı.

Bazin, Louis [and others]. 1965. *Philologiae Turcicae Fundamenta II*. Wiesbaden: Franz Steiner Verlag.

Bombaci, Alessio. 1968. *Histoire de la Littérature Turque*. Trans. Irene Melikoff. Paris: Librairie C. Klincksieck.

Boone, Joseph A. 1995. "Vacation Cruises: or, the Homoerotics of Orientalism." PMLA 110(1): 89–107.

Browne, Edward G. (1902–1924) 1964–1969. *A Literary History of Persia*. Vols. 1–4. Cambridge: Cambridge University Press.

Bülbül, İbrahim. 1989. *Keçecizâde İzzet Mollâ*. Ankara: Kültür Bakanlığı Yayınları.

Burmaoğlu, H. Bilen. 1989. *Bursalı Lami'î Çelebi Divanı'ndan Seçmeler*. Ankara: Kültür Bakanlığı Yayınları.
Çavuşoğlu, Mehmed. 1970. "Zâtî'nin Letâyifi." *Türk Dili ve Edebiyatı Dergisi*. 18: 1–27.
———. 1971. *Necâtî Bey Dîvânı'nın Tahlili*. Istanbul: Millî Eğitim Basımevi.
———. 1973. *Necâtî Bey Dîvânı (seçmeler)*. Istanbul: Tercüman Gazetesi.
———. 1978. "16. Yüzyılda Yaşamış Bir Kadın Şâir Nisâyî." *Tarih Enstitüsü Dergisi* 9: 405–416.
———. 1981. *Divanlar Arasında*. Ankara: Umran Yayınları.
———. 1983. *Yahyâ Bey ve Dîvânı'ndan Örnekler*. Ankara: Kültür ve Turizm Bakanlığı Yayınları.
———. 1986a. "Divan Şiiri." *Türk Dili: Türk Şiiri Özel Sayısı II* 52 (415-416-417): 1–16.
———. 1986b. "Kasîde." *Türk Dili: Türk Şiiri Özel Sayısı II* 52 (415–416–417): 17–77.
———, ed. 1987a. *Hayâlî Bey*. Ankara: Kültür ve Turizm Bakanlığı Yayınları.
———. 1987b. "Kasidelerinden Örnekleri." In *Nef'î*, 80–135. Ankara: Atatürk Kültür Merkezi Yayını.
———. 1987c. "Kaside Şâiri Nef'î." In *Nef'î*, 79–89. Ankara: Atatürk Kültür Merkezi Yayını
Çavuşoğlu, Mehmed, and Ali Tanyeri, eds. 1981. *Hayretî Divan*. Istanbul: İstanbul Üniversitesi Edebiyat Fakültesi Yayınları.
———. 1987. *Zatî Divanı III*. Istanbul: İstanbul Üniversitesi Edebiyat Fakültesi Yayınları.
Cengiz, Halil Erdoğan. 1972. *Divan Şiiri Antolojisi*. Istanbul: Milliyet Yayınları.
———. 1986. "Divan Şiirinde Musammatlar." *Türk Dili: Türk Şiiri Özel Sayısı II* 52 (415-416-417): 291–429.
Chittick, William C. 1983. *The Sufi Path of Love*. Albany: State University of New York Press.
Dilçin, Cem. 1986. "Divan Şiirinde Gazel." *Türk Dili: Türk Şiiri Özel Sayısı II* 52(415-416-417): 178–247.
Dvořák, Rudolf, ed. 1911. *Bâkî's Dîwân: Ghazallijjât*. Leiden: E. J. Brill.
Erünsal, Ismail. 1981. "II Bâyezid Devrine Ait bir İn'âmât Defteri." *Tarih Enstitüsü Dergisi*. 10–11(1979–1980): 303–342.
Fuzûlî. 1950. Fuzûlî Divanı: Gazell, Musammat, Mukatta' ve Ruba'î kısmı. Ed. Ali Nihat Tarlan. Istanbul: İstanbul Üniversitesi Yayınları.
Gâlib, Şeyh. 1994. *Dîvânı*. ed. Muhsin Kalkışım. Ankara: Akçağ Yayınları.
Gibb, E. J. W. 1900–1909. *A History of Ottoman Poetry I–VI*. London: Luzac and Company.
———. 1901. *Ottoman Literature: The Poets and Poetry of Turkey*. Washington and London: M. Walter Dunne.
Glünz, Michael. 1991. "The Poet's Heart: A Polyfunctional Object in the Poetic System of the Ghazal." In *Intoxication Earthly and Heavenly: Seven Studies on*

the Poet Hafiz of Shiraz, ed. J. Christoph Bürgel and Michael Glünz, 53–68. Bern: Peter Lang.

Gökyay, Orhan Şaik. 1974. "Bakî." *Türk Dili: Mektup Özel Sayısı*, 274: 44–46.

Gölpınarlı, Abdülbaki. 1953. Nesîmî-Usûlî-Rûhî. Türk Klâsikleri 24. Istanbul: Varlık Yayınevi.

———. 1954. *Divan Şiiri: XVII. Yüzyıl*. Türk Klâsikleri 39. Istanbul: Varlık Yayınları.

———. 1955. *Divan Şiiri: XVIII. Yüzyıl*. Türk Klâsikleri 41. Istanbul: Varlık Yayınları.

Halman, Talât S. 1987. *Süleyman the Magnificent Poet*. Istanbul: Dost Yayınları.

Holbrook, Victoria Rowe. 1992. "Originality and Ottoman Poetics: In the Wilderness of the New." *Journal of the American Oriental Society* 112(3) 440–454.

———. 1994. *The Unreadable Shores of Love*. Austin: University of Texas Press.

İpekten, Hal-k. 1973. *Fuzulî*. Ankara: Atatürk Üniversitesi Yayınları.

———. 1986. *Nâ'ilî*. Ankara: Kültür ve Turizm Bakanlığı Yayınları.

———. 1989. *Enderunlu Vâsıf*. Ankara: Kültür Bakanlığı Yayınları.

———. 1990. *Nâ'ilî Divânı*. Ankara: Akçağ Yayınları.

———. 1991. *Fuzulî*. Ankara: Akçağ Yayınları.

İsen, Mustafa. 1994. *Künhü 'l-ahbâr'in tezkîre kısmı. I. İnceleme, II. Metin*. Ankara: Atatürk Kültür Merkezi.

İsen, Mustafa, and Cemâl Kurnaz, eds.. 1990. *Şeyhî Dîvânı*. Ankara: Akçağ Yayınları.

Işık, Ihsan. 1990. *Yazarlar Sözlüğü*. Istanbul: Risale Yayınları.

Kalkışım, Muhsin, ed. 1994. *Şeyh Gâlib Dîvânı*. Ankara: Akçağ Yayınları.

Kalpaklı, Mehmed. 1991. "Osmanlı Şiirinin Edisyonunda Bilgisayar Kullanımı Metoduna Giriş ve Fevrî Divanı'nın Elektronik Formu." Dissertation. Istanbul University.

Karaalioğlu, Seyit Kemal. 1973. *Türk Edebiyatı Tarihi*. Istanbul: Inkilap ve Aka Kitapevleri.

Karahan, Abdülkadir, ed. 1966. *Figânî ve Divançesi*. Istanbul: İstanbul Üniversitesi Edebiyat Fakültesi Yayınları.

———. 1972. *Nef'î Divanı'ndan Seçmeler*. Istanbul: Millî Eğitim Bakanlığı Yayımları.

———. 1986. *Nef'î*. Ankara: Kültür ve Turizm Bakanlığı Yayınları.

———. 1987. *Nâbî*. Ankara: Kültür ve Turizm Bakanlığı Yayınları.

———. 1991. *Les Poétes Classiques à l'Époque de Soliman le Magnifique*. Éditions du Ministère de la Culture. Ankara: Kültür Bakanlığı Yayınları.

Kınalızâde Hasan Çelebi. 1989. *Tezkiretü 'Ş-şuarâ I–II*. Ibrahim Kutluk, Ed. Ankara: Türk Tarih Kurumu Yayınları.

Kocatürk, Vasfi Mahir. 1967. *Divan Şiiri*. Ankara: Edebiyat Yayınları.

Küçük, Sabahattin. 1987. "Bâkî'ye Dâir Notlar." *Fırat Üniversitesi Dergisi (Sosyal Bilimleri)* 1: 147–156.

Laṭîfî. 1314. *Teẕkîre-i Laṭîfî*. Ed. Ahmed Cevdet. Istanbul: Ikdam Matbaası.
———. 1990. *Latîfî Tezkiresi*. Ed. Mustafa Isen. Ankara: Kültür Bakanlığı Yayınları.
Mazıoğlu, Hasibe, ed. 1962. Fuzûlî: Farsça Divan. Ankara: Türk Tarih Kurumu Basımevi.
———. 1988. *Nedîm*. Ankara: Kültür ve Turizm Bakanlığı Yayınları.
Meisami, Julie Scott. 1987. *Medieval Persian Court Poetry*. Princeton, N.J.: Princeton University Press.
Menemencioglu, Nermin, and Fahir Iz, eds. 1978. *The Penguin Book of Turkish Verse*. Harmondsworth and New York: Penguin.
Menocal, María Rosa. 1994. *Shards of Love: Exile and the Origins of the Lyric*. Durham and London: Duke University Press.
Nâ'imâ. 1280 (1863). *Târîḫ-i Nâ'imâ: Ravżatu 'l-Ḥüseyn fî Ḫulâṣatı Aḫbârı 'l-Ḫafıḳayn*. Istanbul: Ṭab'ḫâne-i Âmire.
Nasr, Seyyid Hossein. 1964. *An Introduction to Islamic Cosmological Doctrines*. Cambridge, Mass.: The Belknap Press of Harvard University Press.
Nicholson, Reynold A. ed., trans., commentary. 1925. *The Mathnawí of Jalálu'ddín Rúmí* 1–8. London: Luzac.
Ocak, Fatma Tulga. 1987. "Nef'î ve Eski Türk Edebiyatımızdaki Yeri." In *Nef'î*, 1–44. Ankara: Atatürk Kültür Merkezi Yayını.
Onan, Necmettin Halil. 1941. *İzahlı Divan Şiiri Antolojisi*. Ankara: Maarif Matbaası.
Onay, Ahmet Talât. 1992. *Eski Türk Edebiyatında Mazmunlar*. Ed. Cemal Kurnaz, Ankara: Türkiye Diyanet Vakfı Yayınları.
Özgül, M. Kayahan. 1990. *Yenişehirli Avnî*. Ankara: Kültür Bakanlığı.
Pakalın, Mehmed Zeki. 1971. *Osmanlı Tarih Deyimleri ve Terimleri Sözlüğü, vols.* 1–3. Istanbul: Millî Eğitim Basımevi.
Pala, İskender. 1989. *Ansiklopedik Dîvân Şiiri Sözlüğü, vols. I and II*. Ankara: Kültür Bakanlığı Yayınları.
Sâlim, Mîrzâzâde Memed Emîn. 1315 (1897). *Teẕkere-i Sâlim*. Ed. Ahmed Cevdet, Istanbul: İḳdâm Maṭba'ası.
Sehî Bey. 1980. *Tezkire*. Ed. Mustafa Isen, Istanbul: Tercüman Gazetesi.
Shaw, Stanford. 1976. *History of the Ottoman Empire and Modern Turkey, vol. I*. Cambridge and New York: Cambridge University Press.
Tâhir'ül-Mevlevi. 1973. *Edebiyat Lûgatı*. Ed. Kemal Edib Kürkçüoğlu, Istanbul: Enderun Kitabevi.
Tanpınar, Ahmet Hamdi. 1956. *XIX Asır Türk Edebiyatı Tarihi, Vol. I*. Istanbul: İstanbul Üniversitesi Edebiyat Fakültesi Yayınları.
Tarlan, Ali Nihat, ed. 1945. *Hayâlî Bey Dîvânı*. Istanbul: İstanbul Üniversitesi Edebiyat Fakültesi Yayınları.
———. ed. 1950. *Fuzûlî Divanı: Gazel, Musammat, Mukatta' ve Ruba'î Kısmı*. Istanbul: İstanbul Üniversitesi Edebiyat Fakültesi Yayınları.
———. ed. 1963. *Necâtî Beg Dîvânı*. Istanbul: Millî Eğitim Basımevi.

———. ed. 1966. *Ahmed Paşa Dîvânı*. Istanbul: Millî Eğitim Basımevi.
———. ed. 1970. *Zatî Divanı, Vol. II*. Istanbul: İstanbul Üniversitesi Edebiyat Fakültesi Yayınları.
———. 1985. *Fuzûlî Divanı Şerhi, Vols. I–III*. Ankara: Kültür ve Turizm Bakanlığı Yayınları.
Timurtaş, Faruk K. 1985. *Osmanlı Türkçe Grameri*. Istanbul: Umur.
———. 1987. *Bâkî Divanı'ndan Seçmeler*. Ankara: Kültür ve Turizm Bakanlığı Yayınları.
Tolasa, Harun. 1973. *Ahmet Paşa'nın Şiir Dünyası*. Ankara: Atatürk Üniversitesi Yayınları.
———. 1979. *Şeyhülislam Bahayî Efendi Divanı'ndan Seçmeler*. Istanbul: Tercuman Gazetesi.
———. 1983. *16 Y. Y.'da Edebiyat Araştırma ve Eleştirisi*. Izmir: Ege Üniversitesi Edebiyat Fakültesi Yayınları.
Tulum, Mertol, M. Ali Tanyeri, eds.. 1977. *Nev'î Divan*. Istanbul: İstanbul Üniversitesi Edebiyat Fakültesi Yayınları.
Ullah, Najib. 1963. *Islamic Literature*. New York: Washington Square Press.
Ünver, İsmail. 1987. "Övgü ve Yergi Şair Nef'î." In *Nef'î*, 45–78. Ankara: Atatürk Kültür Merkezi Yayını.
Yılmaz, Mehmet. 1992. *Edebiyatımızda İslamî Kaynaklı Sözler*. Istanbul: Enderun Kitabevi.

www.ingramcontent.com/pod-product-compliance
Ingram Content Group UK Ltd.
Pitfield, Milton Keynes, MK11 3LW, UK
UKHW030900120525
458415UK00001B/70

9 780295 985954